The Altruists

The
Altruists

ANDREW RIDKER

JONATHAN CAPE

LONDON

1 3 5 7 9 10 8 6 4 2

Jonathan Cape, an imprint of Vintage,
20 Vauxhall Bridge Road,
London SW1V 2SA

Jonathan Cape is part of the Penguin Random House group of companies
whose addresses can be found at global.penguinrandomhouse.com.

Penguin
Random House
UK

First published in the United Kingdom by Jonathan Cape in 2019

Excerpt from "Apology for Want" from Apology for Want by Mary Jo Bang
(A Middlebury/Bread Loaf Book, University Press of New England, 1997).
Reprinted by permission of The Clegg Agency.

penguin.co.uk/vintage

A CIP catalogue record for this book is available from the British Library

ISBN (Hardback) 9781787330450
ISBN (Trade paperback) 9781787331686

Printed and bound in Great Britain by Clays Ltd, Elcograf S.p.A.

Penguin Random House is committed to a sustainable future
for our business, our readers and our planet. This book is made
from Forest Stewardship Council® certified paper.

MIX
Paper from
responsible sources
FSC
www.fsc.org   FSC® C018179

For Paul and Susan Ridker

Among animals, we're the aberration:
want appropriates us,
sends us out dressed in ragged tulle, but won't tell
where it last buried the acorn or bone.

—MARY JO BANG, "Apology for Want"

The Altruists

The Alter family was beset by fire. All autumn there were flare-ups, happenings, the kind of uncoordinated auguries that look ominous only in retrospect. In September, Ethan singed his thumb trying to light a cigarette. Three days later, a faulty burner caused the range in the kitchen to malfunction; the igniter made an anxious sound, a string of desperate ticks, before sparking a flame that caught Francine's cuff. And at Arthur's fiftieth birthday, a modest gathering on the back lawn of the house, a trick candle fell from the carrot cake and set a few dead leaves alight, which Maggie stomped out with her foot.

The largest of that fall's infernos occurred one Thursday evening in November. Francine was in her office with Marcus and Margot Washington, a pair of married intellectual property lawyers with a boutique firm. It was their first session—they had been referred to Francine by a mutual friend—but the couple's reputation preceded them. The previous April, they had successfully defended an emerging peer-to-peer file sharing service against a hip-hop crew behind a popular song with an unprintable title. But the Washingtons did not look like two people at the peak of professional success. Margot's foot bounced restlessly in place. Marcus stared at his lap. They had come to Francine in need of mediation.

"You understand the delicacy of our situation," Margot said, clutching the handle of her purse. "We can't have anyone knowing about this."

Francine understood clearly enough. Margot's roots in St. Louis were deep, her family history a veritable fable of inheritance and birthright. She was said to be descended from the French grandee Pierre Leclercq. According to legend, Leclercq, a fur trader with a million acres in colonial St. Louis, freed one of his concubines, Bathsheba, and put land grants in her name in order to protect himself from creditors. But Bathsheba flipped the property and took Leclercq to court, inspiring generations of lawsuits over his estate. For years Leclercq's descendants were the embattled, flamboyant characters at the forefront of the city's aristocracy. The Washingtons were visible figures in what remained of St. Louis society, and all the more so for being one of two black couples who lived on Lenox Place, a gated street near the Central West End.

"Of course." Francine nodded.

Margot scrutinized the room. "Do you always work from home?"

"Since we moved in," Francine said. "Four years ago."

"Four years," Margot said. And then repeated it, "Four years," weighing the measure of that time.

Before Arthur moved the family west from Boston, the space that was now Francine's office had been a sunroom, a structural addition on the western end of the house. One wall was made almost entirely of glass, through which Francine watched the scorched leaves of red maples fall one after another all season long. On the office door, facing out, an engraved brass nameplate insisted on its present function. Arthur had protested the cost of the plate, as well as the acoustic panels on the walls, but Francine ignored him. She understood the value of discretion, and of putting up a solid front.

The home office was a consolation of sorts, the primary condition in her agreement to move. She needed a place in which to foster her career, having left behind a well-paid appointment at a private clinic in Newton. Though she had been reduced to working out of a small room in her house, her name was gradually coming to mean something in the suburbs of University City, Clayton, and Ladue.

"I haven't had any complaints yet," she added.

Margot nodded decisively and set her bag beside her. "All right," she said, "I'll begin." She moved herself back on the couch and squared her shoulders. "If you must know, and I suppose you must, my husband has lately cultivated something of a habit, a proclivity, which I refuse to indulge and which threatens to undo our marriage."

"I'd like to hear it in Marcus's words," said Francine. "Marcus? Are you comfortable sharing with me?"

Marcus squinted into the tangerine dusk light shining through the panes.

"He won't tell you."

"Marcus?" Francine tried again.

"He refuses to engage," said Margot. "But something must be done." She paused. "So here it is: my husband likes to play dress-up. He finds this erotic."

Francine looked again at Marcus, but he was silent. She pinched the inside of her cheek between her teeth. "All right," she said. "Marcus, it would really help if you could say something."

"He says he likes the feeling. The confinement. He says the rubber's like a second skin."

"The rubber?"

"Latex, actually. Yes. He likes to dress up in a bodysuit and pretend that he's a household pet."

"So—okay." Francine shifted in her chair. "Marcus likes to dress up like a dog."

"Not dog. Household pet. Sometimes he's a dog; sometimes he's a cat. And sometimes he's a hamster, which is ridiculous, because hamsters live in cages and run on wheels, whereas Marcus, *Marcus*, is a well-regarded trial lawyer with a firm to run." Margot dipped her head inside her bag and rooted around until she emerged with a black face mask, two long ears drooping from the top. "Put it on," she demanded.

"That's not necessary," said Francine.

"He likes it so much, he can show you what he looks like. Put it on, Marcus."

Before Francine could interject, the mask was in Marcus's hands.

She watched as he eagerly pulled it over his head and adjusted it until his eyes were aligned with the holes.

"Do you see? Do you see what I'm dealing with here?"

Francine nodded. She was beginning to get a sense of things. By and large she saw two kinds of clients in the well-heeled suburbs where she made her living: those with legitimate issues to work through, and those whose neurotic temperaments had them convinced that even the slightest change of mood was cause for alarm. That a dose of unhappiness was surely depression, that a swell of panic was no less than clinical anxiety rearing its twitchy head. The Washingtons, she reasoned, likely fell into the latter camp. They were probably just looking to be reassured that they were normal.

Francine had been doling out a lot of reassurance lately, and it bored her. She wanted something she could invest in. She had been preoccupied all day, nervous as she always was with new referrals, eager to make a good impression—and for what? A little midlife kink? Life, with its routine skirmishes, was difficult enough.

Take Maggie. She was throwing a fit over her role in the Thanksgiving pageant. She'd wanted to be an Indian—that nomenclature, however incorrect, still persisted at Captain Elementary in the year 2000—and had been cast, instead, as the cornucopia. Ethan, meanwhile, had taken to locking himself in his bedroom. He had removed himself from the family and replaced them with a computer he'd been cautious enough to purchase only after Y2K turned out to be a whole lot of worry over nothing. He bought it with his own money, which he'd saved toiling each summer at the JCC in Creve Coeur, and this defense—"It's my own money, I can do what I want with it"—had successfully foiled Francine thus far. And on top of everything, earlier that week the university had dismissed Arthur's request to be considered for a tenure-track position. He'd been a visiting professor in the engineering department for four years now, though he hardly felt like a visitor. He taught more courses than any of his colleagues, sat on innumerable committees, and most importantly had, perhaps too hastily, taken out a hefty mortgage on the house. Despite all this, his dean of faculty, Sahil Gupta, informed him that nothing could be done until the budget resolved itself. For days now Arthur had been stomping around the house, cursing under his breath and periodically stating, like a mantra, "Budgets don't resolve themselves."

Marcus spoke from behind the mask. "Do you smell that?"

"Stay on topic," Margot snapped.

"Hold it—" Marcus sniffed through the mask's snout holes. "Something's burning."

"Dr. Alter, he's ducking the issue. Isn't he?"

Francine cocked her head. "He's right. I smell it too." The air inside the office grayed. "Okay," she said. "Everybody out."

Francine and the Washingtons stepped out into the hall, where they found Arthur, Ethan, and Maggie, and soon both families stood in a semicircle on the front walk beneath a rapidly purpling sky. The elastic hoot of sirens could be heard somewhere beyond the walls of Chouteau Place.

"Who's that?" Maggie asked, pointing at Marcus.

Margot's eyes narrowed. "Take off the mask. You're scaring the girl."

"I'm not scared."

The sirens grew louder. Arthur began to pace. "What did you do?" he asked, of no one in particular.

"Nothing. I wasn't doing anything," rushed Ethan.

"*I* was practicing my lines," said Maggie.

"I thought you were a cornucopia," said Arthur. The block was overtaken with blinking flares. A fire truck pulled up behind them. "Cornucopias don't talk," he muttered to himself, hustling to confer with the men climbing out of the truck.

"I talk!" Maggie shouted after him. "I have lines!"

"He knows," Francine cooed. "He knows."

Lynn Germaine, who lived in the craftsman next door, took a tentative step out of her house. "Everything okay?" she called helpfully from underneath the eaves. "Something burning?"

Francine waved her away. "We're fine, Lynn," she said, cheeks flushing with every passing minute that her life stood on display.

Margot sent Marcus to start the car. He sighed and shuffled off. Margot fixed her gaze on her husband, then on Arthur. She turned to Francine. "So," she said, nodding at the fire truck. "How long have *you* been married?"

Before Francine could answer, Arthur was back by her side. Three of the firemen were already storming the house. Two others unfurled a long hose and made for the hydrant in front of the Germaines'. Francine's heart stuttered as she watched them rush her home.

"What did you do?" Arthur asked again. He chewed his cuticles, and looked back at the truck and then at the house. "I should go in there."

"Let the men do their job," Francine said.

"They don't know their way around. They won't know how to triage our valuables."

"They're not going to triage anything," she said. "They're going to put out the fire."

"Oh, look!" said Margot. "You can see the smoke rising up through the window!"

Arthur made a break for the house. Francine leapt and snagged his collar. Her grip was firm, and held him in place. She was used to this. *This is what I do*, she thought as she restrained him, ashamed to be doing so in front of Margot, ashamed to be holding Arthur back, preventing him from certain death while her life went up in flames before her, thinking all the while: *What would this man do without me?*

PART I

ONE

You're coming with us."

Maggie had known Emma since braces, but the awkward girl who'd played saxophone in their high school jazz band with enough enthusiasm to redeem the instrument—and, for that matter, jazz—was now in her second year of law school. A dozen of her classmates stood clustered in Emma's living room, hands hooked around significant others or planted confidently on their hips. In the kitchenette, handles of vodka with frosted-glass insignia shared counter space with plastic jugs of Simply Orange. Maggie swore she knew the song piping through the apartment, but each time she came close to identifying it, an incoming text would ping through the phone that was hooked to the speakers and throw her concentration. "You always show up at the start of things," Emma continued, "but then you sneak away like no one's going to notice."

"No I don't," said Maggie.

"Well, good. Because you're coming out with us tonight."

Maggie ground her teeth and stared at the orange ring of residue at the bottom of her Solo cup. Across the room, a toothy boy in fashionable glasses was doing an impression of someone Maggie didn't recognize.

"There are a lot of interesting people here," Emma added, gesturing to a huddle of her classmates.

Maggie scowled. The whole scene felt staged. Everyone was too put together, too self-assured. A jolt of paranoia seized her. Had this party, this Lower East Side gathering of marketing associates and financial analysts and almost-lawyers, been arranged for her benefit? Maggie couldn't shake the feeling that this conspicuous display of upward mobility was intended to send her a message.

"What are you trying to say?"

Emma put her hands up. "I'm not trying to say anything!"

Maggie relaxed her shoulders. She was doing fine, after all. She made rent working for the good people of Queens. Her only boss was her conscience. Most days this meant running errands, or babysitting, or liaising with city government on behalf of her Spanish- and Russian- and Chinese-speaking neighbors. Odd jobs. Over the course of five months she'd cultivated a small network of clients, mostly immigrants who considered her US citizenship to be a marketable skill. It was satisfying work, though it didn't pay particularly well. She was always a little bit hungry.

The toothy boy sidled up to them. "We were talking about Ziegler," he said.

"Oh my god," said Emma. "Ziegler!"

"Who's Ziegler?" Maggie asked.

"He's one of our professors," said the boy. "Torts."

"What are torts?"

"It's when an injured party—"

"Oh. Never mind."

The boy looked hurt. "Okay," he said.

Emma introduced them. "This is Maggie. We went to high school together."

"What do you do?" the boy asked, squinting.

Recently, a Polish woman on Himrod Street hired Maggie to talk at her newborn son. She was told she could say anything she liked, as long as she said it in English, the idea being that the baby would assimilate the language into its burgeoning subconscious and grow up fluent. But on her first day, once the mother left the room, Maggie blanked. She muttered *erm* and *um* and *uh* the whole session, paralyzed at first by nerves and then by guilt at the prospect of making ten bucks an hour without having earned it. "I can't take your money," she told the woman at the session's end. "But I'll be back next week with a lot to say. I promise."

Okay, so the hunger wasn't dire, but to be honest? Denying oneself a full belly kind of felt a little bit saintly. Maggie kept enough money on hand to afford to feel saintly, to afford to turn other money down. She regulated her spending with scrupulous discipline, consuming only what she needed, only what she felt she deserved. The problem was that her body couldn't differentiate between self-inflicted hunger and the other kind. It, a body, knew only "hunger"—the nutritional deficiency, not the ideological assertion—and, accordingly, she'd slimmed. Six pounds over two years. Which wasn't nothing, especially when you weren't much to begin with.

It was nice at first, feeling light and wobbly all the time. She walked the streets of Ridgewood with a mild buzz that blurred the boundaries of her consciousness. But then her cramps grew claws and the hunger pangs turned violent. She became concerned after passing out in a five-flavor cloud behind the Hong Kong Super Buffet, her legs buckling in mutiny against her. In the first semester of her freshman year at Danforth University in St. Louis, Maggie took two weeks of Philosophy 101: Foundations of Western Thought before dropping it for something less theoretical, which was long enough for her to learn the phrase *mind-body problem* but not its definition. Now, she felt she was experiencing, if not *the* mind-body problem, then at least *a* mind-body problem. Her body was making its own demands, while the part of her that made her Maggie—she supposed this was the "self"—seemed to hover above it like a tethered balloon.

Emma waved a hand in front of her. "Maggie? Brian asked you something."

Weight aside, Maggie was a credible likeness of her late mother. She had Francine Klein Alter's hair, reddish brown and prone to curl, and a subtle spritz of freckles across the bridge of her nose. But where Maggie was small, her mother had been (not big, or stocky, but) *solid*, with a density that bespoke firm moral conviction. From her father, to whom Maggie refused to acknowledge a resemblance, she'd inherited a partially protruding forehead, a skull hammered into shape by a mind that couldn't make itself up.

"Is she okay?" the boy, Brian, asked.

"We need to put some food in you," said Emma. "I think I have tortilla chips around here somewhere."

"No, no." Maggie waved her off. "I'm fine."

"Are you sure?"

She nodded. A little light-headedness was all. "Positive."

"Okay. Well—all right. Get your stuff together. We're leaving in ten minutes."

"Where are we going?"

"Out."

Maggie scanned the room. Every few minutes someone would excuse themselves from their cluster and join another, which invariably caused someone in that cluster to depart in short order for yet another, the groups always shifting but remaining the same size in some kind of social thermodynamics that struck Maggie as both deliberate and alienating. "That's the problem," she said. "Everybody here is on their way somewhere else."

"What are you talking about? We're going to a bar. All of us."

Maggie raised her eyebrows. "Don't lump me with this 'us.'"

Emma sighed. "Everyone here is super nice. And smart!" She poked Brian with her elbow. "Brian is a genius."

Maggie shook her head. "I can't."

"Mags. It's my birthday." She smiled desperately. "You've known me longer than anyone here. Can you please? This once? For me?"

Maggie was flattered—did she really know Emma the longest, and therefore best?—but she could already see how the evening would play out. She'd buy one sixteen-dollar cocktail and spend the rest of the night regretting the expense, enduring conversations about how 1L had been much harder than 2L while refusing drinks from boys with disposable incomes who all wore the same blue button-down shirts.

"Sorry," she said. "I can't do it."

Emma's smile slanted. "You can, but you won't. You don't have to make things so difficult on yourself, you know. Life doesn't have to be that hard."

But Emma had it wrong. Life *was* hard, for almost everyone, and it was the duty of those for whom life was easy to impose difficulty on themselves before they rotted from the inside out. If there was one thing Maggie couldn't stand to see, it was people with plenty to lose enjoying themselves.

All at once she felt dizzy. Sick. The music in the room began to slur. Was anyone else hearing this? A drop of sweat landed in her cup. She extended a hand and reached for Emma's shoulder, but her fingers never made it all the way.

Though she knew she shouldn't have skipped lunch, Maggie blamed her fainting spell on the wear and tear she suffered at the hands of a twelve-year-old boy.

Twice per week, she visited Bruno Nakahara at his parents' apartment, ostensibly to help him and his brother with their homework. But Bruno's newfound interest in mixed martial arts had resulted in a constellation of bruises spread across her body, hard-won blemishes the color of stale steak. He maintained that pummeling his tutor was a necessary exercise in service of his craft.

"Ground and pound!" he'd shouted earlier that day, knocking Maggie to the floor.

Though this particular job hardly paid, Maggie tolerated, even welcomed, Bruno's abuse. His assaults were evidence that she was engaged in the kind of work that required sacrifice. Think Mother Teresa, frail and stooped. Gandhi and his jutting ribcage. Maggie's were legitimizing bruises. Proof of character. Because that was the thing about trying to do good: you always wound up knuckled in the gut.

The Nakaharas lived in cramped, if cozy, quarters. The apartment overlooked the awkward heart of Cypress, Myrtle, and Madison in Ridgewood, Queens, a pavilion of negative space where you could hear, on quiet Sunday nights, components of the neighborhood in isolation: church bells logging hours, the zip of flickering neon signage. The thirty-year-old feud between a bald man and a pigeon.

"Oh-kay," she'd grumbled, worming out from under him. She limped inside the apartment. "I see we're still working on our anger issues." She used the first-person plural with the boys. It helped establish unity and trust.

The Nakahara living room invariably stunk of burnt taquitos or pizza rolls or whatever frozen thing Bruno was eating that week, cut with the farts of their infirm yellow Lab, Flower, who had long since planted himself in the corner of the living room to die. The wall-to-wall carpeting was dirtied beige like street-side snow. Above a brown pleather couch, a pair of portraits hung side by side: one of Michael Jackson, the other (she had asked) of Petro Poroshenko.

"I don't have anger issues," Bruno said. "I have ODD." He meant oppositional defiant disorder, an affliction he'd read about on the internet.

"It's a real disease," he said, "and you know that." But the accuracy of his diagnosis did not mitigate its effects.

"Disorder," she corrected. "Not disease."

In the six months that she'd worked with him, Maggie had watched Bruno exhaust a variety of interests, including but not limited to switchblades, extreme eating, and pyromania. Though MMA was, as far as Maggie could tell, little more than an excuse for deranged boxers to dispense with the philosophical elements that supposedly made pugilism a "gentleman's sport," she maintained it was a better hobby than the others. It was athletic, after all, and there was tangible proof of its impact. The fruits of Bruno's labors were evident on his body—and extended now to hers.

"I'm already done with homework," called Alex from the kitchen table, his voice twinkling like a concierge's bell. Where Bruno was all chunk, his limbs puffed out and cinched at the joints like those of balloon animals, his brother was small and sleek, streamlined, with clear skin and ink-black hair.

"If you're finished, you can do your MathBlast. And, Bruno, please remove whatever's smoking in the oven right now."

She unbuckled the belt that latched her messenger bag to her chest, and it fell, with a soft shower of zipper clinks, onto the carpet. Liberated, she began stage-managing the apartment, laying three sharpened pencils by Alex's dominant hand before sliding into Bruno's chair to minimize a knockout game video and open Microsoft Word.

Then, as if on cue, the boys' father, an unkempt Japanese man to whom Maggie had never been formally introduced—and who spoke little English, which was weird, because she didn't think the boys knew Japanese—poked his head into the kitchen. He bestowed a long, concerned look upon the scene and disappeared again into his bedroom.

"Bruno, *now*."

He grunted and headed for the kitchen.

Maggie was a tentative disciplinarian. Beneath her strict rules was a deep well of tenderness for the boys. She didn't enjoy punishing them. She would've preferred they obey her out of sheer respect. She wasn't asking for total reverence. But she maintained that they did respect her. Preteen-boy respect could look a lot like disrespect sometimes. It was how they showed affection. And, she thought, recalling the work of a seminal anthropologist she'd read in college, earning the natives' respect was always step one. Or, not "natives," but—whatever.

"Who wants mini calzone pizzas?" Bruno asked, pulling a tray of blackened dough rolls from the oven. He code-switched to his rap voice. "Just kidding, mothafuckaz. These bitches is *mine*." He tipped his head back and let one of the saucy pockets fall into his mouth.

Maggie's wayward path to Ridgewood had begun with the idea, conceived of in childhood, that the world was not just small but responsive to her efforts.

As a girl she took frequent walks through Forest Park in St. Louis, collecting errant golf balls that had flown off course. When she'd amassed enough to fill the blue fourteen-gallon recycling bin her parents kept in the garage, she hosed them down and hauled them to the sidewalk by the teeing ground. An entrepreneurial instinct compelled her to erect a sign: GOLF BALLS. $1 PER. She made forty dollars her first day, selling more than half her stock. But when she showed up the following weekend, Maggie had a change of heart. She decided to give her goods away for free. And why not? She liked taking walks, she liked collecting golf balls—she even liked the purifying act of cleaning them! Although she found golf itself to be a total joke, an uninspired, white-male pastime of the most antiquated kind, she discovered, out there on the green, that she also liked the act of giving.

This was a revelation. If generosity was so euphoric, why did people sell things at all? Why engage in the give-and-take (and take-and-take) of commerce? In the span of two weeks, she had created and destroyed a marketplace. And learned a valuable lesson: the boundaries erected between people and their systems were never as insurmountable as they seemed.

She arrived at this conclusion in spite of a father with a deep reserve of doubt regarding all things philanthropic. A few years after outfoxing capitalism in Forest Park, Maggie expressed an interest in donating her allowance to a hurricane-clobbered New Orleans. But Arthur discouraged her, lecturing his daughter on the dubious fetishism of victimhood and the Red Cross's tendency to squander all its money on overhead.

"They don't do anything with all that cash but sit on it," he said.

There was no convincing him otherwise. One Thanksgiving, after Maggie's aunt Bex proselytized for an hour on behalf of her favorite cause, he exploded with rage: "What on earth does Israel need *trees* for?" It was practically the Alter family credo, an anti–Hippocratic oath: First, Do No Good.

She refused to capitulate. Upon graduating from Danforth two years earlier with the rest of the class of 2013, in the wake of her mother's death and the chaos that ensued—and she couldn't pretend those facts were unrelated to what followed—Maggie made a concerted effort to work the lowest-paying nonprofit internships available. She followed her college boyfriend, Mikey Blumenthal, to a Midtown apartment that was walking distance from the financial firm where he sat all day before two ticking monitors, shifting large sums from one to the other. Crashing with him rent-free above a noisy, tourist-infested street near Madison Square Garden allowed her to pursue more ethical work: an unpaid three-month stint at a global children's health initiative, followed by a five-month run at a clean water advocacy group.

But she never liked the women—it was almost always women—with whom she worked. They were all nonprofit lifers, sad foot soldiers in the war on injustice with puffy eyes and long, carved-out faces like the ceremonial masks of the third worlders they were ostensibly determined to help. But they had no stories, no heroic tales of evil conquered. Their lunchtime conversations were ordinary, their grievances generic. They expended more energy over the faulty office Keurig than they did pushing legislation. Where, Maggie wondered, was the energy? The heart?

To make matters worse, she couldn't even distinguish herself among the interns, couldn't even stake her claim as the Devoted One, for at both organizations there was at least one disturbed girl who agonized over every dollar she spent on herself, every minute wasted not helping others. A girl who seemed to actually believe that her life was no more nor less valuable than anyone else's, the kind of girl who preserved water by skipping showers, forcing the rest of the office to savor her generosity with their noses. A staunch defender of microloans, unless you needed a few bucks for the bus, in which case, no, sorry, because wouldn't that money be more effectively spent on an antimalarial net for a baby in the Congo? Maggie seethed. There was simply no arguing with the Congo.

She loved her third job, though, infiltrating a Mexican restaurant in a strip mall in Paramus on behalf of labor organizers. (By then she had broken up with Mikey, who, in his first year out of college, had developed a substantial paunch, lost a hoop of hair, and registered Republican, claiming that the latter development "made going into work easier.") Her mission was to pose as a waitress, earn the respect of her fellow employees, and slowly but surely sow the seeds of revolution in their minds. To encourage them to unionize without appearing to have encouraged them at all.

There was something thrilling about being undercover. When she was undercover, nothing she did, said, or thought could be definitively attributed to her, even if she wasn't feeling especially undercover when she did or said or thought the thing. Like, for instance, "I recommend the enchiladas" (she didn't), or "I've come to terms with my mother's death" (she hadn't). No matter. At last she'd found it. Yes, at long last, she'd found it: relief from the burden of being oneself.

Meanwhile, she became a phenomenal waiter—courteous, efficient, and witty—which was funny, because she wasn't *really* a waiter. She was an undercover operative. Still, she never broke a glass. She bought cigarettes for the overburdened dishwashers. She learned to spot big tippers. It was physically exhausting but satisfying work, and it felt good to put her brain on hold all day. As a waiter she lived simply and without ambition.

Seven months in, having begun to casually drop the word *organize* around her unwitting colleagues, Maggie's real employers called her cell.

"Hey, Maggie," said the voice on the other end. "This is Brenna. From—you know. I'm here with Jake and Trish. Look, we're all sorry about this, but we're going to have to cut you loose."

"Cut me what?"

This was in September. She was taking the call on break, standing by a Dumpster outside the restaurant, her phone clamped to her cheek, her breath visible in the cold, polluted Jersey air.

"It has nothing to do with your work. We can't afford to employ you any longer."

"I'm fired?"

"From your position with us? Yes. But from the waitressing

job—well, that's still yours, obviously. We can't fire you from the restaurant. And we wouldn't want to! I'm sure you're doing great."

"Super good," echoed Trish.

The labor org supplemented her income. Their contribution was modest, and wouldn't be too sorely missed, but without the knowledge that she worked for them, without the undercover status they granted her, Maggie was just—just—

"I'm a waiter," she said. "Not an activist pretending to be a waiter. Just . . . a waiter."

Jake chimed in. "There's no shame in work—"

"—of any kind, I know," said Maggie, completing their slogan. "Can I at least tell people I still work for you?"

She thought she heard Brenna gasp. "Have you been telling people that you work for us? That's not okay. Um, Maggie? That totally undermines the point. Shit. Have you told anyone you work for us? Have you told anyone what we do?"

"No," she lied.

"Okay. Phew. Phew! You had me there for a second."

Maggie hung up and returned to the kitchen through the back door. The gas grill stunk of burning flesh. The two line cooks were laughing and cursing at each other in Spanish, slipping and bobbing, swatting at each other's groins. She took one step forward and a taco shell crunched underfoot, shattering with a dry, desperate pop.

She quit Taqueria Insufrible and moved to this "up-and-coming" neighborhood in Queens, where she found a room on the sixth floor of a building under stalled construction by a Hasidic shell company. She wondered what she'd do for work. What was her skill set? What was she qualified for? She buried Ridgewood in flyers, offering her services as a babysitter and dog walker. Her phone refused to ring. What, she wondered, had been the point of a degree in American studies if she couldn't parlay it into a life as a gainfully employed, worked-to-death American? For two anxiety-ridden weeks she fretted over her inertia. Then came the call from Oksana Kozak-Nakahara.

A transplant from Ukraine, Oksana, both the eldest and most

in-shape EMT on her squad—in Ukraine she'd been a prizewinning shot-putter and physician—was looking for a college graduate of these United States to monitor her sons' academic progress and improve their English. Maggie eagerly accepted. At their first meeting, Bruno punched her in the abdomen. Oksana scolded him with three enthusiastic slaps. Maggie accepted anyway.

The boys, Maggie came to learn, were perfectly fluent. They just needed help getting through middle school without blowing it up.

"If I finish MathBlast, can I go to my room and tinker with my robotics kit?" Alex asked.

"Gaylord," Bruno said. At *MathBlast* or *tinker*, Maggie wasn't sure. Alex rolled his eyes. "Get a girlfriend."

"Bruno, language," Maggie said. "Alex, kindness. That's a dollar in the jar. For each of you."

The jar had been Maggie's idea. More than a swear jar, Maggie's was a goodness jar, broad enough to include most forms of misbehavior. She didn't mind how the boys treated her—the more they misbehaved, the more she felt justified in setting them straight on what was pretty much a pro bono basis—but she would not stand for cruelty between them.

"I have two girlfriends, and you don't see me acting out," Alex muttered. The boys surrendered their money to the jar on the kitchen counter, where it sat between a corner and a knife block.

Bruno returned to his math homework, using his pencil to turn pie charts to penises. Alex went to tinker. Maggie slumped down in Flower's corner to nuzzle him for a minute before rising and meandering over to the kitchen. Her eyes found their way to the jar. It was three-quarters full, moss green and tickseed yellow, a thicket of bills above a bed of copper and zinc. Her little fiscal terrarium. She coughed and under cover of the sound removed a flutter of singles and stuffed them in her pocket.

Like all economies, Maggie's was rife with paradoxes. Necessary evils. This was one of them: in order to charge the Nakahara family so little for her services, she was forced to occasionally take from them.

The real question was whether the boys were also plundering it. They almost certainly were—the jar sat unattended all week—but what could Maggie say, without being a hypocrite? She would steal, but she refused to be a hypocrite.

Two hours later she bid the boys goodbye and headed home. Maggie lived a few blocks over on the Bushwick-Ridgewood fault line where the elevated M train thundered overhead, metal wheels gnashing the tracks as it passed. The border between Brooklyn and Queens was bustling and tectonic, as though the two boroughs understood their identities to be both distinct and in conflict.

Her apartment building, in which entire floors were boarded up, stood opposite a Food Bazaar and beside a pit. The pit was massive, and comprised the view from her sixth-floor window. She often found herself staring at it. Into it. It was better than TV, she thought—though she didn't own one—better even than the Wi-Fi paid for by her roommate's parents. The pit! Sometimes she saw little men in helmets walking its perimeter, pointing at each other, shouting instructions. The pit might become a parking lot, more apartments, a commercial strip, anything. But things were moving slowly. For now it was a pit, Maggie's pit, a cavity of tremendous potential to be developed in the future.

In the entryway to her apartment, she found her mailbox stuck shut with a grimy compound. Maggie forced the lid and it popped open, revealing a rubber-banded bundle of bills and catalogs. She sorted through them as she climbed the tall staircase. The electric company wanted money, her alma mater wanted money. Maggie wondered why she bothered checking mail in the first place.

She wedged the bundle in her armpit, damp from hiking six flights, and let herself into the apartment.

Her roommate, who was inconveniently named Maggie, too, sat slumped in the blue canvas camping chair that our Maggie had brought in from the street a few months prior.

"Long day?"

"Insane. Three student birthdays. The sugar intake alone. My kids were wired. Totally off-the-wall."

Other Maggie was a teacher with AmeriCorps. She hated it. Her third graders were constantly scuffing one another's sneakers and resorting to violence. It was weird to see her sitting out like this, sunk into the canvas seat's deep pocket. Most of the time she holed up in her room, her existence little more than a series of clicks and latches, light at the bottom of the door.

"Yeah, yeah, I get that. You should've seen my boys today. Bruno tackled me again."

"Maggie," intoned Maggie. "You tutor two boys. I teach three classes of twenty students each. It's exhausting work. You have no idea."

"Relax. I'm not being competitive."

Maggie resented her roommate's superior tone. Other Maggie didn't have a teaching degree and was almost certainly making things worse for her students. The last thing they needed was a bumbling white savior at the head of the classroom.

She scoffed as she made for her bedroom. She was already dreading Emma's party. Now she was in an awful mood. She tossed the mail onto her bed, where it landed in the shape of an outstretched hand.

Something bright drew her attention. Beneath a misaddressed *Working Mother* magazine she found a crisp white envelope, her father's name in the upper-left corner above the name of the street where Maggie grew up.

As she lifted it to her face, Maggie had two thoughts almost simultaneously. One was: *What?* And the stranger thought—which beat the other by a fraction of a second—was that physical mail was such a formal thing, and so last century, the envelope like a little white tuxedo.

TWO

Ethan leaned on the lap of a bay window, the afternoon sun warm at his back. A tome was parted open in his hands. Learning philosophy had lately seemed like a noble means of self-improvement, an antidote to all the screens, a diversion from the Crate and Barrel spirits cabinet with its lacquer exterior and liquor interior. But he quickly found that you couldn't understand Foucault without Marx, and you couldn't understand Marx without Hegel, and so on, all the way back to the Greeks. When he realized that he couldn't understand the Greeks, he bought a Cambridge Companion, which he was currently mired in, wondering if there existed a companion to the Companion.

He returned to the introduction. *Compare the following two questions*, he read, for the fifth time, *both of which greatly exercised ancient Greek and Roman thinkers:*

1. What is a good human life?
2. Why isn't the earth falling?

Ethan was puzzling over the former when he heard the mail come through his slot.

He could not imagine why his father would write. Why he'd go to pains of actually writing, with a pen on paper, to his son. It had been five months since Ethan's last fleeting contact with Arthur on the phone. After Francine's funeral, Ethan had returned to New York for good, his sister—who'd graduated from college that same week—close behind. Neither had seen their father since. It had been almost two years.

He turned the envelope in his hands and worked the lip open. The note itself was characteristically withholding:

> E.—
>
> Would be good to have you home. You (&Maggie) can visit midapril. (spring break.) Important to see family, remember roots, &C.
>
> —A.

Two years.

A lot could happen in two years.

Little had.

The letter scrambled his head. For Ethan, home and humiliation were inseparable. Reading his father's note glitched his system, caused shame memories to unspool like loose tape from a VHS cassette. Here was one: Ethan, fifteen years old, sitting nervously across from Arthur and Francine at the dining room table like it was a Senate judiciary hearing. Like he was defending a thesis. Silk flowers flanked his parents, stemming from fishbowls with glass marbles lining the base. He cleared his throat and told them he was bisexual—not gay; it seemed a safer bet, like dipping one foot into a freezing lake—and his father snorted.

"Arthur!" Francine yelped, but it was too late.

That had been a sweltering, murky August, a St. Louis August, the stink of brow sweat and the sour smell of deet so entwined that it only took the presence of one scent to invoke the other. Ethan's third summer in St. Louis and he still wasn't used to it. The move was his father's doing. In Boston, Arthur had published the odd paper and lectured at MassBay Community College. When he let it be known that he was tired of life in the private sector, an old mentor who'd had the same thought a decade earlier put in a good word for Arthur at Danforth. Then he drowned himself in the Missis-sippi River, and Arthur was called on to replace him.

Though the offer was rife with words like *visiting* and *in-residence*, Arthur believed he could parlay the appointment into something permanent. He'd spent the last few years working for one of the civil engineering firms managing the Big Dig, a plum contract spoiled by inefficiencies, corruption, and design flaws. He complained to his family endlessly. Corrosive salt water leaked through fissures in the I-93 tunnel. The metal barriers intended to protect construction workers from cars had sharp, squared-off edges, earning them the designation "ginsu guardrails." It was only a matter of time before someone was beheaded in a traffic accident. What should have been a dream job quickly turned into a game of pass the buck, Arthur scrambling to dodge responsibility for mistakes that weren't his, to keep his name away from the mounting toxicity associated with his office, until Francine caught him murmuring the Nuremberg defense—*I was just following orders!*—in his sleep. He wanted out. When the invitation came, to teach engineering rather than practice it, a flattering proposition that reinforced Arthur's belief that he was smarter than his colleagues, he decided to move the entire family west, like the pioneers did, in search of opportunity. He frequently played up this angle. They were like real and true Americans, for-tune seekers blazing a trail to a distant, less competitive environ-ment. Francine, a couples and family therapist, could start a small home practice and even volunteer at the university where he'd work. "When you get tired of listening to those upper-crust couples drone on about their lives," he'd laughed, "you can take a break and listen to their kids."

Though anyone familiar with Arthur knew his snorts were stifled snickers, Ethan's adolescence was rocked by a problem of interpreta-tion. Where Francine correctly assumed that the snort suggested Ar-thur knew his son not to be straight, Ethan thought it was a wholesale denial of his confession.

Arthur elaborated: "No, you're not." It didn't clear anything up.

Ethan jumped to his feet, toppling his chair. He fled up the stairs and into his bedroom. He fell down to his mattress and threw the duvet over his head.

The overhead light was dull through the duvet. Ethan's breath gathered in the dark, warm and dense. He wondered how long he could stay under there before he would be forced to come up for air.

There was a knock at the door a few hours later; Ethan had fallen asleep. He tentatively crossed his bedroom. Arthur stood in the doorway. Between his right thumb and forefinger was a little wire key. "We have to do it," Arthur said, "every night, no matter what."

Ethan's eyes welled with tears of anticipation. He swallowed hard, making an audible gulp that caused him to blush. He made his way back toward the bed and sat on it, staring at the wall opposite.

Arthur sat beside him. "Open," he said.

Ethan opened his mouth and tipped his head back. He tried to envision what his father was seeing: the rapid palatal expander. It was a metal bar jammed up in the roof of Ethan's mouth, held in place by branches that extended from it like spider legs, anchored to his back teeth. Arthur inserted two furry fingers into Ethan's mouth, fit the key into the screw hole at the center of the expander, and twisted. Ethan winced. A needle of pain pierced his skull. He dug his fingernails into his thighs. Bitter, metallic saliva pooled at the corners of his mouth as Arthur slowly turned the key, Ethan's jaw stretching wider with every crank. Knuckle hairs tickled his gum line and he coughed, spraying the surface of his father's reading glasses with a fine mist of saliva. Arthur wiped them dry with the sleeve of his shirt.

"I don't like it either," Arthur muttered when he finished, removing the key. Ethan tried to close his mouth but his jaw felt locked in place. A high-pitched sound whistled through his brain. His teeth were ringing. He tried to speak but Arthur was already at the door, closing it behind him.

Later that evening, Ethan slunk downstairs. His parents were in the living room, reading on the couch.

"I'm gay," he said. "Not bi."

Arthur looked over his glasses at his wife. He raised his eyebrows before lowering his gaze back to his book. Francine nodded at Ethan sympathetically. Standing there in tremendous pain, the nerve endings in his gums crying out for relief, it was hard not to feel as though the information had been tortured out of him.

Despite it all, he had to admit there was a small thrill in receiving a letter from his father. An invitation. You waited ages for your father to invite you anywhere. But when it happened, you had to wonder: Is it too late?

Ethan tossed his Companion onto a chair and tucked the envelope in his back pocket. He scanned his apartment, decorated in exactly the spare style he'd wanted. Right angles and clean surfaces. Naked brick. No photographs. Against sentimentality. He wondered what to do—with the letter, with the rest of the day. His eyes fell on the floating shelves of reclaimed pine. They stood there dumbly, parallel and bare like an equal sign on his wall.

Ethan's retreat inward had accelerated in the twenty-two months since his mother died—since he quit his job and bought the place on Carroll Street. He had ceased to be a public person, in any meaningful sense. He disliked how he was in public. His creaking voice, the timid gestures he caught sight of in reflective storefront glass. He was not at ease around people and regarded those who were with envy and suspicion. Whenever Ethan caught someone looking at him on the subway, his first thought was that he was doing something wrong. Standing wrong. Breathing wrong. Then his cheeks would flush with anger. Why should he doubt himself? Why should he make himself small, when lesser souls sat on life with their legs spread open?

Stepping out into the world had begun to feel like a shameful concession. An open admission of dependence. Whether it was food or sex or toothpaste, coming face-to-face with that refrain—*I need, I need, I need!*—made him physically ill. His fantasy of self-reliance was a bunker full of endless shelves, a lifetime supply of everything. His mother, his money—he had coped as best he could, shielding himself from need, girding himself in comfort.

It didn't help that so many public places were objectively unpleasant. Laundromats he hated in particular. The penetrating fluorescence, the pools of rusty water. When his machine went bust and he learned that the blue-awninged Suds & Duds on Union was offering a not unreasonable delivery service—the prospect of a mechanic *in his home* was unthinkable, to say nothing of fixing it himself—Ethan caved. He hadn't washed his own clothes since.

The grocery store, the deli—all delivered for a fee. In making these arrangements he found fewer and fewer reasons to go out. He streamed movies and TV. His phone brimmed with podcasts and music on demand. He ordered books online that arrived in half a day. The apartment, spacious by Brooklyn standards, multiplied in size when you considered all the media available within it.

His lifestyle had come at a cost. Strictly speaking, Ethan was in debt. He'd dropped $150,000 on the down payment for the apartment, a one-bed Neo-Grec that shared a wall with an Episcopal church, gutted the bathroom and kitchen, and redecorated with unusual pleasure, which left him with enough money for a year of voluntary unemployment and compulsive online shopping. He spent enthusiastically on housewares and other nonnecessities: Bernardaud china, a Le Creuset he never used, Waterford Lismore candlesticks, a white marble bread box, an electric corkscrew. A Williams Sonoma subscription to Six Months of American Cheese. Ethan had read somewhere that holding on to money was like clutching an ice cube, which inspired him to buy an aluminum mold from Hammacher Schlemmer that yielded perfectly proportioned balls of ice. Like a comatose patient with no DNR, his sedate lifestyle required a steady drip of funds.

He was an attentive debtor. He tracked his losses and kept meticulous files of receipts and credit card statements, his wallet growing fat with plastic. He knew exactly what he was doing when he ordered the stone-top coffee table with the hand-forged iron base. He knew what it cost to run errands in the back of cars captained by

Somalis without papers, and the price tag on the Tom Ford suit he'd ordered, though he had no occasion to wear it.

And yet for all his attentiveness, for all his foresight, the debt felt completely unreal. Numbers in columns. Debt was immaterial, a figurative abyss—and did the depth of an abyss matter when the abyss was only figurative? Metaphors were flimsier than the actual pleasure he derived from the purchases he made: Egyptian cotton bedsheets, a La Pavoni espresso machine. Financial institutions spoke in the language of community—membership, relationship, belonging—and to Ethan these words were significant. It was good to be wanted, to feel as though he belonged.

If the debt seemed illusory when Ethan was sober, it was all the more so when he was drunk. He enjoyed cocktails, but the upside of beer, thanks to the nationwide surge in microbrewing, was that it could be passed off as a hobby. He drank the spectrum, from the palest yellow wits on through to night-black stouts, pilsners and pale ales and lagers, brown ales and dunkels and porters. He was democratic in his drinking, more consumer than connoisseur, un-concerned with specifics. He'd experimented with other vices: ciga-rettes in high school, cocaine twice in college. But St. Louis was a beer town. Drinking reminded him of home.

It wasn't serious. Not really. Because of his cloistered lifestyle, he was never drunk in public, rendering him incapable of harming any-one but himself. He could stop when he wanted to. But he didn't want to. He lived according to the wisdom of those novelty T-shirts: he didn't have a drinking problem—he drank, he passed out, no problem.

At thirty-one years old, his twenties officially in rearview, he found himself alone. It was an awful realization and he seemed to make it fresh each morning. Whatever friends he'd had at the con-sulting firm where he used to work had fled the city for suburbs with better public school districts, or else were only interested in talking shop, the petty squabbles and betrayals in which Ethan was no longer invested. He recalled a time when he'd been invested—in bonuses, colleagues' weddings, the way his supervisor pissed with his hands on his hips like he was trying to intimidate the urinal. But that era was done, finished. A few months out of the loop and you realized how insubstantial all that was. It was only the buoyant shouts of the hedge funders balling in Carroll Park on Saturday mornings that made him wonder whether he was wasting his life.

His twenties. A decade of sexual internships with attractive, interesting men he should've counted himself lucky to date—men who saw in him a handsome vessel to be filled according to their wishes.

The first boyfriend he lived with, years before Carroll Street, was by all accounts a catch, fresh off the Theatre Arts track at Brown. Long-limbed and gorgeous, Shawn sported a high-and-tight undercut long before the white nationalists reclaimed it, his excellent grooming inspiring heretofore-unseen bouts of jealousy among Ethan's female coworkers. Shawn was on flirting terms with every bartender in the borough and brought Ethan to club nights with no digital fingerprint, events you had to hear about the old-fashioned way, by living in the world. That he'd grown up poor in Appalachia made his commitment to the privileges and follies of his cosmopolitan contemporaries permissible—more than that, he was a veritable success story. Being poor in pastoral Pennsylvania was not the same as being poor in New York. To be poor in New York was still a form of "making it," especially to bitter family back home, who, when asked, would simply say of Shawn, "He's in New York," which never failed to explain everything.

They met when Shawn mistook him on the sidewalk for an actor friend. "Oh, whoops," he'd said as he turned to face Ethan on the street.

"What?"

"Nothing, I—thought you were someone else."

"Oh. No," he said. "I'm me."

Shawn's eyes twinkled. "Hey. I'm on my way to this thing . . . it's at a restaurant. A bakery, actually—a boozy bakery, you know? But at night it turns into an after-hours place. Do you like dancing?"

Ethan was too startled to respond.

"Oh, come *on*, it'll be fun!"

And that was that.

Ethan was more escort than boyfriend. When Ethan wasn't out of town for work, Shawn brought him to screenings, galleries, and block parties, unable to comprehend why anyone would live in such an expensive city if they weren't going to get their money's worth. Shawn thought youth was for hoarding experience; Ethan found most experiences draining and ephemeral. Nonetheless, two months after they had met, Shawn's apartment was fumigated and he spent one awful week at Ethan's then-place in East Williamsburg, where it became clear that Ethan lacked the energy to keep up with him on weeknights, which Shawn treated like weekends, in part because he was a half-employed stage manager and in part because Ethan suspected that Shawn, shark-like, would die if he ever stopped moving. Shawn returned home a day early, eager to get back, to get away, even though the exterminators had cautioned against it, advising he wait until the toxins had aired out.

Teddy, two years later, was a better match. He was short and olive-skinned with whey-enhanced triceps and legs like matchsticks. All ambition, he'd landed a prestigious job clerking for a judge Wolfe, who was known for his staunch utilitarianism and his belief that the so-called adoption racket could be improved if couples selected children via auction.

The job gave them plenty to talk about. "Oh my god," Teddy would shout above the braggy din of a Financial District pub. "You would not *believe* what Judge Wolfe said today." He worked insane hours that almost rivaled Ethan's. When they did share a bed, every other weekend, Teddy, who thrice mentioned his "kinky side" during their first date, would lose himself in a Fleshjack while Ethan gave him a shoulder massage, after which he'd pass out, blaming his exhaustion on work and leaving Ethan in a state of rebuffed arousal. "I'm sorry, babe," he'd say, drooling into his pillow. "Next time, I swear."

The relationships soon soured. Ethan's passivity, which had allowed his partners to project such dazzling colors on him in the first

place, did not make for easy cohabitation. A canonical family anec-
dote concerned the time that a young Ethan was sitting on the
ground, drawing with crayons, when a family friend stepped on his
hand. But the man didn't notice, and stood there a good minute
while Ethan suffered quietly, trying to keep his face from publishing
his pain.

"You'll never see me again!" Shawn cried the day he left for good,
appropriately theatric, lingering at the door of Ethan's place. He
stood there a while, waiting to be called back. "You're never *present*,
Ethan. You're all hung up!" Ethan sat on his tufted love seat, toes
pointed out at mirrored angles, staring at the V between his shoes.

He liked to think he'd given up on dating before Carroll Street.
On work and being in public too. But it was the last two years on
this enviable block, where sun-gilded microgardens fragranced every foot, that had made a hermit of him. That had sealed him shut
inside his life.

THREE

While in his senior year of college, a classmate of Maggie's named Kevin Kismet invented a location-based dating app, RoseBox, which paired potential significant others on the basis of shared traumas. His idea was that race, class, educational background, taste in movies, and physical appearance were superficialities at best, and had nothing on the bonds between people who understood each other's suffering: veterans, addicts, survivors of abuse. With the help of some friends in his Mobile App Development 300 course, he built an exhaustive list of adversities and wrote them into a simple matchmaking algorithm. Users built profiles based on their collected hardships. For example: If you never knew your father, the app would seek out other users who had grown up in a single-parent home. If you once endured a difficult surgery, RoseBox would find you a partner who had also gone under the knife. If you were picked on in school—and so forth. To pretty much everyone's surprise, the app, which had begun as a homework assignment, exploded in popularity. Now, almost two years after he graduated, his company was valued in the tens of millions.

A week after fainting at Emma's birthday party, Maggie sat in a Bed-Stuy café, reading about Kismet's upcoming IPO on her phone and ignoring a string of texts from Emma. She looked up from the screen with the world-weary sigh of a much older person.

The café was squarely Warm Industrial, its walls paneled with salvaged wood beneath a maze of exposed ceiling pipes. Cage brass pendant lamps hung over crate shelves bearing burlap sacks of coffee beans. The word *boulangerie* was painted in arching gold copperplate across the street-facing window. She had chosen the café because it was roughly midway between her and Ethan's respective neighborhoods, and because it was the kind of place he would like: upscale, and resembling his apartment. (He'd allowed her to visit him there only once. The interior was stylish but impersonal, a slick aesthetic that did not permit feeling.) On the exposed brick wall behind the counter, the café manager was hanging a Warholified portrait of Toussaint Louverture as a tribute to the neighborhood she was gentrifying.

Maggie was beginning to worry that Ethan wouldn't show at all. He wasn't above bailing on her last-minute. He'd blame his absence on "social anxiety," though Maggie didn't find that defense convincing. It was a fine line between self-loathing and selfishness. They shared more than a prefix. Intelligent, sensitive, tall—here was a man with all the advantages. But what had he done with them? People with less than Ethan had accomplished much, much more. Besides, getting coffee with your sister hardly counted as "socializing," and as someone who propelled her angst outward, she had trouble understanding her brother, the private multitudes he seemed to contain. She suspected that his desperate need for privacy and his bottomless well of ennui were merely symptoms of loneliness. She thought he needed someone he could be alone *with*. All his can't-pick-up-the-phone evasiveness, all the tortured, you-wouldn't-understand posturing—it was the cri de coeur of a social animal in isolation.

She redirected her irritation back toward Kismet, then catapulted it at society writ large. It did not speak well of society at this still-early stage of the newish millennium that an idea like his was worth so much. RoseBox, with its "iconic" red heart-shaped profile border, had started as a joke. She'd heard Kismet say as much herself! At a Sig Nu charity benefit outside the student parking complex! Now that he was rich, though, Kismet had become a real cupid, proselytizing on behalf of love every chance he got, appearing on *Anderson Cooper* to preach the bonding properties of shared victimhood and rebut detractors who wondered what he did with all that data.

Maggie eyed the freelancers seated throughout the café, busily tapping their devices on the brushed-steel tables before them. Chances were that some of them were scrolling through RoseBox right now. She zeroed in on a handsomely stubbled guy by the counter with an Eye of Providence tattooed on his forearm. Maggie wondered what his issues were. OCD? Child of divorce? Touched by a priest? There were countless possibilities, all of them intriguing.

She returned to her phone and after a minute of futzing found herself on the RoseBox download page. Well, she thought, now that she was here . . . And suddenly the app was downloading and Maggie's checking account balance dropped ninety-nine cents, the money flickering between server farms before it disappeared.

Holding the device close to her chest, she built her profile. TRAUMATIC PUBERTY? Of course. ANXIETY/DEPRESSION? Not clinically, but a definite yes. HISTORY OF BEING BULLIED? Well, she *had* chaired an anti-bullying campaign in middle school. Never mind that she'd mercilessly bullied people into joining.

As the hardships grew increasingly niche and she arrived at LOSS OF PARENT AT FORMATIVE AGE, the person with whom Maggie shared this specific trauma crept through the café door.

Ethan had become handsome late enough in life that it still surprised his sister. His short hair verged unexpectedly on blond. He had the rosy cheeks of a child. He was cocooned in a cozy, shawl-collared sweater that looked as soft as handled money. His belly seemed to bulge a bit, a slightly pregnant protrusion. She hadn't seen him in at least two months, but Maggie knew him by his walk. The way he carried himself. Or failed to carry himself, hunched, like his body was a little bit much.

She stuffed her phone in her pocket and stood to greet him. They hugged across the low table, forming a letter A in profile. She felt his stomach against hers. She thought to comment on it, but she didn't want to draw attention to her own body, how fragile she'd become. But he was too wrapped up—in the sweater, in his thoughts—to notice. On the table between them, forks and knives were swaddled in napkins beside a paper card that bore the impotent command NO LAPTOPS.

"Thanks for meeting me," she said. "Did you walk here?"

"No, no," he said, tugging on the tail of a thin scarf wrapped around his neck. It unspooled on his lap. "I called a car." His eyes darted warily back and forth across the room.

"A car? That's kind of a waste, isn't it? Of money? And carbon, um—fossil fuels?"

Ethan didn't answer, and dropped his gaze to the menu. "Do you know what you want?" he asked.

"Because the G runs right by here." She crossed her arms over her chest. "You could've taken the train, is what I'm saying."

A yawning waiter took their order. Ethan asked for a black coffee, and Maggie, who wanted creamer but now felt unable to admit it, took the same. Her phone shook in her pocket, emitting a whining sound she'd never heard it make before.

"How's the place?" she asked. "Still liking the neighborhood? Are you seeing anyone?"

"Maggie, please," he sighed.

"What?"

"Ease up on the mothering."

"I'm interested! I want to help!" She drummed her fingers on the table. "What about job stuff?" she pressed. "Still just—"

"Enjoying myself," he said flatly.

"But by now you must—"

"Maggie."

"Because the cost of—"

"*Maggie.* Drop it."

"I don't understand," she said, shaking her head. "Even with everything that happened, I still can't believe you quit."

A consulting firm had hired Ethan out of college to "implement transformation imperatives," which meant explaining to business leaders twice his age how to streamline their operations. The firm sent him around the world to conduct research and present it to the Fortune 500s that could afford their services. He pinned a software company's failures on the weakness of its brand recognition; he fingered thirty employees at a healthcare NGO ripe for "vocational displacement." He'd worked a memorable case for Dr. Scholl's that involved interviewing 1,500 rural Chinese farmers on their footwear preferences. He thrived at first, the interminably long days leaving little room for introspection. He passed out in hotel beds, too exhausted to dream. But the job was taxing, and each passing year he felt increasingly ridiculous for the power he wielded, as he had little experience with software, or healthcare, or orthotics. His team's findings had been used to justify the dismissal of countless employees at companies with which Ethan had only a fleeting affiliation. The hotel beds left a stiffness in his neck. Unfortunately, his colleagues were not as tormented about their roles. They all moved up or out to brighter careers, while a continuous supply of recent college grads assumed their posts and Ethan, who was not adept at the politics of self-advancement, became something of a reluctant elder statesman.

"You called me a sellout the whole time I worked there," he said.

"You *were* a sellout! But you had something to do all day, at least."

"All that travel—"

"You didn't seem to mind it at the time. You were extremely high functioning. Okay, things got out of hand. Mom died. You crashed. But you've been down for how long now?"

"The more I thought about it, the more I realized how miserable I was."

"There's such a thing as too much thinking."

"Let's just talk about what we came here to talk about."

"Fine." Maggie dove into her coat and emerged with her father's letter, which she dropped on the table. Ethan produced an envelope of his own, which he placed on top of hers.

"You got snail mail, too, huh?" she asked. Her phone whined again.

"He went all out for sure."

"So what do you think?"

"I don't know," he said. "I'm not thrilled about the idea."

"Because of him?"

"Because of him."

It was not what Maggie had hoped to hear. Though she had no interest in seeing her father, she wanted to pay respects to her mother, and on top of that there were some items she hoped to collect in St. Louis and bring back with her to New York. Some personal effects. A thing or two of Francine's. Arthur's invitation provided her the opportunity to return home without seeming to have wanted to, and raid the house for keepsakes. "Oh," she said without conviction. "He's not so bad."

"I was thinking over what you said after the funeral. About how he's had plenty of opportunities to be present in our lives. About how it's time I realized he isn't going to change."

"Did I say that?"

"You did."

Whine.

"Well," she said, twisting a curl of hair. "I mean, sure."

"You said, and I quote, 'You spoil him with second chances.'"

"That doesn't sound like me." She couldn't go to St. Louis alone. She needed Ethan with her, to act as a buffer between her and her father. A whole weekend with Arthur, just the two of them, was unthinkable. Without Ethan, the chemical composure of the family skewed volatile. "Maybe this time it's different. He wrote us, after all. *He* invited *us.*"

"I'm honestly shocked to hear this from you."

"We can visit Mom."

"'Spoiled with second chances,' you said."

"That doesn't sound like me at all."

The waiter reemerged, clanking their coffees on the table with botched flourish. Maggie raised the mug to her mouth, blowing folds across the dark surface.

Ethan took a sip and drew in a sharp breath. "Oh, *shit.*"

"Hot?"

"No," he said, lowering his head and making a visor of his hand. "Behind you. Coming out of the men's room. Don't look."

Maggie jerked around in her chair. A tall, muscular blond with the sides of his head shaved was taking his seat at a table in the back.

"I said, don't look."

"Who's the neo-Nazi?" she asked.

He shushed her. "Keep it down."

She turned to look at him again. "He's cute. If you're into Übermenschen."

"Let's go," Ethan said.

"We just got our coffee!"

"Fuck, fuck, fuck." He ducked his head.

Whine.

"Is that you?" he asked.

"No. Yeah. I don't know. Promise you'll think about it." Her phone whined again.

"Will you turn that thing off?" he snapped.

"Hey," called a voice from behind her. "Ethan!"

"*Shit,*" he whispered. Ethan sat up in his chair. "Shawn!" he said, waving.

The blond sauntered over to their table. "It's good to see you!"

"You too." Ethan stood and put one arm around Shawn's shoulder before sitting again. "This is my sister, Maggie."

"Hey."

"Hey." Shawn cocked his head. "Been a while, handsome!"

"Yeah."

Maggie coughed.

"I'm actually glad I ran into you," Shawn said. "I dropped my phone in the toilet last week and lost, like, all my numbers. But I'm having a little get-together . . . well, not so little—I'm actually getting married this spring?" He raised his left hand. A gleaming gold band hugged his ring finger.

"Congratulations."

"Well, and so, there are these boats? They leave from Hell's

Kitchen and go down the Hudson, to the Statue of Liberty and back. Really slow, though. You're on the water for six hours. So we're doing that. A little, not-so-little party. To celebrate. You should come, Ethan. I met my fiancé on one of these things. It's kind of full circle for us."

"Thanks, but I'm not sure that's my type of—"

"You haven't changed a bit! Come on, Ethan. It'll be *fun*. A boozy cruise down the Hudson. We have at least a hundred people coming. Maybe you'll meet someone!"

"I don't know . . ."

"I won't take no for an answer."

"When is it?"

"Yay! The eleventh. The second Saturday of April."

Maggie's eyes bugged wide. She nodded vigorously at the letters on the table between them.

"Oh!" said Ethan. "I can't."

"No?" said Shawn. "Why not?"

"I'm going to St. Louis with my sister."

Shawn pouted. "Oh, well."

Maggie's phone whined again. She tore it from her pocket, muttering, "What, what, *what!*" A stack of push notifications from Rose-Box informed her that there were six people with matching damages nearby.

"Well, it was good to see you," Shawn said. "You look good. You always looked good, Ethan." And with that he returned to his table.

"Glad to see you had a change of heart," said Maggie.

"Yeah, yeah." Ethan sipped his coffee.

"If you bail on me, I'll tell him you're free after all. I'll find him and I'll tell him. You know I will."

"What did that mean, 'You always looked good'?"

"It's a compliment."

"Did you hear an undertone? I heard an undertone."

"You're insane."

The bell above the café door rang. A large man in a gray hoodie lumbered inside. The hoodie read *Champion* and the kangaroo pocket had been torn off. His beard was thorny and stained yellow at the mouth. In his right hand was a large plastic bag full of other, smaller plastic bags. The manager rushed over and shooed him back out the door.

"Hey," Ethan said suddenly. "What was it you used to call Mom?"

"Huh?"

"You know." He waved a hand around his head, tracing an invisible corona.

"Oh, right. 'Madame Furry.'"

"Because she had that—"

"Coat, yeah." Maggie fluffed her hair. "With the fur-trim hood."

"Madame Furry. Right."

"I thought it made her look aristocratic."

"Yeah."

"Like a queen."

The cardinal regret of Maggie's life was that she hadn't been with her mother when she died. After all the time she'd spent at Barnes-Jewish Hospital, pacing the antiseptic halls of the Monsanto Cancer Center, falling asleep at her mother's bedside, she was absent at the moment that mattered most. Even worse was where she'd been instead: on a river in the Ozarks, lying tipsy on a raft, floating lazily toward graduation.

If there was a better portrait of civilization-threatening entitlement than two hundred wasted undergrads in inner tubes clogging the Meramec River in Missouri, Maggie couldn't name it. Boys with dad guts and girls in tan-ready positions, tops unhooked and asses gently raised. Coolers full of sun-soured beer. Coolers with their own rafts. Entire floating apparatuses devoted to the coolers, loose cans floating downstream beside them like obedient pets. Cozies and anklets and tank tops, sunglasses in any one of six different colors with the Danforth University logo stamped across the temples. Everything snaking down the river, one of the largest free-flowing in Missouri, churning so slowly it seemed almost to be moving backward.

She was riding with Mikey and his best friend, Feinstein, who lay passed out next to her. The boys bought into Senior Week—seven days of tuition-sponsored outings for the graduating class—with shameless sincerity, and after Maggie balked at Cardinals tickets, trivia night, and the gala in the botanical gardens, which Feinstein obnoxiously pronounced *gay*-la, she felt obliged to join them on the float trip.

She should have been at Barnes-Jewish, humbling herself by a hospital bed.

"I don't see why you can't enjoy yourself this once," Mikey had said, catching a mosquito in flagrante and mashing it against his leg. Maggie pretended not to hear him. He went on about his nana being sick some years before, how she wouldn't have wanted him to mope and grumble all day long about it.

"You know," she said, "it's not the same thing at all, actually."

But he was right, in a way. She was determined to hate the float trip. By hating it she could not be accused of enjoying herself for even one moment while her mother slowly perished.

"It's like you're *trying* to be miserable," he said.

She burned at just how right he was, and wondered where those skills of perception had been for the past five months of their, whatever, thing.

Feinstein was a beer snob and had assured them he would "handle it" vis-à-vis float drinks. But his twelve-can bounty of small-batch IPAs was drying Maggie out beneath the fat sun, and there were still three hours left on the trip. The uniformity of their surroundings and the rafts' imperceptible velocity obliterated space. There was only time, and much too much of it. A thread of cloud broke in the distance. A different mosquito kept returning to the same bulbous bite on Maggie's ankle. After Mikey had her pinch a pimple on his back and after Feinstein woke to tan his belly, splotched with moles, she found she could stomach the boys no longer, and vomited over the side of the raft.

Francine died later that same hour.

The float trip was supposed to be her one indulgence. Her one brief respite from the barbed beep of the PCA pump, the groan of convulsing MRI coils, the pervasive smell of puke and the peroxide cover-up. The drips. And she had been—rightly, she felt—punished for it.

After coffee with her brother, she called Mikey and invited herself over to his apartment.

Their breakup had been needlessly impulsive. That much she was willing to admit. He was a good-natured kid, considerate and generous, but one afternoon, toying with his laptop, she'd discovered an endless YouTube cache of interviews with prominent New Atheists. She endured forty-three seconds of measured Islamophobia before storming into the steamy bathroom of their Midtown apartment and announcing to Mikey that she was moving out. The shock caused him to slip in the shower. He brought the curtain down with him.

He'd taken the breakup pretty hard, though she knew he had grievances of his own. He hated when she reduced the heroes of his favorite movies to disorders from the DSM. ("Scarface isn't a narcissistic personality!" he'd shout. "He's just Scarface!") In any case, she gathered that he was doing well for himself, having moved from Midtown to Williamsburg.

"Williamsburg?" she said, when he opened the door.

He was doughier than when she'd seen him last, and balder, though he looked, somehow, younger, less like a man than a toddler with baby fat to spare and hair still growing in. "You know when people talk about this neighborhood being 'over,'" she said, "it's because of people like you."

"Good to see you too."

"Sorry. I'm in a mood."

"We're all in moods. You can't not be." He leaned in for a hug.

"Maggie!" came a voice from the couch.

"Well, shit," she whispered into Mikey's shoulder. Behind him, in the living room, she could see Feinstein's nest of curly hair jutting

out from the far end of a beige IKEA sleeper sofa. A movie was playing on the TV in front of him, a documentary following an American violinist on a cultural tour of China. "What's *he* doing here?"
she asked.

"Visiting," said Mikey. "I took the day off to see him. You know
I work, right? You can't just barge in on a weekday afternoon."

Maggie shrugged. "Worked this time."

Feinstein sat up and made room on either side of him. Mikey sat
on his left. Maggie stood on the other side of the sofa.

"Grab a seat," said Feinstein. His eyes were hidden underneath a
fringe of hair, his cheeks sooty with stubble.

"I'm fine," she said.

"Feinstein's visiting from Boulder."

Maggie feigned interest. "What are you doing out there?" she said.

"Guess," Feinstein smiled.

Maggie rolled her eyes.

"I work at a holistic dispensary."

"Got it."

The American violinist was berating a group of young Chinese
musicians on the television. "It's not just about technical profi-
ciency!" he shouted.

"Yeah," said Feinstein. "There's a lot of money to be made out
there. I mean it, Maggie. A *lot*."

"Since when are you so entrepreneurial? Weren't you a chem
major?"

"My parents think I'm in med school."

"Jeez," said Maggie. "How have you kept that up?"

Feinstein shrugged. "It's easy. They don't ask a lot of questions."

Mikey mouthed the word *divorce* across the couch.

"Oh. Sorry to hear that," Maggie said aloud.

"Hear what?"

Mikey looked away.

"This time, with *feeling*!" raved the violinist.

"Um, nothing," Maggie said. "Hey, Feinstein, do you mind if I talk to Mikey alone? In his room?"

"Sure thing," said Feinstein. "Whatever you say."

Maggie gestured to Mikey. He rose, slowly, and led her down the hall.

"I didn't know Feinstein was in town," said Maggie, as soon as the door shut behind them.

"He's having a hard time," Mikey explained. "Divorce proceedings. Both of his parents summoned him to testify on their behalf."

"I don't want to talk about that."

"Okay." He scratched the back of his neck. "I'm actually glad you're here. It's good to see you. I know you said we're meant for other things and other people, but—I still like seeing you."

Her eyes watered. Spending time with Mikey—and Feinstein, for that matter—made her feel as though she was still an undergrad at Danforth. As though his presence alone sent her back in time, back to college, to St. Louis. Back before her mother died.

"Do you ever talk about me?" he asked.

"Come here," she said, and kissed him.

"But . . . Feinstein . . . ," he muttered, as she pulled his shirt over his head. They shed their clothes and fell onto his mattress, sheeted with the baby blue blankets that she recognized from college.

She climbed on top of him and drew him into her. She brought her face to his and kissed his neck. But no matter how much she shut it out, her mind returned to the Meramec. The heat. Her parched mouth.

She closed her eyes.

There had been a time when Maggie enjoyed sex. She'd slept with a few other boys in college, and while she could appreciate the informality of campus hookups, the culture turned you into an emotional puritan. Mikey had been the rare guy who wasn't afraid to show interest. They quickly fell into a routine, the sex decent and about as mutually beneficial as it could be with a young conservative. But since her mother's death, she'd become all too aware of the harm a body could cause, the damage it could do to itself and others. For nearly two years now she'd been chasing the unburdened pleasure she'd once felt, enveloping Mikey in search of it, and coming up short each time.

"Have you lost weight?" he whispered.

She put a hand over his mouth. A prickling heat crawled up her body. She looked up at the *Scarface* poster on the wall before her, the books piled on the bedside table. *The Alchemy of Finance. The Case for Israel.*

"I'm sorry," she said. "I can't."

"Can't what?"

Her vomit sloshing into the river.

Maggie swallowed. "*The Alchemy of Finance?* Not exactly a turn-on."

"Says the trust fund baby."

"What was that?" She rolled off him and lay on her back, crossing her arms over her breasts. "Shut up."

"I'm sorry."

"Why would you say something like that?"

"Maggie," he pleaded. "I'm *sorry.*"

"You can finish yourself off."

He shut his eyes and placed a hand on Maggie's thigh. A minute later, with a groan and a twitch, he stopped moving.

"I don't know what I'm doing," she said.

They lay side by side in silence. Mikey's breath slowed to a normal pace. Then he asked if her dad was in town.

Maggie made a gagging sound. "I'm naked. You're naked. What kind of question is that?"

"Is he?"

"No . . ."

"Did you recently see him?"

"No."

"What about your brother?"

She turned red. "Why do you care?"

"Just wondering."

"Wondering."

"Because in college, you only initiated sex when you wanted to blow off steam."

"Not true!"

"I'm thinking post-Thanksgiving, post–winter break, Parents' Weekend . . ."

"Okay, okay, okay!"

There it was again, that perceptiveness. Maybe she had underestimated Mikey. Though, in fairness, he was easy to underestimate. Or, at least, to estimate. He was a Jewish boy from White Plains. She never had to ask about his past because she could assume it: summer camp, Maccabi Games, bar mitzvah speech co-authored by helicopter parent. SATs, Birthright, *Portnoy*.

"You know," she said, "It's not a 'trust fund.' My situation does not make me a 'trust fund baby.' You realize that, right?"

"What's the difference?"

"You are so callous!"

"Seriously, what's the difference?"

"First of all, it's not in a *trust*. It's an *inheritance* I received after suffering a *personal loss*. Second, I didn't grow up knowing about it. I lack the trust fund baby *mentality*, which is what people mean when they say 'trust fund baby' in the first place. And, thirdly, I've renounced it!"

"Oh yeah?"

"Yes!"

"Except that you haven't, though, have you?"

"I'm going to!"

"You can't say you've renounced money that's still in the bank. Under your name."

Maggie grunted.

"I'm sorry. Listen . . ."

Mikey's problem, Maggie realized, had less to do with his moral character than it did his trajectory in life. Here was a fundamentally good person who had grown up too fast. Global finance, weight gain, political conservatism: this was not the life of a twentysomething. Whereas Maggie—she was doing it right, capitalizing on her youth and disseminating the perks of her privilege, all in the most effective way possible . . .

"Are you listening?" he asked. "I said, I still care about you."

"I should go."

"Stay. Please. Talk to me."

Maggie shook her head. "I'd rather die than live a superfluous life."

And besides, she was due back in Queens. The M train carried her east past the top floors of ruined warehouses, their windows shattered or blown out, the neighborhoods degentrifying, dilapidating, falling into honest ruin as she went. Debarking at Myrtle-Wyckoff, she ran to meet the Nakahara brothers at their school. Oksana was working late and her husband was in bed with the flu.

The boys attended a charter school housed within a century-old Methodist nursing home, an improbable Victorian pile just removed from the street by a narrow strip of campus as if to say, *Look at me, ahem.* The roof shot up with spikes and spires. Pale stones rippled through the patterned brickwork. Litter clumped throughout the yard where four basketball hoops—no backboards—stretched skyward, slim poles and rims in raw space.

Maggie made it in time, at three o'clock, as children began seeping through the rasping gates, carting their tiny backpacks and lunchboxes. Bruno and Alex were among the last to appear, escorted by a severe-looking authority figure in a wool cardigan and an obvious wig. Alex ran ahead while Bruno walked hangdog beside his captor.

"Do these belong to you?" she asked.

"Um . . . ," said Maggie.

"You're the nanny, yes?"

"I'm more of a mentor-slash-tutor, or think 'life coach' minus the New Age gibberish."

"Well whatever you are, this one here needs to learn that violence doesn't solve anything," she said, one hand clamped to Bruno's neck. "He assaulted a poor little boy today."

"Bruno," Maggie said.

"I take it you'll be punishing him?" the woman asked.

"All right."

"Promise?"

"Excuse me?"

"I'm not comfortable releasing this boy until you promise me that you'll be disciplining him."

"Yeah, okay, fine. Come on, guys." They set off for the boys' apartment.

"It's not my fault," Bruno muttered.

"It's not," chimed Alex. "He doesn't have a girlfriend. I have two, and do I look like the kind of person with anger problems?"

"That's a dollar for the jar," Maggie said. "And we don't have anger problems."

"Yeah," said Bruno. "It's ODD."

"What actually happened?"

Bruno explained. Apparently, he'd been outed during recess when a classmate, Trevor Kwan, correctly identified Bruno's flip phone as being six years obsolete. Worse, Trevor had swiped the clunky thing, which didn't technically work, seeing as Bruno's father had trashed the battery years earlier and Bruno had been using the old phone as a prop, making loud fake calls at recess. At which point the Kwans, Trevor's gang, began chanting "No-phone! No-phone! No-phone!" while tossing the silver Motorola over Bruno's head.

"So," Bruno explained, "I punched him in the teeth." He raised an arm. His hammy knuckles were battered with dents and scratches.

"Guys," she said, "I thought we talked about this. About conflict resolution? And how we handle ourselves at school? You have to know that I worry about you as much as your mom does. And not because it's my job. You guys are like family to me."

"Our mom doesn't worry," Alex said.

"That's not true!"

"No, it is," said Alex. "She told us: 'I don't worry about you.' Two of her cousins got cancer from Chernobyl. She said: 'I have bigger worries than you.'"

"Okay," said Maggie, "well—okay. Just be safe at school, okay? For my sake."

"It's my disease." Bruno shrugged. "Nothing to be done about it."

That evening, having exhausted her patience with everyone in her life, but still feeling terribly lonely, Maggie accepted an invitation to her aunt's house for dinner.

For Ethan, who contrived an excuse not to attend, these trips out to New Jersey were a hassle. Maggie made them out of solidarity. Though her aunt's lifestyle confounded Maggie, Bex was still her closest link to her mother, and a companion in grief.

You could never grieve too long for women like her mother. Eagle-eyed but never critical, intelligent without the need to show it, Francine had selflessly sacrificed career advancement for the preservation of her family—for which she'd served as moderator, referee, and peacekeeping body. She was, to Maggie, both a role model and a cautionary tale. A case study in what women were expected to be, and what they had to give up to be it.

An hour before sundown, as Maggie surfaced at 175th Street, Bex pulled up in a military-grade SUV. "My baby!" she gushed, stamping Maggie's cheeks with kisses. Her skin was taut and fragrant, tugged back by a ponytail and viscous from her liberal application of a guava-enriched moisturizer. She ran her fingers through Maggie's coiled hair.

"God, it's soft."

"Thanks."

"Like your mom's is. Was."

"Bex . . ."

"Ahh," she said, dabbing at her lashes with a tissue. "Look at me, all emotional. This is a happy occasion."

"Occasion?"

"Everyone's excited to see you, gorgeous."

"Everyone?"

"Everyone! It's Shabbat, beautiful."

"Oh," said Maggie, "I guess I forgot. I'm not exactly . . ." She looked down at her black jeans, months unwashed and crusty with line-of-duty splatter from the Nakaharas. "It's been a long day."

"Don't worry. You can borrow some clothes. You look thin!"

Maggie shrunk in her seat, the prickling heat returning to her cheeks.

Bex looked her over as they crossed the George Washington Bridge. "Your mother used to give me a hard time when we were girls. I would skip meals before a big date, that kind of thing. Francine wasn't having it. She was a therapist before she was a therapist, you know?"

"I know."

"And that's all I'll say about it."

Bex had Francine's warm, dark eyes. Her head down, Maggie stole glances at her aunt's uncanny face while the civilian tank rolled through the open-air Lexus dealership that was New Jersey.

Maggie liked her aunt, or at least took a sociological interest. Bex Goldin of Bergen County, born Rebecca Klein in Dayton, Ohio, had, some thirteen years earlier, married Levi Goldin, heir to the tristate area's largest asset appraisal and liquidation company. In addition to the Jersey palace, he and Bex kept an Aspen house, where he had once made Maggie's father plunge a steak knife into the frozen earth because he'd sliced cheese with it.

"What's new?" Bex asked, nearly running a sedan off the road.

"Not much. I'm thinking of going to see my dad in St. Louis."

"Arthur? Oh, Maggie . . ."

"You don't think I should?"

"Look—he's your father, not mine. You can't shut him out forever. Although I wouldn't blame you if you did."

"I can handle it."

"I know you can, gorgeous. But stay on guard, okay? I don't want you getting hurt. You can never be too careful."

A tall iron gate permitted them into the compound. The Goldins' tremendous house, protected from the street by a long, narrow driveway, concealed behind it a swimming pool and clay tennis court. An engraving of a compass rose was etched into the courtside walkway, a concrete circle nested in the brick, with Maggie's cousins' names inscribed beside each cardinal direction: Ezra (N), Lauren (E), Maxine (W), and their dog, Solomon (S). At its end, the driveway widened into a paved plaza where no fewer than three cars were ever parked.

"Come inside," said Bex. "Come come come. The kids are excited to see you."

Mirrors of different sizes and shapes hung assorted near the kitchen entrance. The icy adornments had a chilling effect, populating the space with cool reflections. Maggie saw Lauren and Maxine glide across the surface of a hallway mirror seconds before they appeared in front of her.

"Say hi to your cousin," Bex instructed.

The girls grumbled. They were twins, fourteen years old and hiding beneath curtains of black hair.

"Give her a kiss," said Bex. She'd picked up this habit from her husband's family. It wasn't an unwelcome gesture, but compared to the Goldins, Alters tended not to touch.

"*Fine,*" said Lauren, and the girls pecked Maggie on her cheeks.

"Teens," said Bex, rolling her eyes and making cuckoo circles with her finger to her ear.

The hallway led to an airy salon with a white piano and matching white chesterfield sofas. Maxine scurried to the piano and began plunking random keys.

"Going to play something for Maggie?" Bex called. "No? Okay. Maybe later."

She gestured for Maggie to follow her up the stairs. "Ez-ra," she called. "Your cousin Maggie's here! Come give her a kiss and let her help you with your homework!" She turned to her niece. "You don't mind, do you?"

They found him sitting on the floor of his room beneath a mounted wall-sized chalkboard labeled EZRA'S GRAFFITI WALL in bubble letters. "Come down for dinner in twenty," Bex said. "I'll lay out some things for you to wear."

"So," said Maggie, after Bex had gone downstairs. "What are you working on?"

Ezra groaned and knocked on the cover of a textbook on the floor beside him. *Imperialism Reconsidered: A Primer.*

"You're in sixth grade?"

He nodded. Maggie thought of the Nakaharas' crumbling school, and the penises littering Bruno's homework.

"We're doing Africa," Ezra explained. He waved a xeroxed map of the continent, labeled 1881–1914. "We each get to be a country. I'm England. I have to color in the places that I want and then tomorrow in class we're gonna fight over them."

"The places you want?"

"Yeah. For like, resources." Ezra took a red Magic Marker to Algeria.

"Do you need any help?" Maggie asked.

Ezra looked up. "Can you get me a Capri Sun?"

After begrudgingly fetching her cousin the wrong kind of laminated juice pouch ("Wild cherry? I hate wild cherry"), Maggie wandered the upstairs hall. She counted two, three, four spare bedrooms for guests. Or refugees! Lots were pouring in from the Middle East and thereabouts. There was a civil war on in Syria. It was an incontrovertible fact: there were always going to be people who needed rooms, and there were always empty rooms in Bex's house. It was that kind of opulent waste that frustrated Maggie to no end. The thought was enough to make you loathe your blood relations.

She found her way to the master bedroom. An outfit was laid out on the bed for her. But she gravitated toward a marble countertop instead, where she found a neat row of necklaces displayed on a long velvet pillow. She looked to the doorway behind her. She listened for footsteps. Nothing. Emboldened by her aunt's spacious house and her cousin's entitlement, Maggie justified the swiping of a rose gold chain, so thin and fine it seemed to be made of air, letting it fall into her pocket to be pawned in the name of some greater purpose.

She rearranged the others to fill the vacancy on the pillow. "Maggie, Ez-zie, din-ner!" she heard Bex call from below, in a voice that sounded nothing like her conscience. She ignored the ensemble on the bed and went downstairs in her street clothes.

A mafia of Goldins had gathered in the dining room. Tan women stood leggy in short skirts, heels hoisting them above their husbands. Maggie made the requisite rounds, hugging the rhinoplastied women of Levi's family, all of whom lived in colossal homes nearby and convened for Shabbat every Friday night on a rotating basis. "Maggie," said her aunt, clearly at pains to ignore her niece's crusty jeans, "you remember Sarah, and Alexis, and Adam, and Leila, and Justin, and Madison . . ."

She felt two massive hands on the back of her neck. Her uncle. He turned her around and enveloped her in a robust hug.

Levi was six foot something and extremely fit. Duty bound, at eighteen he had pilgrimaged to Israel in order to voluntarily enroll in the IDF's paratrooper division, a fact that seemed to hover above his slick head, not unlike a tiny paratrooper, anytime she saw him. "I'm glad you could join us," he said.

The room hushed as two sheepskin-boot-clad granddaughters escorted Sol Goldin, paterfamilias, into the room. He paused to lean delicately forward and pet the dog that bore his name. Sol wore a pink shirt with a patterned inner lining and suspenders, his sleeves rolled up over woolly white arms. He greeted heads of family one by one, appraising each of their faces. His wife, Doris, looked on approvingly.

When he reached Maggie, she found herself in an involuntary bow, which he answered by kissing her forehead.

There was something unsettling about the orderliness with which the dinner proceeded, everyone sitting only after Solomon sat, eating only after he began to eat. Talk mostly concerned Ezra's upcoming bar mitzvah. Who would cater, what to wear, how he was progressing with his Torah portion.

"Are you practicing?" Doris asked him.

"Yes, Grandma."

"Good boy."

Across the dining room table, over roast chicken and a London broil—Maggie doubled up on stuffed cabbage—Levi asked after Ethan.

"He's good. I saw him earlier today, actually."

"Where is he?"

"Oh, yeah, he says—he's sorry he can't make it. Something came up."

Her uncle scoffed. "What could have come up? He doesn't have a job!"

Levi was the kind of lesser magnate who believed that everyone should have a job, irrespective of his or her net worth. That there was dignity in neckties, purpose to be found in fishbowl conference rooms. Although, come to think of it, Maggie didn't know how *he* spent *his* time, what actually comprised the day-to-day of a professional vulture. She knew he played tennis. That was all. Before Francine died, Levi used to challenge Arthur every time he visited, though Maggie's father always deflected. "What Levi doesn't understand," he told his family every time they left New Jersey, "is that tennis—played at our level, that is—is a game of skill, not strength. Levi lacks the former. Now the pros, of course, need both." He'd turn to Maggie in the backseat. "Your uncle is a big guy," he said, "but Daddy would wipe the floor with him."

"Oh, well," said Maggie. "You never know with Ethan."

"And you?" asked Levi. "Are you working?"

"Here," said Bex, "let me go get some tea. Does anybody want tea?"

"I work."

"Oh?"

"Babysitting, tutoring, that kind of thing."

"I mean *work* work."

"Work work?"

"You're not going to be an errand girl forever."

Maggie bristled. She knew that Levi was aware of the inheritance. Francine's money meant little to him, his family fortune dwarfing hers by orders of magnitude, but she could tell he wanted to know what she would do with it. What her next move was. The necklace burned in her pocket.

"What's your dream job?" asked Alexis, or Madison. A whole arc of the table was listening now.

"I'm majoring in business!" offered Leila.

Across the table, Sol had fallen asleep. "I think my work is meaningful," Maggie said. "Helping people in my neighborhood."

"Depends," her uncle replied, "on what you mean by 'work.'" He sat up straight the way men often did, to remind you of their physical dominance. "Listen. It's like this. We work to survive. In the jungle, in the desert, wherever, you hunt or you die. You catch food or you don't eat. Survival. But, you'll say, we're not in the desert any longer! Correct. And what comes after survival? Look. I have a saying. 'First survive, then thrive.' It's the same instinct on a different level. You don't understand this yet, because you're not a parent, but once you've ensured your stability, you turn next to your children. *Their* security. And then *their* children. So they never have to work like you did." He considered this, and nodded. "And still, it's necessary, work. I also say: 'You retire, you expire.' Show me a man who quit his job at thirty-five and I'll show you a soul in decay. We were not meant to be idle. See? That's the trick of it. You work and work and work toward the inadvisable goal of never having to work."

Maggie had a strong conviction that her uncle was wrong. That his ideas were self-serving and vainglorious. That he was not accounting for big, out-of-her-depth abstractions like, say, the interconnectedness of the global marketplace and the ethical responsibilities of the wealthy. "Work is—" she began, hoping to refute him, but suddenly she felt as though she'd looked down while crossing a rickety rope bridge. Like she'd noticed the thrashing river below, the fraying cables, the rotten wood.

Mercifully, Bex returned from the kitchen to interrupt her, a silver tray balanced on her palm. "Doesn't she look gorgeous?" she said, stroking Maggie's hair with her free hand. "I would kill to be that age again."

Levi nodded. "Yes," he said. "A girl like her always has options."

FOUR

The previous week, Arthur Alter woke and realized that he missed his children.

Saturday morning. Seven o'clock. An abrasive, scouring sunlight found his face. Outside, pre-meds and math majors and other dermabrasioned nondrinkers milled about the green while the rest of Extended Campus slept off its hangover. A window was cracked open in the bedroom to accommodate the spring draft. Particles of undergraduate chatter blew in through the fissure from the quad.

He sat up slowly, wary of his worsening back, and dragged his legs over the side of the bed. Beside him, Ulrike was still asleep on her stomach. Resting on her bedside table Arthur noticed, for the first time, the cover of the dog-eared novel she'd been reading. In the jacket photo, a proud acacia tree foregrounded an orange sun. He took offense at its earnest, dawn-of-man orientalism, but then again this was Ulrike's apartment, and he supposed she could read what she wanted.

Ulrike lived in a small, faculty-sponsored one-bedroom situated in the basement of a raucous freshman dorm on Danforth's West Forty, a parcel of land for underclassmen housing named for its vast acreage. It was a demeaning existence, Arthur thought—down there, beneath a bed of hormones, Ulrike was a veritable den mother, a chaperone, a bridge troll—but it was subsidized, and he had no grounds to judge. Lately he'd been living there too.

Arthur's shoulders popped as he rolled them. He and Ulrike

were up half the previous night, their voices raw with argument, sparring over a fellowship offer that would take her to Boston for a year. She told him she was seriously considering it, said it was effectively a no-brainer, career-wise. Which presented an interesting opportunity for Arthur. Ulrike leaving town would be the perfect epoch ender, a conclusion to the Two-Years' Guilt. It would spare him the mess of ending the affair himself. (Ulrike was thirty-five, and Arthur did not believe women when they said they didn't want children.) But what would become of him without her? His kids were gone. His house was verging on foreclosure. His career was in a coffin, ignored by even the thirstiest of academic vampires. Without Ulrike around, he'd have to confront the loneliness that had frightened him into her arms in the first place. But she had been party to, and in many ways responsible for, the implosion of his life; he had knit his fate to hers; she seemed to actually *like* him. He had talked her into staying. Into considering staying, at least. "A pedophilic priest and the biomedical industry walk into a bar," he'd said, "and it's a sports bar. That's Boston. That's where you'd be moving. Trust me. You'll hate it there."

He lumbered to the kitchenette. He fished through her cabinet for something to eat and pulled out a box of Cocoa Scabs. His left arm, which he'd slept on, buzzed at his side. He could hear Ulrike breathing into her pillow in long, chunky sighs. The tiny, teen-adjacent apartment, her Teutonic snore—though Arthur had been slow to admit it, these were more than minor irritants. He depended on them. They were the very materials of his life.

The Two-Years' Guilt began with Ulrike, at the faculty mixer where they met. She was beguiling in all the old terrible ways: caustic, young, German. A recent hire. A medievalist in the history department.

"A medievalist," Arthur repeated. He tossed back his pinot grigio and made a fist around the empty Dixie cup. "I thought we only funded the digital humanities now."

"Well," she said, her W something of a V, the German language idling on her breath like an after-dinner mint, "I must be the exception that is proof to the rule." Arthur was intrigued enough not to question her use of the idiom.

The evening was hosted and organized by the Committee for Interdisciplinary Progress. An outgrowth of the cancerous mass that was the university's endowment, the CIP threw mandatory social functions for professors of differing specialties. Attendees were chosen at random, like jury duty. They hated it, like jury duty. But failure to attend was met with the vague threat of "professional probation," which untenured faculty like Arthur couldn't chance. The committee's hope, he could only assume, was that placing tipsy pedants with competing worldviews in a room together would result in some kind of profitable invention for which the university could take credit. Mostly the profs stood around, self-segregated by discipline, humanities congregating by the snack table while STEM clustered closer to the pews. Ulrike had wandered over to the wooden bench where Arthur stood.

Ever since his fortieth birthday, a quarter century ago, Arthur had been coming to terms with the fact that women no longer regarded him sexually. His solution, since he and Francine were rarely intimate, was to ignore sex as best he could. To disregard women as they'd done him. (This was an ambitious self-denial, even for Arthur, but he managed it, thanks in part to a strict regimen of early-morning masturbation, which kept him thinking clearly until at least the afternoon.) But he couldn't help register the lithe medievalist. And she, miraculously, seemed to register him.

"Speaking of digital humanity," she said, raising her phone. On the screen, an image of a flannelled hipster, boxed by the heart-shaped frame of a popular dating app. "I'm thirty-five years old. This is the kind of man they match me with. Do you agree that I deserve better?"

He did.

"Let's have a look," he said.

Arthur put himself behind her, chin hovering above his colleague's sloping collarbone. He watched her swipe left through the pictures. The jersey-wearing, toasted-ravioli-eating beer bellies that filled her phone made him feel overqualified. Confident. Though Arthur was objectively out of his league with Ulrike, who was tall enough to observe the yarmulke-sized crop circle on his head, the two of them laughed their way through suitor after suitor. God, he thought, technology could be beautiful: vanquishing paramours with the swipe of a finger while a German woman's thighs brushed against his.

"I will never understand the men here," she said, tucking the phone into her back pocket.

"Men here?" Arthur asked. "Or men in general?"

Ulrike laughed. "Here, I think."

"American men take a long time to grow up."

"Is this true?"

"'Prolonged adolescence.' I read a *Times* article about it last week. Which means it'll get a write-up in the *Post-Dispatch*, oh, I don't know, about a year from now."

She laughed. Arthur's heart quickened. "I have had bad experiences with the men here," she said.

Arthur bowed. "Then you and I will get along. Provided you don't mind another bad experience."

"Did you know," she said, "that before this I had never heard of a St. Louis, Missouri." She pronounced it *misery*.

Arthur smiled. "Say that again."

"Missouri?"

"Yes."

He was surprised at his enchantment with her, at his capacity for desire. Ulrike was unlike any woman he had ever been attracted to. Though Arthur knew the wanton truth behind the Ass Man vs. Tits Man debate—the answer was always "both"—he made note that this intriguing woman looked absolutely nothing like his wife. Francine was spheroid, orbicular: ample breasted, round faced, curly haired. The medievalist had a stylishly flat chest, braless under her blazer, with less of a butt than the humble culmination of two powerful legs. She was Francine's opposite, in physical terms. No, he thought—more than that. More than an opposite: a repudiation.

Three paper cups of wine later they returned to her dorm apartment and consummated their flirtation.

The night of November 10. A date iron-branded on his brain. He'd been forced to dredge it up, to return to the scene of the crime in his calendar, when his daughter, some months later, accused him of "lining up a mistress as soon as Mom got sick." Which wasn't true in the slightest. The news of Francine's breast cancer had come, fatefully, the *following* day.

And with it, the guilt.

That first night with Ulrike did not even inch the needle of his moral compass. Things had become so antagonistic with Francine that an affair felt more like an evolution than a betrayal. Their marriage had grown stagnant in St. Louis together, she resentful of the move, he resentful of her resentment, and that he had nothing to show for himself at sixty-five, while his contemporaries were retiring to rest deservedly on their laurels. Which is not to say he didn't love his wife in some deep, irrefutable way. But it was the love one has for a colleague, a professional rival with whom one has shared office space for decades. He depended on her, banked on her, needed her to remind him who he was and where he fit. But they did not make each other happy.

As he let himself tip backward onto Ulrike's bed for the first time—as his body bent from y-axis to x and Ulrike positioned her knees at (1,0) and (-1,0)—Arthur, for whom temptation had always been manageable, his lust powerful if easily quenched by a few quick minutes in a faculty bathroom stall, allowed himself, for once, some pleasure. Arthur, he of the hereditary thrift, who denied himself everything, who spent decades flouting material culture, allowed himself the most material pleasure there was. You couldn't think your way out of sex. You couldn't outsmart it. You could only give in or try in vain to spurn it.

He gave in.

They fucked most often at Ulrike's apartment. They did it, occasionally, in his office, twice spilling the real dirt at the base of his plastic dieffenbachia. In these impassioned fits, far away from chemo and head wraps and pills, Arthur reacquainted himself with his tumescence—hot, crimson, spiteful, happy; the unambiguous dumb thrill of a woman whispering *cock* and meaning his. In the surplus minutes of his day, in order to ward off thoughts of death, he imagined Ulrike straddling his face, her nub growing into his mouth like a seedling sprouting in accelerated time.

Doing it at her place had its perks. Down on the basement level of the freshman dorm, there osmosed a youthful energy, his sexual stamina feeding off the eighteen-year-olds upstairs—kids shedding their virginities, honing their skills. And he, too, a little out of practice, honed his.

Ulrike Blau was no mere mistress. For one thing, she was almost certainly brilliant. (Arthur had no way of being sure, lacking as he did any knowledge of medieval history or literature, but her CV, which he downloaded from her faculty profile page, was extensive. Though her credentials were European and meant nothing to Arthur, he could only assume a journal like *Mittelalterliche Geschichte* possessed a high level of prestige.) She was certainly well liked by students and administrators, who wished her a *guten Morgen* as they passed her on the quad. Her intelligence, her likability—these were crucial. It made her more than a fling. She was a woman of substance.

So what was she doing with Arthur?

It had crossed his mind. Her intellectual prowess, his bald spot. The thirty years between them. One night, feeling guilty about Francine's health and drunk on the schnapps Ulrike kept in her cabinet, he asked her. "Why me?" he said. "Why me, when you could've had any young adjunct on campus?"

"Do not go on a fishing trip for compliments," she said. "I am not attracted to this."

"But you're attracted to *me*. I want to know *why*."

"It is personal."

"*Please*."

She sighed. "I can tell you a story about a young German girl who grew up in a subdivision outside of Frankfurt."

Arthur stirred. His penis pushed against the fabric of his briefs. "Tell me."

Ulrike nodded. She began to tell him how it happened. How she was a shy girl, a studious teenage outcast; how she used to bike through Sachsenhausen Süd to visit her only friend, Karin, who lived in a small house near Metzlerpark; how Karin grew breasts and became suddenly popular one spring, leaving Ulrike to sulk outside her house each afternoon, waiting for Karin to part from her new friends and come home; how one night Karin's father found her there, on the stoop, and invited her inside; how she told him everything, the trouble between her and his daughter; how he listened carefully; how he was handsome, with large hands and a sturdy barrel chest—

"Enough, enough!" Arthur's arousal curdled into jealousy. He shook off her story like a dog wicking water off its fur. "Fine," he said. "You're right. I don't need to know."

Considering his wife had recently been diagnosed with breast cancer, the fall of 2012 could have been worse. (Arthur was deeply concerned for Francine. But he was just as concerned with being left alone if she didn't make it. He wouldn't survive one empty hour as a widower, he knew that much. Ulrike was his backup, a need as much as a want.) And the affair itself was so invigorating, so energizing, that his life improved in unintended, unexpected ways. He careened off script during lectures, mocking the scholarly establishment to the delight of his students. Gossip, conflict, backstabbing—it turned out these were all more interesting than torque and the geometry of motion, even to the die-hard kinematics geeks who showed up to his lectures in person even though the talks were live-streamed throughout the university's Wi-Fi radius. He stayed in closer touch with his children, texting them as he walked to and from Ulrike's, full of good cheer.

As a husband he became a model caregiver, a veritable hospice nurse. No longer terrified of being left alone after her death, he devoted himself to caring for his wife.

But Francine had twenty-five years of administering therapy under her belt and had cohabitated with Arthur a decade longer than that. She was wary of his sudden concern for how she was feeling, the long hours logged by her side at Barnes-Jewish Hospital, the tact with which he communicated her condition to the kids. Friends said they'd never seen him so attentive.

She knew something was wrong.

She skipped the accusations and jumped right to the conclusion. "I don't want to know her name and I do *not* want to know her age," she said, half-conscious from her bed in Oncology, before her husband could reply. Tubes joined her to IV sacs, rigged piggyback to a metal hanger. "And I don't want you fawning over me either. Get Maggie in here."

"It's not what you think," he said. "Maybe I'm being nice. Can't I be nice?"

"No," she said. "No, Arthur, I don't think you can."

The most stinging part of her accusation was not that she was right. It was that she knew him well enough to be right in the first place. It bespoke the longevity of their relationship. That thing he'd tossed away.

He felt bad about it. Terrible. Especially now that she knew. Especially now that he couldn't mitigate the guilt of sleeping with Ulrike by smothering his wife with care. Every hour he spent at Barnes-Jewish, every page of *Stand by Her* and *So Your Wife Has Breast Cancer* he read had helped dull the shame itch. Well, now the itch was spreading. As the affair continued, Arthur failing time and time again to end it, he realized that he was not the kind of man who cheated on his dying wife—he was the kind who couldn't stop.

After the funeral, Arthur, who'd grown up middle-class when such a thing existed, and whose congenital frugality had always been balanced by Francine's willingness to spend, expected that without his wife's income he'd have to make some adjustments. Some changes in his way of life. What he didn't expect was the catastrophe.

It troubled him to think about it.

The execution of Francine's will brought to light a secret that was to Arthur's mind vastly more consequential than his promiscuous extracurricular. During the grueling, bureaucratic nightmare that followed, it was revealed that for the past three decades Francine had quietly attended to a private stock portfolio in her name only, an account that narrowly predated her marriage to Arthur. It was worth a small fortune.

Somehow, though Francine had never expressed any skill or knowledge of the stock market, with its balance sheets and dividends and averages (she wasn't a "numbers person"), she had managed to predict the rise of a tech giant while possessing the foresight to invest in less conspicuous areas like whole-grain food conglomerates, including the very recession-proof company that manufactured the Cocoa Scabs that Arthur was presently failing to enjoy.

All of this would have been a miracle, a windfall, had he not been involved with the medievalist. But he had, and Francine knew.

In her final days she'd rewritten the will.

The money was funneled to their children.

Arthur didn't see a cent.

The family home resided in Chouteau Place, an enclosed high-end precinct between Forest Park and the Delmar Loop in University City. Its curvilinear streets were stacked, one behind the next, arranged in a concentric horseshoe and legally owned by the residents, who were tasked with maintaining the roads, sidewalks, and Easter egg hunts held beneath its dense canopy of trees. "Private places," as they were known, were a local phenomenon from a time before zoning, invented by a Prussian-born land surveyor who'd married into city government. They were a suburban dream of quiet walkways and regulated means of egress. Intimidating gateways turreted the Alters' miniature neighborhood at the center of each of its four walls. The walls were high and difficult to scale, originally intended to keep out poor people, black people, and Jews. Now, in 2015, progress: the gates and their turrets had been razed—though the thick stone posts at the corners still remained—and people had come around to Jews.

Their first year in St. Louis, the Alters had rented a two-bedroom in the Central West End. Arthur preferred the academic life to that of a working stiff, and was confident in his ability to stick around. As soon as his visiting professorship was renewed for a second year, he put a down payment on the place, assuring Francine that the job wasn't going anywhere. He'd hustled in those early years, ingratiating himself with the department and even coaxing a few smiles out of Sahil Gupta, the indomitable dean who'd been talked into recruiting him. He volunteered to teach the courses no one else wanted to teach, an ungodly number of courses, and made himself indispensable. He was still nominally visiting but no one ever told him to leave, and each year Arthur's dream of a permanent faculty position swelled in inverse proportion to its likelihood. But fifteen years had passed since his request to be considered for tenure was denied, and each year he was called on to teach fewer and fewer classes, his pay scaled down to the adjunct rate, his contract always renewed last-minute. He grew bitter. He'd begun to see himself for what he was: cheated and underpaid, with a cramp in his neck from all its time on the chopping block. There were twelve long years left on his mortgage. He would have to work at least that much longer.

The house had always been a little too expensive. An inch outside their price range. But it was no grander than Francine's vision of her family, and Arthur's of himself. It was a beautiful wood-and-brick colonial, modest for its surroundings, and, to Arthur's mind, an engineering marvel: the room that would become Francine's home office had a street-facing wall made of glass panes supported by thin iron rods, like a greenhouse, which, on account of its ingenious construction, could withstand winter winds and pummeling hail. The office had been his gift to her, a consolation for moving her family into the heart of the heart of the country.

They sacrificed. The kids saved on college by staying local. All so they could continue living in the gated enclave. So long as it furnished their life.

But the mortgage, given the present circumstances, was not sustainable. Without Francine's income, payments on the house fell to Arthur and his tenure-allergic professorship. He was teaching two courses this semester, earning $5,000 for each. It pained him to think about the extent to which Francine had been carrying the family, financially, though they had moved for Arthur's career. He was falling behind on his mortgage payments. This fact was not lost on his bank, which was currently toying with his credit score like a ten-year-old toys with his penis: inquisitively, and for pleasure.

Not a day passed that Arthur didn't wonder how, and why, his wife had squirreled all that money away. How she got it was beyond him. But why had she kept it secret from him? And what did she *need* it for? An emergency fund? Had she planned to leave him? He'd blazed every path of possibility. None of it made sense.

The Alter family had been lucky enough to come out of the 2008 crisis relatively unscathed. But seven years later housing prices hadn't rebounded, and Arthur couldn't unload the house without losing good money, not even if he wanted to.

And that was the other thing: he didn't want to. He couldn't take another failure, couldn't eat another loss. He was living at Ulrike's while the house that would soon be taken from him sat unoccupied, a monument to defeat, a reminder of both his late wife and his impending eviction in precisely equal measure.

Did he miss his children? It was a question too unbearable to ask, like staring wide-eyed at the sun. The physics of it were all wrong.

What he missed was his old life, and his children had been part of that. His wife was gone. His house was going to be taken from him. The children were all that was left. The children—and the unexpected money in their name.

Ulrike choked on a breath and startled awake. Her hands swept the bed. "Mm? Arthur? Come here. Lie down."

He dropped his bowl in the sink. "I'm stepping out," he said.

"For what?"

"Meeting. Department meeting."

"On a Saturday?"

"Yes. Go back to sleep."

Ulrike sighed and laid her head back on the pillow.

Their affair was well into its third year. It no longer seemed right to call it an affair, and it no longer felt like one. Since Francine died, Ulrike had ceased to be "the other woman." She was something else now. *The* woman. No "other." He knew he was in a relationship because he'd begun lying to her about his whereabouts.

Arthur crept out onto campus. It was a clear, refreshing morning in March, the rarified Danforth air now powdered with perfumes and allergens, no longer winter but the wind still skittish—gathering momentum, agitating trees. Ferrying pollen and rattling windows. Nature thrumming at the molecular level. It was the kind of morning when you didn't loathe being a professor. When you remembered that the purpose of scholarship was to seek beauty. To seek out beauty and truth and to draw lines around them. To live happily within those walls.

Arthur beelined past a gang of slackliners toward Main Campus and stately Greenleaf Hall. He ducked inside and up a neglected staircase into the African Studies Library, lurking through the lengths of citrus light cast through the six lancet windowpanes above him.

The library was in a state of elegant decay. The university, normally fascistic in its regulation of property, had let the African Studies Library fall into disrepair. A spoiled smell haunted the rafters, like something had crawled up into the ceiling beams and died.

The library's odor plus the lagging Wi-Fi and lack of a café conspired to make it an unpopular student workspace, and on a Saturday morning in March, it was practically his private sanctuary. Colleague-free. No students in sight. He inhaled the death smell. God, was it odious. The price for the solitude he sought.

He sat before a long, sturdy table and he wrote.

He could hear the wind gathering outside, sweeping through Main Campus, gusting past the offices of deans and vice deans, provosts and professors emeriti. His pen squirmed between his fingers.

He felt like a pickup artist, a pervert whistling after his life as it passed him on the street in a miniskirt.

Trembling, he folded the two notes and hid them deep inside his pocket.

The other upside to the African Studies Library—and this was no small thing—was that it contained his comfort object. (Francine had named it. She was fond of identifying the comfort objects of her patients and relations. Their totems and fetishes. Their repressions realized in plastic. She'd named Arthur's as a joke, but like all jokes, it was 70 percent true.) Rising from his seat, he made his way toward the back of the room to retrieve it.

Arthur approached the stacks with predatory alertness, running his fingers along the jutting book spines. Leather, board, paper glossy and rough, text flat and embossed. His one solo publication. When asked why he hadn't published a manuscript-length study, ever, Arthur was quick to respond: the world doesn't need more books.

He pounced as soon as he saw it. A slim, jacketless hardcover, pale red, glue cracking at the binding. TOWARD A NEW SYSTEM OF SANITATION IN THE NEW NATION OF ZIMBABWE: A PROPOSAL, 1981, was stamped across the cover. And below, in smaller (but no less dignified) type: ARTHUR ALTER.

There existed fewer than fifty copies in the entire world. Most were probably pulped or in prison libraries by now. Arthur's personal collection had been ruined in a house fire fifteen years earlier. There had been a laundry mishap, a stuffed-up lint screen that had clogged the dryer vent, backing up flammable exhaust gases. The large cardboard box containing Arthur's copies, which rested by the combination washer-dryer, had perished. Fire and water damage both; the machine had leaked as it burned. But as long as Danforth kept a copy he felt safe. No harm could befall him then.

His heart rate slowed to a human pace. He took long, sustained breaths. He lingered on the word *proposal*. Had a word ever held so much hope? He stared at it, the open Os, the Ps like skeleton keys.

The temperature of his guilt sank. Standing there in the old library, turning the thing over in his hands, Arthur found himself shot through with new confidence. He would have to mail the letters before it ran out.

FIVE

It was Arthur who decided that his son would attend Danforth University. Ethan's grades were good enough to get him out of state, but Danforth waived a generous percentage of tuition for the qualified children of employees who had served the university five years or longer. This was Arthur's sixth. He learned of the subsidy through the university's financial aid pamphlet, a glossy document that had the scripture-like effect of converting him as soon as he put it down. He set to calling Danforth "Ethan's school" long before the applications were due. He said it so often and with such certainty that by the time his son's acceptance letters puddled on the floor beneath the mail slot, no one bothered rushing to retrieve them.

Ethan, then a high school junior, wasn't thrilled with the idea. He had nothing against St. Louis, and was flattered at Arthur's insistence that he stay close, whatever the reason. But he longed to go elsewhere, to New York City, specifically, where he could be himself, whatever that meant, far from his father's scrutinizing gaze. Ethan couldn't risk running into him on campus. Not in college. It would ruin him, he was sure of it. But Arthur explained that unless Ethan wanted to spend the next thirty years of his life smothered by debt, he'd be wise to take advantage of the offer. Plus, this was in the wake of 9/11, there were serious concerns regarding national security, and what could be a less desirable target for international terrorists than a city that couldn't even draw international tourists?

"I understand if you want to apply elsewhere," said Francine, who was spearheading a peer counseling initiative on campus, volunteering her time to run seminars on stress, anxiety, depression, eating disorders, and other issues commonly observed in undergraduates. "I can see how you wouldn't want to go to the same school where your parents worked."

Ethan looked at his father. Arthur raised his eyebrows hopefully. "Yeah." He nodded. "I don't know. Maybe I can make it work."

Arthur took his son's maybe as a yes and began applauding the decision every chance he had. "Ethan's joining me at Danforth," he'd tell family and friends, "courtesy of a generous institutional discount." Sometimes he credited Ethan with the idea. "He was wise to cash in on this discount," Arthur would say, patting his son on the shoulder approvingly, as though the savings would be passed on to Ethan and not funneled into the mortgage. Still, there was value, real value, in those pats. But the word remained with Ethan—*discount*—and he forever felt that his education had been plucked from the dollar bin; that the surrounding students in the lecture halls, the ones whose parents paid in full, were somehow learning things he wasn't, convening after hours and receiving bonus knowledge.

Though the Alters lived a short walk from the university, Ethan convinced his parents that paying for him to live in the dorms was the least they could do. "I won't make any friends out here," he told Francine, gesturing through the dining room window at the sober streets of Chouteau Place. He was not without leverage. There was, after all, the $23,280 per year he was saving them by attending Danforth in the first place.

His parents agreed. But living in a dorm meant furnishing it, and subsequently Arthur and Francine made scene upon terrible scene at Tubs & Tupperwares Too in the Promenade at Brentwood. They argued over mattress pads and desk lamps, bulletin boards and book lights, stacking drawers and shoe racks. Whether Ethan needed a shower caddy and a laundry hamper. "I went off to school with a backpack," Arthur huffed, "and that was it."

"I know for a fact that isn't true," said Francine.

"Excuse me. Were you there?"

Nothing upset Ethan's father like things. He was a minimalist. He had never learned, nor yearned, to inhabit that enviable space in the "upper-middle class." The Alters were all too familiar with his position: a refrigerator kept his food cold and a septic system sucked his shit underground. What were all these extra *things* for? Francine spent, Arthur whined. Yin and insufferable yang. He made an inappropriate amount of fuss the day she brought home a bagel guillotine. He cut his bagels with a knife to spite her.

"Okay," he said, looking over the shopping cart. "Tell me why our son needs an electric kettle."

"Because it's nice to have. For tea, when he's studying. He can make instant coffee and hot chocolate too. It's not a crime to have one nice thing."

Arthur turned to Ethan. "Do you drink tea?"

"I mean, not really—"

"See?"

"And instant coffee and hot chocolate," Francine said.

"Do you know how many times I've needed an electric kettle in my life? How many times the words 'electric kettle' even occurred to me before now? Zero. That's how many times. Zero times."

Francine pressed on with all the cunning of a practicing therapist. "It's not just an electric kettle. It's more than that. Think: What if someone walks by Ethan's room, and he's in there making tea, or hot chocolate, and that person says, 'Hey, that looks good, can I have some?' And then they get to talking. Okay? A new environment is hard enough. You have to give people an opportunity to approach you. This"—she pulled the box out of the cart and shook it—"is an opportunity. And I think that's worth the cost of an electric kettle. That's worth *twenty-five dollars*."

Arthur, grumbling, excused himself and went to wait in the car.

Francine smiled. "You see," she told her mortified son, pushing the cart through Kitchenwares, "he's not so tough when you learn to push back."

Danforth's century-old Main Campus sat on an acropolistic hill. It had always impressed Ethan as a boy. Now, as a matriculating student, he found the grandeur hollow. Over dinner Arthur lectured on the problem: Main Campus was purportedly constructed in the Oxbridge fashion, replete with arches, spires, and crenellations, when in truth it had clearly been inspired by the Ivies, themselves aping Oxbridge, making Danforth the knockoff of a knockoff. Worse, all the newer buildings spread across Extended Campus were built to look like those on Main, collegiate gothic outfitted with rosy bricks and energy-efficient windows, causing them to appear both contemporary and hundreds of years old, an uncanny homage that argued in favor of the past as being totally inescapable.

Ethan wasn't as concerned with the architecture as he was with his father. He feared the still-potent possibility that they might see one another out there, on campus, in public. Arthur, anticipating this— or perhaps similarly determined not to encounter his son in the sandwich line at Olin Lounge—approached him before move-in with a proposal.

"Listen," he said quietly. "We'll divide the campus in two. Main Campus, where my office is, that'll be off-limits to you between ten a.m. and five p.m. I'll stay off Extended Campus and the West Forty as best I can. That's where you'll live and take most of your classes this year anyway. Okay?"

Ethan nodded. "Okay."

Move-in went smoothly—Arthur stayed home in protest against the school's coddling, over-the-top student welcoming ceremonies— but socializing was another story. No one at Danforth gave Ethan the opportunity Francine had hoped the kettle would afford him. Impenetrable cliques assembled within days, mostly comprised of East Coast kids who knew one another from high school or theater camp or soccer tournaments. There was an activities fair, predicated on the notion that you already knew what you liked, and that you wanted to do it with people. Athletes roved in packs, and fine arts majors locked themselves in studio all day.

Ethan wandered, untouched by any social passion. He was a strong student, a one-season high school athlete (baseball, right field), and handsome. But he had never parlayed these gifts into a community. They had only ever worked for him.

Freshmen were at the mercy of the frats, who held events with themes like "Snowpants or No Pants" and "King Tuts and Egyptian Sluts." The sororities didn't have houses to throw parties in because of the state laws defining brothels. Ethan stood in the corner of more dim basements than he cared to think about, watching coeds get sprayed with foam and groped. Parties hosted by the LGBT student groups were no better. They played the same music and also had foam machines. The gropers were gender nonconforming. Twice Ethan went home with boys who were eager to cuddle in the morning. Their desperation was too nauseating, and too familiar, to stomach. One of them dragged him to a meeting of the Danforth Pride Alliance. But Ethan couldn't understand what the members had in common with one another, and what he had in common with them, beyond the obvious. So they weren't heterosexual—so what? He thought he might as well start a club for light-haired Jews.

He took a course in the gender studies department, Intro to Sexuality, which was more therapeutic than academic. His classmates were extremely forthcoming with sensitive information, as though intimacy wasn't something to be earned, but baby-birded from one mouth to another. The midterm was a survey you had to fill out listing everything you'd ever done, sexually, and at what age. Ethan had no interest in disclosing his intimate history, but it wasn't a problem for his cohort of Lil' Kinseys. The surveys were anonymous, but Ethan was the only male student in class. His handwriting gave him away. Halfway through the semester he realized they'd been getting dinner after class without him.

Months passed and he had not befriended anyone at school, not even his roommate, whose sole interests appeared to be online gambling and his girlfriend back in Nanjing. Tianyi—Eugene, as he insisted Ethan call him—was the shy son of a high-ranking functionary in the Chinese government. (Eugene raised his voice only once all year, interrupting his and Ethan's global politics professor to denounce, in labored English, the July 1 protests in Hong Kong.) But for all his ideological posturing, Eugene had a weakness for American capitalism. Below his capri-length cargo shorts he sported Nike Dunks. He played 3-D slots long into the night. He owned a Maserati that he kept in the student parking complex.

His constant presence wore on Ethan. Loneliness, it turned out, was perversely addictive. He found the only thing he wanted after a long day of being alone on campus was to be alone in his room. "At least you won't be sexiled," offered Ethan's acne-scarred residential advisor, explaining that an antisocial, crypto-fascist roommate did not warrant a room transfer.

Ethan could avoid his father most of the time, but their decided-upon borders were necessarily porous. Now and then he visited instructors during office hours on Main Campus. Once, after consulting with his professor on an essay—the course was Popular Crime and Early American Anxieties, a new offering from the American studies department, which occupied the former sociology wing on Main Campus—Ethan ducked into Greenleaf Hall to use a restroom. He sidled up to one of two free urinals. As he unzipped, his eyes darted to his left, where, under the aqueous green fluorescence of the men's room, he recognized the man beside him. The man, his father, glanced right and looked back down. He stopped pissing, shook, zipped, and washed his hands. He left without a word.

Now, Ethan thought, it was entirely possible that his father hadn't noticed it was him. Or perhaps he simply refused to speak at the urinals. Which was fine. Procedure was procedure. But one more possibility occurred to Ethan, something at once heartbreaking and petty: the possibility that his father had glanced right, registered his son, and, in accordance with their boundaries, pretended that he hadn't.

At the end of his freshman year, Ethan successfully applied for a room to himself in one of the modern sophomore dorms the university had erected on the West Forty. He had given up on finding a new roommate and worried that Eugene, an international student who might not know better, would assume another year of cohabitation. He tried and failed to initiate the conversation until, to his surprise, Eugene brought it up in April. "We must discuss our dorm placement for next year," he said one afternoon.

"Yeah," said Ethan. "About that . . ."

"I will be in suite with five other Chinese student."

"Sorry?"

"I apologize." He put a hand on Ethan's shoulder. "I am sure you will find a happy place to live."

Ethan wasn't certain. At parties, he felt like he belonged to another species. He didn't know how to approach people. Social life was governed by extracurriculars. There was a Korean a capella group, a black a capella group, and an a capella group that changed the words of popular songs so that they were about Hanukkah. He went to an intramural softball tryout but didn't make it to the diamond. From the parking lot it looked like everyone already knew each other. He realized now that he'd come to count on Eugene as a brother in solitude, a fellow sufferer. It occurred to him that perhaps Eugene had been playing 3-D slots all year with other expat students on campus, forming friendships conjoined by Ethernet cables. He learned then that there are levels of loneliness, as many types as there are people, and that one should never assume that one's solitary condition has anything to do with someone else's.

Though the building was new and its facilities were up-to-date, a stigma had already attached itself to Wrighton, Ethan's sophomore dorm. Consisting mostly of single rooms, it was thought of as "the creepy dorm," a refuge for the friendless and the specially accommodated. The showers were outfitted with seats and handles for the wheelchair-bound students who, per the university's disability policy, were guaranteed spots in Wrighton. Those kinds of flourishes put people off. It didn't help that a clinically depressed econ major had thrown himself from a fourth-story balcony there one year earlier.

By the time his second year at Danforth had begun he'd succumbed to a loneliness that was in part facilitated, if not encouraged, by the structure of the dorm itself. The staggered rooms and lack of common spaces were designed to keep the shut-ins shut in. Ethan even found himself missing Eugene, whom he sometimes saw on campus with a new girlfriend, surrounded by the children of Chinese diplomats and bankers. The 2004–2005 academic year did not look any more promising than the last.

A minor mystery sustained him. Draped over the door of the room across from Ethan's was a banner, white with blue stitched lettering, that read: YOUR FELLOW MAN. It was the only sign of life in Wrighton. The banner confronted him each time he stepped out of his room into the hall, running the height of the door and disappearing through the crevice on top. He obsessed over the banner. He wondered who lived behind it. In the fog of post-lunch lectures, Ethan doodled, his pen loafing carelessly across the page, casting off lines and curves at random, but when he came into consciousness at the end of class, more than once he found the words YOUR FELLOW MAN encroaching on his notes.

One afternoon in late September, the campus cross-breeze ripe and cold, Ethan discovered the electric kettle, boxed, in a duffel bag deep in his dorm-room closet. He recoiled. His chest contracted and his cheeks went hot. It was like he was at Tubs & Tupperwares Too again, watching his parents bicker, the sales assistants judging from a distance. The shame was fresh. He picked up the box and went to dispose of it.

On his way to the large trash bins at the end of the hall, a voice behind him asked, "What's that?"

Ethan turned. A young man was leaning on the banner-draped door, framed by those three mysterious words. YOUR FELLOW MAN.

The fellow man had a plain, matter-of-fact handsomeness to him. He had round cheeks and light brown hair. A stiff cowlick furnished his wide forehead. He stood on the balls of his feet, giving him an extra inch. He wore the well-fitting khaki pants of a guy who "got it," fashion-wise, and the Old Navy T-shirt of a guy who didn't. His eyes were sea-foam green, two lone extraordinaries.

"It's a water heater," Ethan said, scrambling to regain his presence of mind.

"A what?"

"An electric kettle."

"Oh. Ha," he said. "Gay."

The color fled from Ethan's cheeks. Though he had been out to his parents for almost three years now, he usually passed for straight, which put him in the awkward position of having to come out to every new person he met. It was burdensome, dragging sex into the conversation just to let people know—and to what end? So they could put him in some arbitrary category? Eventually he stopped trying. It became a point of pride that no one could read him for what he was. But how had the fellow man known immediately? Then he remembered what was in his hands. The kettle, he realized—the *kettle* was gay.

"I'm Charlie."

"Ethan."

Charlie followed him to the end of the hall. "I'm getting rid of this," Ethan explained.

"Whatever." Charlie shrugged, lifting the lid of the trash bin. "In you go," he told the kettle.

And suddenly he was everywhere. In the dining hall, in the library—they had matching schedules and habits. Ethan must have passed his hallmate a thousand times before they met, never before noticing the skinny kid with the cowlick, the way a pop song can go unnoticed despite repeated passive listenings in supermarkets and malls. They even had a course together, Introduction to Human

Evolution, where Ethan started sitting next to Charlie, helping him with the names of their hominid precursors. *Australopithecus africanus*, he'd whisper. *Homo heidelbergensis.*

Charlie was a physics major and had enrolled in human ev for the social science credit. He was also, Ethan came to learn, a St. Louis native, the fifth and youngest son of Dan and Ellen Bugbee and the only one not currently working at Anheuser-Busch in distribution with their father. "It's what you do in my family," he explained. "Anheuser's been good to us. The brewery? Near Soulard? It feels like our family legacy is there. Like it's our estate. Dad used to say we had horses growing up—he meant the Clydesdales. Put it this way: no one in my family has ever lost a game of Flap-or-Fill." On Highway 40, an orange neon sign flashed between images of an eagle flapping its wings and an empty Anheuser A filling up with beer. Charlie claimed all Bugbees could guess, with stunning accuracy, which image would appear at the moment their car drove past. Charlie's favorite jacket bore a similar logo printed across the back, the eagle and the A.

Charlie was a Bugbee to the core. Unlike the majority of English, history, and philosophy majors, whose studies colonized their personalities, Charlie refused to let Danforth make an intellectual of him. "My parents were surprised that I went here and not Mizzou, like my brothers. I promised them it wouldn't change me. I don't know why it would. I mean, I still watch Tiger football," he said. "I'm not going to *stop* drinking Bud."

"What's with the banner?" Ethan asked one afternoon. Class had ended, the lecture hall was thinning out, and the two *Homo sapiens* were heading back to Wrighton. Ethan walked the walk he'd perfected as a preteen, half consciously humming the song that kept his footsteps heavy and deliberate: *I–am. E–than. Al–ter. And–my. Mid–dle. Name–is. Da–vid.*

"What banner?"

"On your door."

"Oh. Yeah, that. It's from my camp, in Maine." Charlie explained that though his family hardly left the Midwest, for the last ten summers he'd flown east to Brundle Pines, the oldest continuously running boys' camp in America, first as a camper and later as a counselor. The camp was, in Charlie's telling, an idyllic Eden amid a forest of spruces by a warm, sleepy pond. Where boys, he said sincerely, learned to become men. "My dad works double shifts all summer to send me." A pair of wooden monuments to the Brundle Boys lost in World Wars I and II stood at the center of the campground. He spoke rapturously of the place: of paddling at sunrise, dusted with conifer needles, free from the calculating eyes of girls; of the camp's four pillars (brotherhood, nature, leadership, silence); and of the singular luxury of unexploited New England wilderness, his eyes brightening as he did. The underside of the banner on his door, he explained, read COMES FIRST, the Brundle Pines motto.

Your fellow man comes first.

"Sounds awesome," Ethan said.

"It is."

They reached the dorm entrance. Charlie swiped them in with his key card.

"Can I ask," said Ethan, "why are you in Wrighton? I mean, I *wanted* to live alone, but some people don't. I was wondering . . ."

"Fucked over," Charlie said. "By my rich-kid hallmates from last year. Said we could all get a suite together and then bailed last-minute for this place off campus. A three-bedroom in the Central West End. I was like, I can't afford this. Heated tiles in the bathroom."

"Sucks," said Ethan.

"You're not one of them, are you?"

"One of who?"

"The rich kids. Like all the other entitled East Coast assholes at this school."

"I grew up in St. Louis," Ethan said, omitting the name of the gated neighborhood. His heart paced faster as he added, excitedly, "I'm here on a subsidy. A tuition discount." Charlie nodded approvingly.

This was the first of many ways that Ethan Alter, college sophomore, began to unburden himself. After class most days he sat in Charlie's unadorned room and drank Bud Light. They played *Halo* and talked. Side by side before the television screen, Ethan revealed things he'd formerly kept secret—and found, to his surprise, that Charlie had mirror stories. They shared traumatic dental episodes (Charlie had had impacted canines) and a sense of being ill fit to their families. It occurred to Ethan that he'd never been as happy as he was drinking mass-produced pale lager in an unadorned room with a boyish guy on the shorter side of five foot six. Maybe, after a quarter lifetime in the Alter household, this is what he'd always wanted: no cynicism, no pretention, only the wan honesty of being.

Ethan had put a lot of care into his own room. Above his bed hung a framed poster of a foggy Monet bridge he'd seen at SLAM. On the wall opposite was a watercolor landscape his grandmother had painted. Beneath it, an Easton bat, laser cut with the words ETHAN ALTER—2000–2001 SPORTSMANSHIP AWARD was pinned to the wall with brackets. Christmas lights circumscribed the window. His desk was bare. When Charlie walked in for the first time he was silent with awe, pausing to dote on both the Claude Monet and the Nan Alter, and whispered, "Your room is sick."

Ethan knew he meant it. Charlie never said a thing he didn't mean. Irony, sarcasm—these were foreign languages to him. And yet every earnest expression of sensitivity was quickly undercut by something vulgar—"Curtains are kinda gay, though"—that left Ethan dizzy and confused.

Straight men confounded him. Saying the right thing and then immediately the wrong—what *was* that? A side effect of not having to hide oneself? Of a life without filters or amendments?

A student suicide in late October resulted in the canceling of classes on the third Friday of the month—an unexpected three-day weekend. Ethan asked if Charlie had plans.

"I don't. Go home, I guess."

"Yeah, same. I was thinking, though. What if we went somewhere? Like a trip? I can borrow a car." He loathed the thought of spending this impromptu long weekend at home, with his father and without Charlie.

"Yeah. Actually, that could be tight. Where would we go?"

"You pick!" Ethan said, a bit too excitedly. "If we leave Thursday afternoon we can take a straight shot anywhere."

Charlie paused to think. His eyes glazed and shone. After a long minute he turned to Ethan and stated, definitively, "Pittsburgh."

Pittsburgh. That, from the depths of Charlie's mind. *Pittsburgh.* Not Nashville, four and a half hours south, or Chicago, equidistant to the north, but Pittsburgh: the City of Bridges, Steel City, Iron City—nine hours away by car. That Charlie had not (or could not) name a more interesting place was dangerously endearing.

"Okay," Ethan said and smiled. He would have gone anywhere with Charlie. "Pittsburgh it is."

On Thursday afternoon, they set out in Francine's new Toyota station wagon, a sea-green Spero, which she offered to Ethan and his friend.

"Why did you say 'friend' like that?" Maggie asked. She was reading in the living room with her mother.

"Like what?" Francine said.

"You said it like, *friend.*"

"No I didn't."

"You did!"

"You kinda did, Mom," Ethan interjected.

"I'm happy you found someone," she said. "A friend. A friend to take a weekend trip with. A weekend trip to Pittsburgh."

They left at three. Charlie wore his Anheuser jacket. As they approached the Mississippi River, Ethan saw the Arch through his window, the Gateway to the West growing awkward and superfluous as he put it behind him—the massive, stainless-steel catenary shrinking in the rearview as if calling out, *You're going the wrong way!* And then the city flattened, Missouri became Illinois, East St. Louis passed them by and there was nothing. Trees, grass, open sky—a billboard reading LOVE YOUR BABIES, BORN & UNBORN. Rattling in the backseat was a twelve-pack of Bud Select that Charlie had insisted they take with them.

"You know what I like about you?" Charlie said in Illinois.

"What?"

"You act like you're this quiet kid but really you're crazy. You're down for whatever."

"Yeah?" Voltage in his veins.

"Yeah. Like this trip. I said Pittsburgh and you were like, 'Yes. Let's go.' You know what I mean? You're just *down*."

Charlie fell asleep somewhere in Indiana. Ethan sneaked prolonged looks at him—he found he could stare for six seconds at a time before having to check back with the road—as headlights swept Charlie's face. Around eight thirty he pulled onto Route 68 and drove south into Yellow Springs, Ohio. He wound his way through the dark, veering into residential neighborhoods of discomfiting quiet until the road broadened again.

Ethan pulled into the parking lot of a green clapboard pizzeria with a loud sign. He decided not to wake Charlie. He went in, ordered four slices, ate two alone in the restaurant, and boxed two for his sleeping friend. Back on the road, Charlie woke with a smile to the smell of hot cheese.

"What's this?" he said.

"For you."

"You're crazy." Charlie took a bite. "Fuck, this is good."

"I looked it up. Supposed to be the best."

"You went out of the way for this?"

"I'm glad you like it."

"But where did you find it?"

"I did a little research beforehand."

"You're cultured, you know that?"

"I am? Oh, man. Thanks."

"I know I'm not." Charlie wiped a spot of glistening grease from his lips.

"You are!"

"No. I'm not. No one in my family is. We have other good things about us, but we're not *knowledgeable* in that way. I know that. I figured that out a long time ago."

Ethan smiled. "You really know yourself, huh?"

"Don't you?"

"I don't think so."

"Why not?"

"I'm not sure. Maybe I don't want to know. It's scary, I think, to look at yourself that way. That's what's cool about you. You're brave enough to look inside yourself and *know*."

"Some people don't like that," Charlie said. "That's why it's hard for me to make friends. At school, I mean. Some people want you to adjust yourself to fit some bullshit precon . . . precom . . ."

"Preconceived notion."

"Right. See? Cultured. But that's why I love Brundle Pines. I don't have to change who I am."

"I think I do that."

"Do what?"

"Adjust myself. For other people."

"No, you don't."

"No?"

"Not at all. No way."

Ethan swelled.

"Do you think I'm dumb?" Charlie asked. "Because of what I said about being cultured?"

"No," Ethan said. "God, no. I'd never think that. You're not dumb. No. Never."

Ethan checked his reflection in the rearview mirror, his face coming in and out of darkness as he passed through pools of highway light. Though his path to physical desirability was by no means over, in recent years the expander had come out, granting him a handsome, architected smile. His pores had tightened. His shoulders broadened, as if there had been a larger version of himself encased within a narrow body all that time, a self that had finally hatched.

They checked into a first-floor room in a Holiday Inn Express south of downtown Pittsburgh. The room had two double beds. Ethan dropped his bags on the scratchy carpet and fell onto his bed, exhausted. He passed out listening to Charlie recount a news item he'd seen on TV where investigators shone black lights on hotel rooms to disgusting effect.

He woke at sunrise. He could hear the patter of shower spray on plastic from the neighboring room, and smelled the waffle batter bubbling between irons in the lobby's breakfast bar.

He opened his eyes. Charlie was standing by the side of Ethan's bed. In his left hand was a sweating bottle of Bud Select. His right hand gripped his erect penis. Both were extended in offering.

Pittsburgh gave them sun for three days. Or so the view through the windows implied—the boys hardly left the hotel. They fooled around and slept late and drank all day. They hung the PRIVACY PLEASE placard on the doorknob as the room grew provocatively stale. Every now and then they went in search of food. Charlie mispronounced *pierogi* on three separate occasions. The city was unassuming and let them get away with everything. The boys Ethan had previously slept with were fumblers. They were as uneasy in their bodies as he was. Charlie was different. He led with his body. It was, Ethan thought, the best weekend of his life. So it came as a surprise when, after the flames of Pittsburgh cooled and they drove back to Danforth, Charlie too went cold—sitting apart from him in class, shutting the door to his room—and Ethan found his worst fears realized: he was alone again, entirely uncertain as to why, until Charlie returned from winter break that year with a girlfriend and said that what he and Ethan had done was a "camp thing," distinct from the life he wanted in St. Louis, and if Ethan ever told, he'd kill him.

Sophomore spring was chaos, a period of record losses. Loss of appetite. Loss of interest. Loss of energy. He felt faint. A high-pitched sound burrowed in his ears and stayed there. He felt like there was an expander in his chest, rapidly expanding. For weeks his mouth carried the taste of batteries.

He stayed in bed. His heart skittered, little manic bursts puncturing the torpor like a mouse darting from one corner to another. Ethan checked himself into Student Health Services when he knew his mother wouldn't be there. He was given two Tylenol and told to relax. He couldn't understand what had happened. His life wilted like a question mark.

On top of this he lived in fear. Charlie's room was right across the hall, the banner still hanging from the door. YOUR FELLOW MAN. It had a menacing air to it now. Ethan had to plan his comings and goings to avoid his hallmate. At first he spent whole days on campus, leaving early and coming home late. Once, at night, as he stepped through the threshold into his room, he heard the click of a door opening. He could feel a presence behind him. He bounded forward and slammed his door shut.

Senior year, Ethan wandered the botanical gardens. He watched his feet in the footlights. All throughout the green were students in khakis and sleeveless dresses. Pinkies poked out from the stems of champagne glasses. Kids whom Ethan had seen expelling Chinese takeout on the sidewalk comported themselves like gentlemen and ladies. A girl skipped past him, barefoot and giggling. Rival a capella groups harmonized with each other. There was an air of forgiveness across the lawn, the smell of roses and tulips and of no hard feelings.

He was eager to graduate and get to New York. He had dragged himself to the gala out of some misplaced hope that now, in the final week of college, he would find his people. That they would reveal themselves at last, and say: *We've been waiting for you.* But lapping the gardens he felt only shame and confusion, unable to comprehend how kids less attractive, less intelligent, and less talented than he had formed such close bonds with one another in a quick four years. He was surrounded by pairs and groups. The first bus back to campus wasn't leaving for another hour, and Ethan was out of drink tickets.

He rounded a corner. A young man sat on a bench by the reflecting pool, hunched, his head between his knees. He looked like he was sleeping, or possibly ill. The young man raised his head to watch a lilac-colored bubble of glass, pinched at the top like a teardrop, float across the surface of the water.

Ethan froze. He hadn't been this close to Charlie in two years. He'd moved off campus after Wrighton. Whenever he saw Charlie on the quad, Ethan ducked behind a building, as he did with Arthur. He feared for his life, but the more potent fear was that Charlie would hurt him again. What was stopping him from luring Ethan in and then disappearing? Certainly not Ethan, who wanted nothing more than to be lured. But Charlie didn't look so menacing, not now. His hair was mussed. He wore a white button-down shirt tucked into chinos with no belt. Ethan walked tentatively toward him.

"My man," Charlie slurred, pointing at Ethan. "That's my man right there."

Ethan sat beside him. He tried to summon anger at the boy who had abandoned him, but the sight of Charlie, his cheeks full and green, brought out the caretaker in him.

"You okay?" he asked, in a voice that belonged to his mother. "Can I get you something?"

"I know you, man."

"And I know you."

"No," said Charlie. "I mean I *know* you." He burped into the crook of his elbow.

"Are you sure I can't get you anything? Some water?"

Charlie shook his head.

"Okay. I'm just going to sit here, then."

A few stray students milled about the pool. Faint laughter carried through the purple air. Behind him, three bronze angels blowing horns were perched on tall stone columns.

"It's over," Charlie said suddenly. "It's all over."

"College?"

"College . . . man, fuck college." His eyes were half-closed, dimming the light of his eyes like a drawn shade.

Ethan had the urge to pick him up and carry him into a walled-off section of the gardens, lay him down on the grass, and tend to him. He couldn't locate the rage he was entitled to, the rage that Charlie deserved. "What are you doing this summer?" He tried not to sound like he cared.

Charlie shook his head.

"Going back to camp?"

"Can't."

"Why's that?"

"Dad said. Even though I pay for it myself. I guess I'm too old." He looked at Ethan, his eyes narrow and suspicious. "I'm too *old* for that."

"I'm sorry to hear it."

"Yeah, yeah," Charlie said, his head bobbing. He swallowed a sob. His shoulders shook. Ethan was prepared to tell him it was nothing to cry over, but as the last of the sunlight drained from the sky and the overhead lights in the garden flashed on, forcing Charlie's eyelids to flutter, on his face Ethan saw what it would mean not to return.

"You'll be okay," he said. "You're smart. You'll find something." The fear had left him completely. Charlie seemed incapable of hurting anyone. Ethan felt his body fill, like a glass, with tenderness.

"Where are you going?" Charlie slurred.

"I'm not going anywhere. I'm right here, with you."

"Yeah but where are you *going*."

"Oh." Ethan nodded. "I fly to New York on Wednesday."

Charlie leaned in and lowered his voice. "Don't tell anybody . . ."

"I won't."

". . . I want to get the fuck *out* of here."

"You can."

Charlie sniffed. "Maybe."

"Why not?"

Charlie shook his head. "You've got it all in front of you," he said.

"So do you."

"It's different. You, Ethan." Charlie flattened his palm and pushed it out ahead of him, making a whooshing sound with his mouth. "It's all right there for you. I know where you live."

Ethan straightened his back. "What?"

"I know where you *live*," he said again, with less menace than understanding.

"Your life is going to mean something," Ethan said. "You can do whatever you want."

Charlie reached out toward him. Ethan closed his eyes, his lips pursing instinctively. He felt a hand on the tip of his ear. Charlie had stopped short. His fingers slid down the curved helix, landing on the lobe, which he held between his thumb and index finger, rubbing it like a coin, for luck.

SIX

A priest, a rabbi, and an engineer are all lined up for execution. Guillotine. The priest steps up first. He lies down on his stomach, pokes his head through the head hole, and the executioner pulls the cord. Priest holds his breath—but nothing happens. The blade is stuck. 'Divine intervention,' he says. 'An act of God.' And he's released. Okay. Next up is the rabbi. He lies down, and the executioner pulls the cord. The blade begins to fall, but it gets stuck again. 'Baruch Hashem,' he says. 'I'm saved!' Finally, the engineer steps up. Looks the guillotine over. Sticks his head through the hole. And as the executioner prepares to pull the cord, the engineer shouts, 'Wait—I think I see what the problem is . . .'"

Crickets. Or, rather, the rustle of paper, the unified hum of fifty laptops, and the thin snare of a pop song run through dangling headphones. But, otherwise, silence.

"Because he kills himself. That's the joke. The engineer is thinking technically, thinking like a problem solver, and he winds up killing himself. That's why it's funny."

The final slide of Arthur's presentation loomed in LED behind him, a clip-art cartoon of a cat with its head through a guillotine.

That he had been delivering this lecture in the same way for five years and only today tried something new—the joke—and that it failed in no uncertain terms only buttressed Arthur's belief that teaching was an exhaustible art. Lectures could not be tweaked and turned forever as a painting or a poem could. A lecture's perfection was finite.

Not that it was any small thing, mastering a lecture—holding students' attention, knowing when to change gears, change slides. It could take years of fine-tuning. But when you found it, you found it. Subsequent improvements were met with diminishing returns.

A lecture was practical in that way, like a bridge. Arthur constructed a truss bridge in his mind to illustrate the point. He imagined its floor beams, stringers, and struts. It was a thing of beauty, this truss bridge, with its interplay of tension and compression, its manipulation of shear stress, the way the twin forces of each truss worked in elegant tandem. But a bridge had to have purpose before it was beautiful, which is to say a bridge is only as beautiful as it is successful in joining two shores. Embellishments were hindrances in Arthur's field. A stunning bridge that collapsed under the weight of its adornments was no bridge at all.

He made a note to drop the joke.

"All right," he grumbled, "you're dismissed."

A minute hand snapped into place and spring break descended on Danforth. Students fled the lecture hall. This was a profitable time for the university, one full week during which cafeteria staff, adjunct professors, and other hourly employees sat at home, their pay suspended, waiting for students to return from cultivating hangovers at resorts in developing nations.

Arthur snuffed the projector light.

"Professor Alter?" someone said. "Professor Alter?"

He looked up from the small remote control in his hands. Standing before him was a pink boy with a fuzzy blond head and the anxious bearing of a freshman. ESE 103: "Engineering" Social Change was popular with underclassmen. It was supposed to be an idealistic survey, a gut for do-gooding nonmajors, and was advertised as such. In practice, the course was much more cynical. Instead of encouraging civic-minded DIY projects, Arthur railed against technological determinism. Instead of celebrating regional accomplishments in the field, he devoted an entire lecture to the human cost of local endeavors—a lecture he was especially proud of, titled "In the Shadow of the Arch." Still, a fresh crop of young optimists filled the lecture hall each year, and it wasn't unusual for a student to attach himself to Arthur—they were invariably male—in the hopes that he would be their mentor, their guardian, their campus father.

"Yes?"

"I wanted to say, I really liked today's lesson."

"Thanks."

"The whole thing about thinking like an engineer? Super interesting. Not that I'm an engineer, per se. I mean, of course I'm not! I'm still deciding on a major. But what you said about the centrality of . . . um . . . managerialism . . . in the field, which tends to understand human relationships as factors to be exploited . . . a system of inputs and, um . . ."

"Outputs."

"Right. That was cool. I never thought I'd major in engineering but now I'm really considering it."

Arthur's eyebrow arched. "I'm glad you're enjoying the class," he said, tapping his foot. He wasn't keen to foster parent anyone this year, not when he had his children to worry about.

"So, anyway, I was thinking—how can I put my education into practice, you know? And I thought maybe it would be cool to start some kind of extracurricular organization? To help out in the city?"

He squinted. "Like how."

"Like, I don't know, installing some kind of sprinkler system in a, let's say, community garden? And I thought—who better but Professor Alter to be our faculty advisor?"

"I don't know about that."

"It's easy! The school will fund any club with three members and a faculty advisor."

"The way this place spends money," Arthur muttered. "Listen. I'm not your guy."

"I looked you up, Professor. You have loads of experience, here and abroad, with—"

"No."

"But in class you said—"

"Don't you get it? Weren't you listening?" Arthur wiped his

forehead with his sleeve. "These projects always fail. Always. That's what I'm trying to tell you. That's what this class is about. There are costs to this kind of work, understand? Tremendous costs."

"I only wanted to help," the kid squeaked.

"You redesign park benches and the homeless revolt. You build a shelter for them and a year later it's a crack den. You can never foresee the real-life consequences of your work. A community garden—please!"

The freshman hung his head. "It was just an idea."

"Here's an idea for you. Get a master's in social work. Go to med school. You like gardens so much, become a botanist. You want to help in the city, become an urban planner. Or be an engineer, for all I care. But whatever you do, stay in your lane. Don't think you know what's best for other people, because you don't." His hands were shaking. "You can't barge into someone's neighborhood and tell them how to water their plants. I wish you could, but you can't. I promise you, no good will come of it."

The kid's mouth was open, his ears blushing. "I'm sorry."

"Don't say sorry. Just. Don't. Get. Involved."

"Okay. Sorry. I mean—sorry."

Arthur bounced his heel. "Are we done here?"

"Yeah," said the kid, shoulders hunching. He backed away from Arthur, one slow step after another.

Arthur left the building and hustled through Extended Campus, his heart agitated, beating in double time. A sun-shower broke out, the slender raindrops pricking his neck.

"Arthur."

He spun around, nearly slipping on the rain-slick footpath. A wide black umbrella floated toward him, beneath which he could make out the lower third of Dean Gupta, walking dry through the shower in wing-tip oxfords and a navy suit.

"Sahil, hi," said Arthur, pointing over his shoulder with his thumb. "I was heading off, actually—"

"I was thinking." Gupta paused, exploring the silence while rain berated Arthur's bald spot. Though Gupta had been directly responsible for denying his request for a tenure evaluation, Arthur found himself in the cumbersome position of craving the dean's approval. The man's scientific career was legendary: his professional experiments with chemiluminescence in the 1960s had run concurrently to his personal experiments with psilocybin, a fruitful pairing that led to the invention of the glow stick. Gupta's storied past, with its controlled substances and prized patent (3,774,022), had long ago earned him the respect of students and colleagues alike—Arthur begrudgingly included. But lately, his reputation secured, the dean had mellowed out, turned administrator, and taken up golf. Like many successful men, he cherished success itself, and regarded his less-prosperous colleagues with bewildered contempt. Every brush with Gupta, ten years his senior, was a reminder of how little Arthur had accomplished. "Let's set up a meeting," he said finally.

Arthur froze. "A meeting?"

"Sometime after spring break." The dean's leathery voice was gilded with an aristocratic affect he exhibited tastefully, like a gold watch that spends most of its time tucked under a sleeve. "There's something I need to discuss with you."

This was the end. Arthur could feel it. After years of teaching, five classes per semester giving way to four, then three, and now two, he felt the vise tightening all around him. What was the meeting for, if not to finish him off? He blinked away the thought.

"Spring break. Perfect."

The dean folded his arms. He took his time evaluating Arthur. "Everything okay with you?" he asked.

"Everything's fine."

Gupta took a moment to assess him. "Good. Good. Now get out of this rain, hm?"

Arthur nodded and made off for Greenleaf Hall. He took shelter inside, up the stairs, and through the doors to the African Studies Library. He raced toward the book. His comfort object. He imagined it gone, the sliver of space it occupied foreclosed on, squeezed out by the two massive volumes that flanked it.

But it was there, where it always was, between Murdoch Alison's *Debunking Conrad* and Chester Ambrose's *Understanding Apartheid*. Arthur tore it from the shelf. He sat with it for forty-five minutes, poring over its contents, triple-checking that the pages were all present and in order.

The clouds had parted by the time he left. Outside the library, with restored cell service, his phone pinged with an email from his son.

He was coming home.

Arthur forgot all about the dean. He let himself into Ulrike's and cooked a reconciliatory dinner—baked salmon, his only specialty, frugally garnished because "the garlic does a lot of work"—and told her, when she walked through the door an hour later, that she might not see much of him in the coming week.

"Why?" she asked. "I do not understand."

He beckoned her to sit at the kitchen island, which he'd cloaked in a tablecloth.

"It might be cold," he said. "I waited."

"You know I teach on Friday nights."

"Rookie move is undercooking it. You have to wait, trust yourself. Not get overeager."

"Arthur."

"What."

"Is this because of our fight? The stupid fight? The fellowship, I still have not—"

"No," he said. "It's not that. I've—well, listen. I'll tell you. I've invited my kids home."

Ulrike's chin dimpled, the impressions forming an unreadable alphabet of inverted braille. "I told you before, Arthur," she said. "I do not like to hear about your children."

At the start of their affair she'd banned Arthur from discussing his children or his sick wife—*especially* his wife. She'd successfully deferred the guilt of sleeping with a married man simply by waiting it out. It worked; he was married no longer. Still, she couldn't bring herself to imagine anything tangible about Francine. The night Arthur let slip her name the first time, Ulrike promptly got in bed with two Benadryl and a bottle of Malbec in an attempt to wipe it from her memory. Children, on the other hand, tended not to go away.

"I will not be their mother," she said.

"I'm not asking you to! In fact, if you could make yourself scarce while they're in town, that might go a long way toward getting us on track."

"First, I tell you I am leaving," she said. "You tell me to stay. Now you are telling me to go away. Arthur, I cannot decipher you."

"I'm not telling you to go anywhere." He looked at his fillet in the hopes of directing her attention toward the protein-rich sign of his commitment. "I need to get the house ready."

Ulrike's slender brows knit together. Arthur hadn't asked about her life before St. Louis, but had gathered, from offhand remarks, that her parents were both public servants. Her father was a civil engineer—Arthur decided not to read into that—and her mother, he believed, was a schoolteacher. From this grist he'd concluded that her family, inveterate Frankfurters, were plainspoken realists with no tolerance for bullshit—and that Ulrike had inherited these qualities.

"The house? Arthur, what will you get it ready *for?*" Ulrike squared her shoulders as she made—then belabored—her point, asserting that the house was a safety net for him, a means of keeping one foot out the door of their relationship, and that she wasn't going to turn down a career opportunity in a (let's face it) more interesting city for a man who paid a crazy mortgage to dodge commitment to a (frankly) beautiful woman in her prime such as herself, espe—

"For us."

Ulrike paused mid-syllable and swallowed it back down. "What?"

"Give me this time. Let me see my kids. And then, when they're gone—I want you to move in. To live with me."

"For how long?"

Arthur leaned over the table. "For the foreseeable future."

Ulrike set her fork down with a civilized clink.

"The foreseeable future," she repeated. "What does this mean?"

"What do you mean, what do I mean? My kids are coming home. They'll help me with the house. And then I want you to move in with me."

He was not in control of his words. They leapt like lemmings from his mouth. Anything to keep her. Anything to keep from being alone.

"The job market, Arthur," she said. "If I stay in St. Louis I am risking opportunities."

"I get it. The vagaries of academia. But that's why I can promise the *foreseeable* future. The unforeseeable future—well, we can't see it, can we?"

"You do not sound like yourself."

She was right. The unforeseeable future was nothing to scoff at. The unforeseeable future was Arthur's greatest source of anxiety, and a major factor in his coupling with Ulrike. Arthur often felt that his entire life was one long postponement of some future reckoning.

"Give me a chance. Please. It's much more space. A big improvement for you. Cozy. Great neighborhood."

"But my life is elsewhere."

"Where?"

"Everywhere. Berlin. Indiana. I have gone everywhere."

"And it's time to settle somewhere."

"Arthur."

"Stay. Just awhile. Stay in St. Louis. You wouldn't have to live in this hovel. No more campus, no more freshmen vomiting in the hallways. You could live in a real house on a real street. Chouteau Place. Have you been? Probably not. Want to know why? It's *private*. Our own little neighborhood."

"You own this house?"

"Yes. Kind of. It'll be all mine in no time."

"When?"

"After my kids leave."

"How?"

"Don't worry about it. Let me handle it. Trust me."

"I do not know."

"Think of what you'd save, moving in with me. I know how this school treats its faculty. Move in with me and you won't have to pay a penny in rent."

"If I do this, it will not be for the money."

"Sure, right."

"It will be for us."

"I'm saying. As a *bonus*. The savings are a *nice bonus*. Think about it."

"I will."

"Good. Now eat your salmon. I made it special."

The following day Arthur returned to his home for the first time in weeks.

It still surprised him that for seventeen years, from 1996 through Francine's death in 2013 and in patchwork months after that, Arthur had done most of his living here, *here*, in this elegant, self-governing enclave of academics, aesthetes, coastal transplants, and other university affiliates. That for seventeen years his steps were softened by Oriental rugs, his belly full with coq au vin and Ore-Ida oven fries, the kind of irresistible, unlikely culinary marriage he'd strong-arm Francine into making. For seventeen years he'd taken long steamy showers and hardly ever reused towels without at least running them through the dryer. O comfort! It was only now, living as frugally as his principles demanded, that he realized her role in making it all possible. He'd had it both ways for nearly two decades, railing against a culture of commodities while partaking in the comforts with which Francine had insulated his family. Without her, he would never have lived this life, occupied this place.

He put the car in park and stepped onto his property. Birdsong scattered through Chouteau Place. Arthur shut the car door and walked up the driveway, his feet reacclimating to the particulars of its topography, the cracks and ridges and other workmen's errors. He paused over a bloom of dandelions rooted in a pavement crevice. He kneeled to get a closer look. Serrated leaves cut upward through a growth in the ground. Two yellow flowers wavered with his breath.

One would be forgiven, considering the undisturbed calm of the private place, for losing world-historical perspective while within its bounds, for devoting oneself entirely to intimate ruptures, bubbles, and tears in the asphalt.

Arthur bunched the weed and tore it from the earth.

He rose, stretched, and then surveyed the small yard. Frowning, he nabbed a trowel from the garage and brought it back out where, along the property line, he scooped and flung the pithy leavings of his neighbor's poodle mix so that they landed, decisively, in that selfsame neighbor's garden.

The kitchen appeared as it had been when he last left: clean, almost sterile. The freezer was still stocked with shiva casserole and shiva kugel, a genre of food that belonged, in Arthur's opinion, permafrozen. The fridge was still covered in newspaper clippings and one of Ethan's middle school drawings. The revised USDA Healthy Eating Pyramid. And a flowchart Francine had found and taped up:

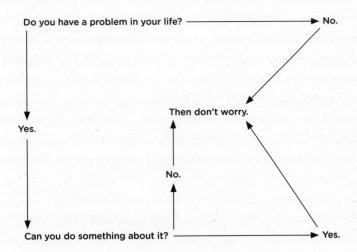

It was only the rotting mangoes and pears in the wire fruit basket, and the tiny flies that swarmed them, that signified a place where no one lived anymore.

In the living room, he vacuumed. He cleared mousetraps and chucked the corpses out into the bushes that lined the backyard. He spritzed and wiped down glass with citrus-saturated ammonia, beginning with the kitchen windows and then working room to room. The basement carpet had assimilated the smell of smoke from the house fire, but this could be used to his advantage. The olfactory bulb was closely linked with memory and emotion. While restoring Ethan's and Maggie's bedrooms, he accidentally touched his face, his fingers fresh with disinfectant wipe, compelling a stream of chemical tears to blur his vision.

He refocused. As Arthur saw it, the success of his children's visit depended on the formula

$$(P + N)(\tfrac{1}{2}A) + G = M$$

where P = Pity, N = Nostalgia, A = Apology, G = Guilt, and M was Money, or Mortgage. He tried to keep this in mind.

He began with N. He hunted for stuffed animals, plus security blankets and beloved picture books and other trigger objects, which he deployed like land mines throughout the house. As a final, pitying touch, Arthur assembled all the letters from his bank and put the first notice on the counter in the kitchen, the second notice on the tiered accent shelf between the dining room and foyer, and the third notice at the foot of the stairs. That way, if his children entered the house through the side door, as the Alters always did, the path to their bedrooms on the second floor would tell a story.

In the morning he returned to his work on the house. After breakfast he climbed atop Maggie's bed and pulled on the knot at the end of the string dangling from the center of the ceiling. A rectangular panel teased open. Arthur pulled harder and an angled ladder with red rungs stubbornly descended, touching down with a *pfft* on his daughter's white shag rug.

The Alters' attic was a black hole for family miscellany. Entering and exiting through that retractable ladder was just difficult enough to ensure no one ever went to retrieve anything, even though Arthur had ingeniously rigged an overhead light bulb to flick on when the ladder stretched to full extension. As his head crowned into the attic, he saw the mess his family had accumulated there: reference books and CD-ROMs, stereo equipment, tennis balls in plastic chutes. Three generations of internet routers. By a small triangular window, a half dozen leather-bound photo albums were splayed seductively open. Beside them, a papier-mâché pharaoh's mask shared a bin with bundled socks. The interned body of a once-beloved hamster, wrapped in a towel and odor-sealed in Tupperware, sat awaiting burial beside *D'Aulaires' Book of Greek Myths*. To Arthur's left, a pile of dinosaur figurines, a disassembled telescope, stacks of Maxwell House Haggadot, finger puppets representing the ten plagues, a Ziploc bag loaded with marbles, and doubles of canonical board games: Monopoly, Risk, the Game of Life. And dust. Dust over everything. Coating it, claiming it.

In a far corner Arthur found what he was looking for. A cardboard box marked MEMORIES—written with or without irony, he couldn't remember. He lifted a rotting flap. Inside, as he'd hoped, was a slide projector.

Arthur parked himself before the box. Methodically he removed each 35 mm slide from its carousel, raising them one by one, squinting to preview the images. The closer he aligned them with the light, the more defined the image; the more color flushed within the borders of the black film, the sharper the lines around the faces and landscapes depicted. Most slides he returned to the carousel, but some, some he dropped into a shoebox. When he'd worked his way around the carousel at last, he descended from the attic, which darkened as the ladder slid upward.

That afternoon he visited an office supply store in Brentwood with the shoebox under his right arm. With no help from the mega-retailer's stable of incompetent high school employees, he eventually succeeded in converting the little black slides into digital files, which he then printed in color on glossy photo stock. "Is that *you*?"

one of the nametagged burnouts asked, pointing at a print. "Don't smudge it with your fingers," Arthur said. He had the best four photographs framed at a nearby shop and hung them in the dining room on fresh nails that he drove into the wall himself.

He stepped back to behold them. One, two, three, four. All in a row. Standing in their presence, he felt the dining room transformed into a volatile space. Electrified. The photographs made a powerful statement. About what, exactly? Generosity, kindness, the many selves a body could hold. He stood proudly before them until the sun set and the room went dark.

Arthur's stomach groaned. He had forgotten to stock the refrigerator. He hopped in the Spero and drove south to the Schnucks in Richmond Heights. He parked in the vast, crowded lot and approached the supermarket, which resembled a giant brick mausoleum. Bags of fertilizer were piled out front and the woody, fecal smell caught Arthur off guard as he passed them. He hurried by stacks of plastic lawn chairs and a rack of flowerbeds.

Schnucks was mobbed. Students were stocking up for spring break, darting across the checkered floor toward the liquor aisle, descending on corn chips, and tossing packages of grill meats from freezer to cart. Geriatric customers made their slow, intimidated way through the frenzied traffic, pausing to check the price on frozen vegetables in bags or to sniff a block of cheese. Arthur road-raged his way toward the produce and began filling a plastic clamshell with the most exotic and pungent olives he could find.

A thought occurred to him. *I should get some food that* they *like.* Yes! This was good parenting! Arthur smiled, leaning over the olives to bow in deference to himself.

But what do they like?

He and Francine had never agreed on anything as much as they agreed on what to feed their children. Francine, who had struggled with her weight from time to time, was the first mother in Chouteau Place to regularly make the drive to the Soulard Farmers Market. She wanted the best for her children, decidedly *not* the Jell-O molds and marshmallow fluff she'd been raised on, which meant feeding them large quantities of greens and plenty of seafood, which she called "brain food," as fresh as she could find in a landlocked state. Arthur, who loathed waste, was happy to do his part, diluting his children's fruit juices to a ratio of 1:1. No one could make sixty-four fluid ounces last like Arthur could. When Ethan had his first cup of uncut apple juice at a friend's house in fourth grade, his eyes almost fell out of his head.

Arthur made his way through the mob. He remembered coming here with Maggie, the tantrums she threw over what he bought. She wanted the sweet, radioactive snacks that her friends' parents bought. Well, she was grown up now, and he would get her what she wanted. But when he steered his cart down the cereal aisle, and was confronted by the endless rows of blindingly bright boxes—the lime greens, the hot pinks, the sun-vivid yellows; the eye-popping text, the cartoon mascots—he had to squint to keep his balance. He couldn't stomach the sheer variety. The *loudness* of the boxes. Who needed this many options? The Soviets had been onto something with those bare, gray markets, drab and half-empty. Take your allotted rations and go. No more, no less—no *choice*. Consumer choice was a ridiculous and overvalued freedom.

A little girl riding in her mother's cart knocked a box off the shelf across from Arthur, sending candy-colored balls of puffed grain rolling across the floor, where they gathered at his feet. The girl began to cry, and her mother, those ubiquitous white buds stuck in her ears, kept pushing her cart, leaving Arthur standing over the mess. He shook his head. No. This was all too much. He turned around. The kids would have to go without.

In the evening, Arthur took a walk. He proceeded east along the length of Trustee Row, the procession of McMansions and stucco palaces and gingerbread castles that lined Forest Park on Lindell. He kept his eyes on the beautiful homes and the lunatic dissonance of their architectures. He thought about the foreseeable future.

Still, the past provoked him. The Barnes-Jewish Hospital complex loomed beyond the park's tree line, a towering city of the sick, individual buildings linked by aerial walkways as if trying to draw each other closer.

The pride he took in his work on the house—and it was a singular pride, truly, the kind borne from hard work with one's hands, a type of work not typically afforded Arthur, who lived, as his colleagues and neighbors did, in the triple-mint estates of their minds—failed to ward off second thoughts about his plan.

His plan: What *was* his plan? When his children touched down in St. Louis—what then?

He'd have to split them up. Separate them. Get Ethan alone first, try to win him over. Then Maggie. But how? Arthur didn't know. Who *were* his children? What were their lives? As far as he could recall, Ethan was living in Brooklyn somewhere, working at some kind of consulting firm. Maggie hadn't spoken to him since the funeral. Arthur shook his head. He hadn't been paying close enough attention. He didn't have access to their hearts.

But he needed them. He could cover himself for another few years, sure, but with each passing semester he inched closer to a retirement that might never come, and a death that most certainly would. And now that the dean wanted to sit down with him . . . Something would have to be done.

What was he supposed to do, walk away? A bolder man might have. Men of Arthur's generation were supposed to rabbit-run away from problems like this. But where would he go? What would become of him?

He followed the road until he reached the end of the park, puzzling over his situation, when the trees vanished and he was confronted with the Chase Park Plaza hotel. Standing before the tremendous sand-colored pyramid, that monumental Jazz Age ziggurat, Arthur realized, suddenly, how exhausted he was—he'd been walking over an hour—and turned back toward University City.

SEVEN

D o you like living here?"

"Here meaning . . ."

"Meaning here. This house. St. Louis. I don't know. 'The Midwest.'"

Maggie sat on her bed, shoulder to shoulder with Francine, hunched over *Fundamentals of Abnormal Psychology*. She was two finals away from completing her freshman year. One exam was in her mother's field, and she'd walked home from campus for help.

"Why do you say it like that?" Francine asked.

"Like how?"

"In scare quotes. 'The Midwest.'"

"Because I mean it as a, like, *construct*, an idea, more than I mean the . . . the . . ."

"Geographic region."

"Right."

"As in, 'the heartland.'"

"Yeah."

"'Real America.'"

"Right."

In this memory of Maggie's, her mother's wild curls were pinched back by a silver barrette the same shining color as her favorite watch, which clung to her wrist, ringed by an assortment of loose, jangling bracelets.

"Why do you ask?"

Maggie tugged at her ear. "I guess I can't imagine moving for someone like you did."

"You don't like it here?"

"It's fine. I mean, my life is here. I don't know anything else."

"But . . ."

"But we're not 'midwesterners,' are we? We're like, 'university people.' We have this *university milieu*."

"You're not wrong. Though I am from 'the heartland' myself."

"That's true. But no offense, you and Dad only know professors. And they all live in Chouteau Place. And *you* just said 'heartland' in scare quotes."

Francine smiled. "None taken."

"Anyway, that's not what I'm getting at."

"What are you getting at?"

"I guess I mean to say I can't imagine moving for anyone, period."

"You're independent. I admire that in you. I'll take credit for it, if you don't mind. Good parenting."

"But *you* did that. *You* moved."

"It happens."

"Why did you do it?"

"Lots of reasons."

"Like . . ."

Francine drummed her fingers on the underside of the textbook. "Like when people say that marriage requires a certain fluidity, adaptability, compromise, they often mean on one party's behalf."

"The woman's."

"That is certainly the case most often."

"What does Dad think about it?"

"What does he think about what?"

"Moving us out here. Your sacrifice. Doesn't he feel guilty or something?"

Francine fluffed her hair. "Your father feels guilty about a lot of things. But not that. No, I don't think he feels bad about that."

"What *does* he feel bad about?" Maggie asked.

"Well," she said. "I suppose it's not easy to be as ambitious as he is. Was. Because when you're that ambitious and things don't work out as you envision them—that can be hard to stomach."

"What didn't work out?" Maggie closed the textbook, more interested now in her father's abnormal psychology.

"He had this idea," Francine said. "It was his life. And in a way, it became mine." She sighed and shook her head. "When I was young, there was nothing more appealing to me than a man with an idea."

"What was the idea?"

Outside Maggie's bedroom window, a branched cardinal ruffled its feathers. Francine watched it take off with a flutter. "Well," she said, clearing her throat. "What do you know about African waste management?"

B efore Arthur had his idea, he had ambition, and that was when he met Francine Klein. He was pushy and determined, qualities she found attractive, especially when he was pushy and determined on her behalf. In Arthur she saw a fiery and productive mind at work, the kind of mind she dreamed of possessing herself. Fierce. Uncompromising. Their attachment was heightened by a series of pregnancy scares—a broken condom, problems with the Pill; fate, that Jewish grandmother, was ever pushing for a baby—and by the summer of 1977 they were sharing a cramped one-bedroom in Kenmore Square. Before Boston University's multimillion-dollar urban renewal project facilitated the closing of the Rathskeller and the opening of a Barnes & Noble, Kenmore had been the kind of blighted neighborhood missed only after it was gone, a punk assembly of greasy spoons and methadone clinics. It was a good place to be young and in love.

Francine was earning her PhD, acquiring a vocabulary that she applied with great enthusiasm to her parents. She'd spent her childhood longing to be anywhere but Dayton, to belong to any family but hers. But now, six semesters into her degree, Francine nurtured the one remaining seed of sympathy she'd saved for her mother, whom she realized was merely a maladjusted histrionic with perhaps some mild dermatillomania who had lost the best years of her life managing her husband, a unipolar depressive with a whole host of oedipal issues that Francine couldn't even broach. Naming things provided an unexpected relief. She decided that her mother, though still fundamentally unforgivable, had been a victim of her mind, and of the times in which she lived.

With this newfound sympathy came another, more disturbing revelation. Maybe Mrs. Klein, who called biweekly to ask whether Francine was pregnant yet, was onto something. Maybe fate had a point. Maybe they were in cahoots, it didn't matter: in December of 1980, at twenty-seven years old, Francine decided—realized?—that she wanted a child.

Arthur wasn't convinced. "I thought," he said, "that you hated your mother. All mothers, in general."

"I never said that."

"You say that all the time. Yesterday, in the kitchen, you said, 'The older I get, the less I think of my mother as the exception, but the rule.'"

"What I meant was that I realized she suffered as much as other women of her generation, many of whom had undiagnosed issues brought on genetically or exacerbated by the systems that confined them, so when she acted out it was more a symptom than it was—"

"And you said how that was both extremely irritating and a great relief, because it meant you were normal, but it also robbed you of the right to complain."

"Arthur! I didn't say 'the right to complain.' I said, 'the feeling that I'd overcome something as the daughter of a sufferer of mental illness.'"

"That's not how I remember it. In any case, this conversation can wait. I can't engage. There's no room in my brain for this right now."

She rolled over in bed and almost toppled out, crowded as she was by his ambition, which was beginning to colonize his attention, in her prescient thoughts, like a mistress. She wished he wasn't so aloof. She wished he'd focus on what was in front of him—her, for instance. But that long view was what she envied, and was drawn to. She couldn't imagine what it was like to see yourself as a potential agent of history, a Great Mind. When he was in good spirits, his ambition was exhilarating. It was like being wonderfully drunk. When he was unhappy, as he was now, he seemed arrogant and quixotic, giving Francine nausea and the spins.

She attributed his sour mood to work stress. Until recently he'd been developing a pet project at the engineering firm, creating an inexpensive, fast-setting substance that he hoped would one day replace concrete. It involved a special paste that Arthur had concocted that reduced the amount of cement required to make the mixture. He'd been at it for the past year, consulting with material engineers around town, staying late at the office to run stress tests, and falling behind on his other assignments. But the result of this experiment, while cheap to produce, turned out to be weaker than concrete, and unable to support larger structures like bridges and ships' hulls and shopping malls, even when reinforced with mesh and rebar. Arthur had been furious when his supervisor canceled the project. "It's *new*," he'd pleaded. "A novel substance. You're not going to give it a chance?"

"It doesn't matter if it's novel," his supervisor told him, "if it has no applicable use."

"We can find a use. Bear with me. I'll come up with something."

"It doesn't make sense. There's no need for faster, cheaper concrete. There's no demand for it. No one has a problem with concrete as it is. I let you see this through because you were enthusiastic, and because you promised it wouldn't interfere with your work, which it clearly has."

"I *was* enthusiastic. *Am* enthusiastic. I think I'm onto something here."

"I'm going to ask you a question," his supervisor said. "Answer honestly. Are you pursuing this because you think it could meet a real need? Or are you pursuing this to have something to pursue?"

"I reject the premise."

"In other words: Are you doing this for anyone besides yourself?"

"I'll find a use for it."

"It's too fragile, Arthur. It'll never pass code. Not in this country."

He was in a men's room stall when it happened, the mid-January issue of *Time* spread open on his lap. The idea! It electrified his whole body. If only he could make use of his experimental substance somewhere else—somewhere hot and dry, where it would set quickly; somewhere with few regulations; somewhere in dire need of development, where his contributions would go appreciated—if only that were possible, he'd be more than just an engineer. He'd be a humanitarian genius. He looked down at the bespectacled face of the newly minted Zimbabwean prime minister staring up at him from the magazine, smiling below his toothbrush moustache. He raised the magazine to his face and kissed it.

He flushed and fled the men's room. It was only four thirty but instead of returning to his desk, he went straight to the break room where he stored his cross-country skis. He carried them outside and strapped in. The snow in Boston had piled up, bleaching the city, disappearing cars. He sped through the unplowed streets, tripping wildly over the fresh powder, limbs flailing. When he reached the Kenmore Square apartment, he kicked off the encumbrances and left them at the door, clambered up three flights, and breathlessly told Francine his plan.

"You're going to do *what*?" She was sitting at the table, her books and papers sprawled out before her.

He huffed, his cheeks pink from the cold. "I'm going to build sturdy, sanitary, low-cost outhouses all across the Zimbabwean countryside."

Francine blinked. "You're serious?"

"I'm serious. What do you think?"

What did she *think*? She didn't want him to go, is what she thought. But she didn't want to be the kind of woman who kept her boyfriend from pursuing his dream. It was too early in their relationship to sow that kind of long-term resentment. And, she had to admit, there was something exciting about it, about him, standing there all bright-eyed and dusted with snow, charged with purpose. It was a better look on him than vague, unrealized ambition. If she permitted him this trip, she thought, cosigned on this adult rumspringa, he would realize what he had in her. In a few months he would return, sick with freedom, ready to start a family.

"Okay," she said. "I think you should do it."

With her blessing, he wrote a proposal and applied for funding. She helped compose and mail the grants, missing her academic deadlines in service of his. But no sooner had the applications gone out than Arthur was swiftly and mercilessly turned down by nearly every organization he'd solicited: Save the Children, the Southern Africa Development Community, Samaritan's Purse, Doctors Without Borders, Engineers With Passports. Months melted with the snow, and Arthur grew despondent. Francine had never seen him drink more than two beers in an evening, but here he was having three, four, five, six. He put on weight. This from a man who never indulged, who practically accounted for individual grains of rice, who imposed hunger on himself, who wasted nothing and wanted only to unleash himself on the world.

She took some small, private relief at his rejection. It meant that he would stick around. Things would improve once he bounced back. He'd given it a shot, and it hadn't worked out. Maybe now he'd put his ambition toward their relationship. Maybe now they'd make a family.

In the fall, their lives resumed some semblance of normalcy. Francine studied hard, strategically scattering mentions of friends with new babies in conversation. Arthur returned to work, pretending not to hear her.

Then, that spring, an unusual letter landed in his mailbox. The envelope was addressed to Arthur from an organization called the Humble Brothers in Christ. In their typewritten note, they described themselves as "a group devoted to eradicating poverty; to abolishing hunger; to utterly pulverizing treatable illnesses worldwide."

Arthur nearly wept with relief when, at the end of the letter, they stated their intention to fund his project.

Francine was devastated. "Are you sure about this . . . church?" she asked. "I've never heard of it. I don't want to put a damper on things, but I'm saying, it might be wise to keep from getting over-excited."

"I have to take whatever I can get," he snapped.

What the Humble Brothers lacked in name recognition they made up for in enthusiasm—and money. Their tax-exempt church's newly minted publishing wing even printed up a hundred copies of Arthur's detailed proposal, pocket-sized red hardcovers with his name embossed on the front. Arthur was so proud of them that, for the first time since meeting Francine, he cried.

The bound proposals had an outsize effect on Arthur, who'd grown up in a home without books. As a boy he was a natural thinker with precocious critical faculties, but his parents weren't readers. Arthur spent his Sundays in the Sharon Public Library, losing himself in the stacks. His was the typical syllabus of the preadolescent male—biographies of geniuses, novels about baseball—but his favorites were the swashbuckling, empire-defending adventures of Lieutenant Giles Everhard (VC, GCB) as documented in T. S. Worthington's Everhard novels. The good lieutenant was a scoundrel, a rake, a hot-blooded antihero who sailed and slept his way around the world on behalf of Her Majesty Queen Victoria. Drab, cold Sharon, Massachusetts, could not compete with the exotic islands depicted in *Everhard in the West Indies*, nor the American Southwest of *Everhard and the Redskins*. Arthur's parents couldn't have cared less. His mother, a severe woman with undiagnosed Tourette's and an unrelated habit of reminding her son what a little shit he was, threw away whatever books he brought home. She didn't see the value in them. His father, the only cash-strapped dentist in the world, was hardly any help, consumed as he was in self-loathing and the drinking problem that endeared him to the local Irish and made him a Barnum freak show among his fellow Jews. To have a book, now, with Arthur's name on it—it was a rebuttal to them both. If only his father were still alive to see! He drove to Sharon and left a copy with his mother. She never called to follow up.

"This is typical," he fumed. "So typical that she would do this."

"Calm down," said Francine.

"The least she could do is lie to me! Tell me she gave it a once-over! I called her this morning, and guess what? No mention. You were right about mothers. They're the worst. Can't trust 'em. Period."

"That's not what I said. Besides, you know how she is. You can't rely on her for positive reinforcement. She's never given it to you. You're going to have to be proud of yourself. *I'm* proud of you."

Arthur covered his face with his hands. "It's not enough."

More letters followed, details hashed out. It was settled: Arthur was going to Zimbabwe.

There was a lot of hope for the country then. It was newly independent, the breadbasket of Africa, a chief exporter of wheat, corn, and tobacco, all thanks to a charismatic militant named Robert Gabriel Mugabe. In March of 1982, Arthur Gabriel Alter flew from Boston to London, London to Salisbury, which would soon be renamed Harare, landing in the capital city of the country in which he would bring his idea to fruition.

Arthur had upgraded his flight in London for a nominal fee. Before takeoff, Air Zimbabwe provided him, a Club Class passenger, with hot hand towels and complimentary champagne. Once airborne, Arthur enjoyed a ten-hour open bar and a dinner of smoked fish and cornmeal cake, a service that would suffer drastic cuts in the coming months. Across the aisle sat an English-born Zimbabwean, a portly Kipling with a permanent tan. The man had a coarse moustache and a stumped foot. A pink scar extended from the base of his neck to where his shirt was buttoned halfway down his chest. He caught Arthur staring and said, "The war." A couplet occurred to Arthur, something from a poem he'd memorized as a boy in school: *Spicy grove, cinnamon tree, / What is Africa to me?*

In the baggage claim at Salisbury (soon Harare International) Airport, a slender man in a boxy suit and tinted shades displayed a slab of cardboard bearing the name ALTER. Arthur followed the man to a white Mercedes-Benz.

Back in Boston he'd arranged to stay a couple of days at the home of the family of a Zimbabwean colleague, Louis Moyo. On Arthur's last day at the firm, Louis took him out to lunch. When the bill came he passed Arthur a fist of hundred-dollar bills. "Did I loan you money?" Arthur asked. "No, no," his colleague said. "This is for my parents. Give it to them for me, please. American dollars go much further than you think. And also, because I will forget"—and here he pulled a *Playboy* from his briefcase, a creamy-skinned red-head on the cover, topless and leaning over a bottle of spilled red nail polish, her nipples airbrushed into oblivion. "As a token of my thanks," Louis said. He added, "Out in the bush? You might need it."

What is Africa to me: / Copper sun or scarlet sea.

The Moyos lived in an expansive yellow-brick home in Salisbury with a lawn as manicured as any in the tony suburbs of Boston. They were waiting up for him when he arrived.

Louis Moyo Sr. was a jowly, amiable man quick to cut himself down with a playful aside. He made a point to say things like, "You must be exhausted," in kind acknowledgment of Arthur's state. His wife, Promise Moyo, was more assertive, plying Arthur with tea and cakes. A fiercely independent woman, before meeting her husband she built and operated a clothing manufacturing plant. Louis Sr., who, by his own admission, possessed government connections but no particular skills, had arranged a contract for his wife's factory to provide the Zimbabwe National Army with their uniforms. "The world is who you know," he told Arthur, one hand around Promise's waist.

That first night, after leaving him to the guest room, Louis Sr. knocked on Arthur's door. "I would like to wish you good night," he said. "But first, I must ask—did our son give you anything for me?"

Arthur had forgotten about the money. "He did," he said. "One minute." He crouched before his bag with his back to Mr. Moyo. After quietly peeling three Benjamins from the wad—he hadn't forgotten Louis's remark about the value of American dollars—he turned around and passed the rest of the money to his colleague's father. Mr. Moyo's face relaxed into a smile as he wished his guest a good night's sleep.

Arthur spent two relaxing weeks with the Moyo family. Mr. and Mrs. Moyo had both been educated abroad—Louis Sr. in Rochester, New York, and Promise in Toronto—and were curious about the state of American politics. Arthur fielded their questions about Reagan. How could the US elect a Hollywood actor to the office of president? Arthur explained that the average American voter was basically a pampered child with an insatiable appetite for entertainment.

He in turn learned about Zimbabwe. The Moyos were optimistic about independence. Arthur, impressed with their well-appointed kitchen, the Whirlpool washer-dryer, and their high-pressure shower, found himself optimistic too. Between their hospitality, the modern conveniences, and the consistently sunny weather, Arthur was beginning to prefer Salisbury to Boston.

He slept wonderfully there—*Africa? A book one thumbs / listlessly, till slumber comes*—and woke each morning to find hot tea and milk waiting on a tray outside his door, left there by the Moyos' house servant. Over his daily breakfast bowl of bota, Arthur read the *Herald*. Promise taught him how to cook with the coarsely ground maize known as *mielie-meal* in preparation for his time in the country. In the evenings he smoked imported cigars with Louis Sr. One night the Moyos took him to a football match at Rufaro Stadium, where they pulled past throngs of people and into a private lot jammed with Benzes, leading him into the presidential box via a roped-off entryway.

"These were some of his happiest times," Francine told her daughter. "His letters home during those early days were so confident, so certain."

After two weeks Arthur bid the Moyos goodbye and thanked them for their hospitality. Promise hugged him and insisted he come back to visit. He boarded a thirty-year-old Soviet bus with chipped paint to Chiredzi, the small town 400 kilometers south where the Humble Brothers awaited him. As the bus pulled out of clean, modern Salisbury, with its concrete high-rises and purple jacaranda trees, the brutalist skyline dressed in flowering buds, Arthur finally felt homesick, a deferred sadness that he hadn't had the time to process while he acclimated to the country. He thought of Francine, back home, alone.

The city collapsed behind him. The buildings thinned out and gave way to rocky kopjes and scrappy huddles of marula and mopane trees. The air smelled of petrol, wood fire, roasted meat, and soap. A red-brown road shot through the hilly landscape, travelers waiting on either side of it. The bus rattled along, slowly filling to capacity. When the bus broke down, somewhere in Masvingo Province, Arthur and the other able-bodied men got out and pushed.

It was evening when he reached his destination. Chiredzi was a small administrative center in the Lowveld, economically dependent on the sugar estates near the Mozambique border. The Humble Brothers had constructed an outpost a few miles south of downtown.

Arthur walked until he reached the outpost, a one-story cinderblock structure with a red tile roof. In the distance stood clusters of thatched huts, some of them raised on stilts above the blushing earth. He was greeted at the entrance by a twiggy church representative who introduced himself as Rafter Benson.

"Is it just you out here?" Arthur asked.

"Just us," he said, confirming Arthur's worst fears. "Here, let me get your bag. Oh, gosh, this is heavy, huh?"

Rafter had straw-yellow hair and the spindly legs of a cartoon bird. He said he had been living there for two months, preparing the place for Arthur's arrival. "I've read your book a thousand times. Can't say I understand it. But you sure sound like you know what you're talking about."

"Are you a missionary?" Arthur asked.

"Oh, no, no no no," Rafter said. "The Humble Brothers in Christ do not condone proselytizing. Not explicitly. We prefer a more humanitarian approach. We bring aid to those in need. And if, during that process, those in need come to feel that it's prudent to adopt our way of thinking, well, then, we certainly wouldn't stop them."

"You're familiar, then?" Arthur asked. "With this part of the world?"

"Personally? No. This is my first volunteer post."

"And the church? Do the Humble Brothers have any ties to the region?"

Rafter looked confused. "What do you think *we're* doing?"

"*We're* the ties?" He shook his head. "I was hoping you might know your way around. Or at least you might be able to connect me with some other aid workers nearby who might—"

"Nope! Uncharted territory. So to speak." Rafter smiled. "It's going to be an adventure for the both of us. Now, let's go inside and you can tell me what we're going to be doing out here."

It was, above all else, a mission to restore dignity. As Arthur understood it, many parts of rural Zimbabwe still lacked basic sanitation. The poorest citizens did their business out in the bush, contaminating god knew how many wells and water sources, while those fortunate enough to live in walking distance of pit latrines—the kind of shoddy, makeshift outhouses constructed above holes in the ground—were hardly better off. Pit latrines were expensive to construct properly and often fell apart, sinking under their weight into the overfertilized earth. They stunk terribly and required so much maintenance that most were eventually neglected, left to rot as totems to human waste. But in a country eager to modernize, Arthur made the case that every citizen—not only the Moyos and their well-to-do friends—deserved the dignity and privacy of a long-lasting, easy-to-clean outhouse. They deserved to live full, productive lives, without fear of preventable illnesses.

"Gosh," said Rafter, setting down Arthur's bag. "I can already tell it's going to be a privilege to work with you."

There were no distinct rooms in the outpost. It was one long ranch-style corridor. At one end were two cots. Stores of canned foods, flashlights, batteries, and other supplies were stacked at the other. Halfway between them was a sink, and below it, a bedpan.

"You can have whichever bed you want," Rafter said. "Or both. You can push them together and make a double. I don't mind. I'm happy to sleep on the floor."

In the weeks that followed, Rafter made himself useful, gathering sand and cement to mix with Arthur's special paste, whose consistency was not unlike that of mielie-meal mixed with water. He scouted locations and helped plan the prototype. He was pathologically servile, which made him an excellent assistant but irritating company. He was always asking Arthur whether he was comfortable and whether there was anything he could do to accommodate him. He thought himself a mere serf on God's great earthly property—but out in Zimbabwe, with few churches or other reminders of His existence, he directed his devotion toward Arthur. To paraphrase a song that was just then reaching Zimbabwean radio, a decade late: If you can't serve the god you love, serve the god you're with.

One night, Arthur made the mistake of asking Rafter how he found his way to the Humble Brothers in Christ. Rafter talked long into the night about his childhood in West Virginia and the snake-handling church where he had been ordained a child preacher at the age of six. He ran away from home at fifteen and discovered Buddhism in an empty freight car while train hopping north, which he practiced until he was taken in by a sect of Messianic Jews in New Jersey. "But the Humble Brothers," he said, "they're the ones for me."

"How can you be sure?" Arthur asked.

"Oh, I'm sure. This time, I'm sure."

"I have to admit, I hadn't heard of you guys before."

"We're pretty new."

"It's strange to hear about a 'new church.' You don't think of churches being 'new.'"

"There was a time when Jesus was just a guy walking around Galilee."

"I suppose that's true. Where are you based out of?"

"Montana. Butte, Montana."

Arthur had his doubts about the organization, but the work was going well, and the church supported him. Anytime he wrote requesting materials, they arrived in Chiredzi two weeks later, no questions asked.

And yet, and yet. He missed Francine. Her company, her sense of self, her belief in him. He missed Boston. He grew dependent on Louis's *Playboy*. He marked time by the clunky Save the Children pickups that drove along the road past the outpost every two weeks—Arthur regarded their staff bitterly; *You could have had me*, he thought—and by the Coca-Cola trucks with their refrigerated trunks, carrying medical vaccines along with soda in a long cold chain of delivery.

If Arthur wanted to call home, he had to walk into Chiredzi, pray the phone lines were up, wait half an hour, argue for fifteen minutes with operators in Salisbury and Nairobi, and pay upwards of fourteen dollars, all for two patchy minutes with Francine. When they did connect, he found himself at a loss for words. He had to be careful. The distance heightened everything, imbued cursory conversations with heavy subtext. Casual asides could be interpreted and reinterpreted in countless, unexpected ways. Silences were deathblows. It was almost impossible not to become a paranoid on the phone, not to wonder why she didn't pick up when she didn't pick up, or if that static hiss across the wires wasn't a whisper, her playful silencing of a man lying next to her in bed. He frothed with anxiety.

Because they only spoke roughly once every two weeks, when they did reach one another they were pressured into presenting their best selves. There was no time for expressing sadness or frustration—not daily frustrations, like how a scarcity of rebar mesh was causing a delay in production, and certainly not the frustration of the distance itself. (The distance itself was unsolvable, and therefore unspeakable.) There was only time for happiness and romance. Sometimes, those feelings showed up. Sometimes not. In lieu of actual feeling, it had to be performed.

Quickly they fell into platitudes. *I miss you*, she would say after a few seconds of unendurable silence, and he would parrot it back. It was something to say. *I miss you. I love you.* How awful, to hear *I love you* and know it was only said to fill the silence. But what else was there to talk about? Day by day they lost common ground, their lives forking in different directions. What did she care about lavatories? He couldn't personally give two sanitary shits about *The Interpretation of Dreams*. Every minute on the phone was strained. Was this all it took to fall out of love? A handful of weeks and 7,600 miles?

When he wasn't calling Francine or working on his prototype, Arthur made his presence known to the families who dwelled in the huts outside Chiredzi. They spoke Shona, primarily, some Shangaan, and piecemeal English. Arthur did his best to explain, in simple terms and with hand gestures, what he was doing there, but the bodily aspect of his project did not lend itself well to mime. After struggling to communicate his mission, Arthur would play soccer with the children who'd strung up mosquito netting between goalposts outside their homes. Some of them had Shona names, but others, on account of the language imported by British colonizers and American aid workers, were named in English. In addition to Kudakwashes and Kunashes, Emmanuels and Jonathans, Arthur met kids named Sugar (in honor of the nearby plantations) and Nixon (for the American president), Blessing and Goodlife. One young boy, Jamroll Matimbe, named for the sweet dessert a touring English med student gave his mother on the morning of his birth, took a liking to Arthur, and began paying visits to the outpost. A few days per week he'd come by dressed in western hand-me-downs, plaid or paisley shirts with wide lapels, and watch Arthur work.

Though Jamroll didn't know much English, and Arthur couldn't speak a word of Shona, they enjoyed each other's company. Arthur lectured to Jamroll about his project while he worked. Explaining his thought process got him out of his head. Jamroll listened patiently, occasionally replying in his own tongue. Though neither understood the other, Arthur took comfort in the familiar rhythms of conversation, grateful to be talking to someone who wasn't Rafter.

More than the language barrier, their friendship was complicated by Jamroll's weight. Arthur had learned of the two types of hunger plaguing rural Zimbabweans—marasmus, the kind that vanishes flesh, and kwashiorkor, the protein deficiency that causes bloat— and could plainly see that the boy suffered from the former. The center of his chest caved inward, and through a drape of skin Arthur could see his sternum and the contours of his ribs.

Arthur endeavored to understand the boy's condition through the power of the empathetic imagination. They were both human beings, after all. Arthur recalled a summer he spent with his aunt Terry, his mother's sister, when he was roughly Jamroll's age. Terry had never married, and lived alone in East Boston where she had amassed a stunning quantity of pewter figurines. She spoke incessantly about the upcoming election, and the compromising position it put her in. She was a staunch Democrat but believed Kennedy to be an undercover operative for Opus Dei. She was capable of preparing one meal, a dish of her own invention called "fish pizza," which she served Arthur every night for dinner. He never saw her eat, but she invariably sat at the table and watched Arthur. He became sick of the foul taste and began scooping the cheesy fillet into his napkin when she wasn't looking, excusing himself to the bathroom to flush it away. He went without dinner all summer. He lay in bed each night, his stomach roaring, unable to sleep. One night he sneaked into the kitchen to scour her cabinets, but they were empty save for a jar of mustard. The refrigerator, too, was bare. At the time Arthur had been unable to imagine why his mother had placed him under the care of this bizarre woman. Years later, he surmised that he had been serving as some kind of suicide watch. In any event, he returned to Sharon that fall with an understanding of true hunger. It was precisely this experience that allowed him to project himself into Jamroll's body and bridge the distance between their lives. Empathy! He understood the boy completely. He shared his rations of nonperishables with Jamroll, beans and applesauce and powdered milk, though he knew this was only a temporary solution to a systemic problem. Things would improve for the boy, he thought, just as they'd improved for him once he left his aunt Terry and ceased to be her colonial subject—so to speak.

By July a prototype stood proud, a half mile from the outpost and downhill from the nearest well. A wide cylinder, nine feet tall. A vent on top for light and air. Of the four families who lived nearest to the outpost, Arthur had placed it closest to Jamroll's.

"'Moses built an altar,'" Rafter said, looking upon what they had made, "'and called it The Lord Is My Banner.'"

Arthur spent the next few weeks camped out by the latrine, demonstrating to curious locals whom Rafter had recruited how the site was built and how it might be maintained. He showed them how to mix his special paste with the cement, sand, and water, and pour it over the chicken mesh. The paste, he stressed, as best he could, allowed them to save on cement. The latrine had a wooden door with spring hinges, and the whole thing sat atop a round slab with an aperture that led down to a deep pit. The total cost of materials per latrine was twelve dollars. He displayed how the structure could be cleaned with a little water and soap. He watched with pride as one after another stepped inside to take their turn. Never again would the rural peoples of Chiredzi District have to shit in some ramshackle outhouse. Or worse, in the open, by a river.

Rafter photographed Arthur standing beside the latrine, posing with Jamroll. Arthur kept one roll of film and Rafter sent the rest to his superiors. In turn the Humble Brothers sent more money. Arthur was to build more toilets to the west, near Chiredzi's sister town of

Triangle, and south, in the Hippo Valley. He recruited some young men from town and trained them in the construction process. He delegated more and more to Rafter and the men from Chiredzi. Alter Latrines began appearing all across Masvingo.

In September, a telegram reached Arthur at the outpost.

> ARTHUR—
> PLEASE JOIN US FOR A PARTY THIS WEEKEND. YOU CAN RELAX
> FROM ALL YOUR WORK.
> YOURS,
> LOUIS MOYO SR.

The white Mercedes picked him up a few days later. "What should I do while you're gone?" Rafter asked.

Arthur laid two light taps on Rafter's cheek. "Just keep building."

He slept the whole ride back to Salisbury. The brown leather seat back was cool on his neck; the chauffer didn't utter a word. When, at sunset, the Mercedes slowed to a stop in the Moyos' driveway, Arthur stirred awake. He saw the Moyos' yellow-brick house, and his stomach sank with shame. When he'd first come to Salisbury, his nearest point of comparison was Boston. But having spent a few months in the country among Zimbabwe's poorest, he was no longer impressed by the Moyos' plenitude. It made him sick.

The nausea stuck with him through dinner, which Promise had prepared with the help of her house servant. Arthur was too hungry to refuse the food, but eating it only made him feel worse.

"It's wonderful to see you again, Arthur," Promise said over dinner.

"You really cleaned your plate there, boy," said Louis Sr. "They're not feeding you out in the bush, are they? Ha!"

Arthur glared at the beef stew growing cold on Louis Sr.'s plate.

"Are you making much progress with your work?" Promise asked.

"I am," he said. "Our prototype is functional. The next step is to expand. You wouldn't believe how grateful people are."

"Oh, I believe it," Louis Sr. said.

"Well, I for one think it's wonderful what you're doing, Arthur." Promise smiled. "An American coming all this way—for toilets! Who knew?" She laughed.

"It's bad out there," Arthur said.

"There's a real unwillingness to modernize," said Louis Sr. "You've got to keep up or else you'll fall by the wayside."

"He's right." Promise nodded.

Arthur finished his tea with a grimace. "I'm going to go to bed, if that's okay." He tossed in his sleep all night.

The party, which took place the following afternoon, was honoring the birthday of a ten-year-old girl, the daughter of a close family friend. The party was held on the lush green lawn of the girl's house. Buffet tables offered top-shelf liquor and shrimp cocktail to the guests, the plump pink crustaceans arched over the rims of the glasses with their heads dipped in as if gorging on the sauce themselves. Roasted guinea fowl and springbok fillets sat on silver trays. Arthur managed to set aside his anger for twenty minutes while he ate. Then, after two Johnnie Walkers, he discovered it again.

"Mr. Moyo," he said, as the lawn began to tilt. "Excuse me, but where did these people get all this *stuff*?"

Louis Sr. smiled. "What do you mean?"

"In the south I can't get *anything*. Shampoo, razors, batteries . . . even toilet paper is scarce. If I need something I can have it shipped over by my backers, but I see these villagers and I think, how can they stand it? Do they know about all this? The shrimp and the whiskey? And I thought—I thought this was a *socialist country*."

Louis Sr. laughed. "Oh, my friend," he said, his smile suddenly despicable. "This is socialism in Africa: what's mine is mine, and what's yours we share."

Arthur excused himself to the corner of the lawn and threw up in the bushes.

That night he dreamed he was a member of the Royal Navy,

with a harem of sun-bronzed women to defend, but every time he reached for his sword, he found, to his embarrassment, that it was missing.

He didn't return to Chiredzi on Sunday as planned. Shaken up, he took a detour to a Trappist monastery and hospital he'd heard about in Chisumbanje, where he stayed for an entire week, helping patients where he could, assisting the monks in their production of bread and beer. He returned to the Humble Brothers' outpost with a hangover and a renewed belief in his mission.

"What took you so long?" asked Rafter, who was kicking a Humble Brothers–branded soccer ball with Jamroll in front of the outpost when Arthur returned.

"I made a stop on the way back. What'd I miss?"

Jamroll kicked the ball to Arthur. Arthur caught the ball beneath his boot. A drop of water landed on the shell toe. He looked up at the darkening sky, then back at Jamroll.

The boy shrugged. "Rainy season," he said, in English.

By December the showers were heavy and frequent. Construction on the Alter Latrines slowed. But when the sky cleared for a week in the middle of the month, none of the young men Arthur had enlisted to help him reported for work. Jamroll, too, was nowhere to be found. He sent Rafter into town to see what was going on.

Rafter returned to the outpost from a trip into town, his shirt pulled up over his mouth. "Sleenph niphnis!" he said.

"What?"

Rafter uncovered his mouth. "Sleeping sickness." He pulled his long sleeves over his hands.

"What are you doing?"

"Reducing surface area. Arthur, we've got to protect ourselves."

"I left a cement mixer by the prototype. Walk with me."

"Arthur . . ."

"Come on. Walk and talk."

"Sleeping sickness," Rafter repeated, following Arthur and looking nervously around him. "It's a disease. Carried by tsetse flies. It feeds on your central nervous system."

"And it's going around?"

"Chiredzi General is at capacity. They're turning people away."

"Is that where our guys have been?"

"I don't think you understand, Arthur. It's everywhere."

"Is it fatal?"

"Can be. Depends. They ran out of beds. People are sleeping on the floor."

"You don't think Jamroll . . ."

Rafter threw his arms up. "Right now? I'm more concerned about us. About you."

"So what, then?"

"I don't know. We quarantine ourselves, I guess. We see if this blows over. I put in a call to HQ and left a message. I'll try again tomorrow. We need to keep away from anything that could . . ."

He trailed off as they reached the prototype. A faint buzzing sound surrounded it.

"Arthur," Rafter said, extending a shaking arm. "Look."

He followed Rafter's finger to the top of the latrine. A cloud of black dots had settled around the superstructure.

Rafter's jaw slacked open. "They're drawn to the smell," he said. "Oh, God."

Arthur took a step forward.

"What are you doing?" Rafter asked.

"I want to look."

"Are you insane? It could be a breeding ground in there!"

"I need to know," he said flatly. "I need to know for sure."

"I won't let you!" Rafter grabbed him by the collar. "I won't let you get sick."

The following weeks unfolded like a horrible dream. Rumors spread throughout the region. Locals grew suspicious of the white men in the outpost. Children gathered to throw rocks at the Alter Latrines before their mothers rushed in, swept them up, and warned them never to go near one of those things again. Rafter stopped speaking, afflicted by a depression against which no amount of faith could inoculate him. His belief—in Arthur, in whatever the Humble Brothers preached—was irreversibly shaken. He must have said something to his superiors, because in late December the church sent a strongly worded letter and promptly cut Arthur's funding.

He needed to book a flight home, and fast. A few days after the letter from the church arrived, Arthur took the long way into town, hoping to go unnoticed. He felt gutted, carved out, hollow. He couldn't face the Moyos. He could hardly face himself. While walking, the path looping and curving its unhurried way to the bus stop in Chiredzi, adrift in despair, Arthur stubbed his toe on a rock and fell forward, landing flat on the ground. Minutes passed. He made no effort to move. It felt right, lying there. *You're shit*, he thought. The ground was where he belonged.

But the sun was setting, and the phones in town were inaccessible at night. He sighed and picked himself up. He dusted off his elbows and wiped his hands on his jeans. That's when he saw it.

Up ahead, by the side of the road, was an Alter Latrine. But what was it doing here? Who had erected an outhouse on this winding road, and this close to town? He had no memory of approving this location.

He approached it with caution. The outhouse resembled his, though the superstructure was round edged and spiraled. There was no need for a door. The walls were constructed from some kind of ferro-cement. Spiral shape aside, it was practically an Alter Latrine. But with one major difference: extending from the base on which the structure was built rose a black ventilation pipe, roughly nine feet high. And this latrine, he realized, was not new. The surface was scarred with chips and blemishes.

It took Arthur a moment to comprehend what he was looking at. When at last he understood—that airflow from the squat hole was pushed up through the vent pipe; that flies could enter through the spiral opening but were drawn to the light at the top of the pipe; that the top of the pipe was fitted with a fly screen; that this was a vast improvement on his design; and that the outhouse had been standing in this spot for at least a few years—he realized why funding had been difficult to secure.

His idea was not his idea. He'd proposed a solution to a problem that had already been solved. The Humble Brothers, in their ignorance, were unaware. And Arthur, in his vanity, had missed it. His knees shook and he fell, once again, to the ground.

PART II

EIGHT

The Kleins were by no means the unhappiest family on Folsom Drive, but they weren't the happiest, either, the mean of their contentment crashed by Francine's depressed mathematician father. He slept sixteen hours each day, and even while awake he worked from bed, getting up only to make loud, tortured urinations or to sit, frowning, in his mock-leather living room chair. Whenever one of his daughters dared to ask what he was doing, sitting with that distant look on his face, he answered in his duskiest voice, "I'm working on my book." It was like being married to a corpse, her mother complained to friends on the phone, and Francine, eavesdropping from the next room, supposed she wasn't wrong; burly Papa Klein had the soulless stare of a dead man. Still, at eight years old, she was disturbed to hear her mother state her plight so plainly. Until then she had believed her father to be merely lost in thought, wrestling with some high-order theory, forever solving for X.

There was nothing remarkable about the Kleins' ranch home, other than its size. It was one of the smallest on the street, which irritated Mrs. Klein to no end. She compensated by meticulously managing the interior. Throughout the house, above the wall-to-wall carpeting and scratchy furniture, she hung pastel paintings of harlequins that she herself had made. She guarded the space like it was a museum, and enforced exacting rules for household decorum. Be Quiet. No Shoes in the Family Room. Don't Breathe on the Art.

It was Mrs. Klein you had to watch out for. A needle-thin woman with a beehive held in place by Aqua Net, she was a keen observer of social dynamics, a genius of criticism with an arsenal of back-handed compliments, given to saying things like "It's a miracle you photograph well" or "You have the broad shoulders to pull off that blouse." She joined every group and association for women in town with the sole intent of slagging off her fellow members. Francine, who learned to anticipate her mother's comments and adapt herself accordingly, got off easier than Rebecca. Her younger sister, who went by Bex, was not as amenable as she was, had no gift for com-promise, and fought with their mother constantly.

Mrs. Klein's cruelty only wavered once per week, on Shabbat, when she insisted that her husband join the family in the kitchen. She'd light the candles and then quickly shut her eyes to pray in Hebrew. When she opened them, the Sabbath inaugurated by her words, the first thing she saw was the light. She also behaved during the High Holy Days. Francine looked forward to autumn for this reason, when for ten repentant days her mother acted with the ut-most kindness, making public and private displays of goodness with the aim of being inscribed and sealed in the Book of Life.

When the girls were young, their father's book—no tractatus, it turned out, but an undergraduate calculus textbook—was published to some acclaim, and course-adopted all across the country. This sudden windfall resulted in the purchase of the vacant house next door and a second car, a green Impala. The house was for Papa Klein's mother, a decision that infuriated Mrs. Klein, who wanted a bigger place for herself on Folsom Drive, and who did not find her mother-in-law worthy of her charity.

Around this time Francine became preoccupied with fairness. If she asked her mother why they had two cars while her friend Ellie's family had only one, Mrs. Klein would say, bluntly, "Because Ellie's father drinks his paychecks." It was from her grandmother, who now lived next door and did more than her fair share of parenting, that Francine learned a sense of justice. "Your father has been lucky," Grandma Ruth would say in response to that same question.

"I propose this: from now on, you will give Ellie half of your cookie every day at lunch."

"Why?" Francine asked.

"To make things right. To make things equal."

"But half a cookie doesn't equal a car."

Grandma Ruth smiled, her eyes shining with the hereditary twinkle that graced all the women in her line. "You're very bright, you know that?"

"But the car—"

"Yes, you're right. Half a cookie doesn't equal a car. But enough cookies, over time, can count for something else entirely."

The lessons stuck. When Bex took a beating from their father—they weren't called beatings then, but "spankings," which implied an open palm that Bex wasn't fortunate enough to receive—Francine was outraged.

"What happened?" she said, inspecting the bruise on Bex's arm.

Bex sobbed, her shoulders heaving. "I used the phone after six o'clock." It was one of their mother's rules. "I was calling Marie about homework, I swear!"

The following evening, Francine waited until 6:01 and dialed Information. When her father lumbered to the scene, Francine hung up, shut her eyes, and extended her left arm. "Now me," she said, with the hope that a matching bruise would cheer her sister up and restore a kind of balance to the household.

Papa Klein's pupils swiveled behind milky cataracts. He stood before her a moment, then returned to his study, grumbling.

When Francine told her grandmother what had happened, Ruth's breath cut short. She raised her hands to fix her cloud of white hair, tears precipitating below it. "Sometimes there are limits," she said, "to what a person can mend."

The Klein girls had a thing for themed outings. Their favorite restaurant, the site of many a childhood birthday party, was a smoky, blue-lit lounge on North Main called the Tropics. The Tropics, with its thatched pagoda roof and nudie matchbooks and Polynesian-looking waitresses, was a thrill for the girls. They loved anything exotic, anything non-native to Ohio, but more than that they loved the idea of a themed restaurant—somewhere you could disappear into a conceit, somewhere with a whole new set of customs. Their house had so many rules, enforced with the erratic ferocity of a tyrant. What pleasure, then, to inhabit a different space, whose existence challenged the dominant culture of their home. When the girls were eight and ten, respectively, and got the Disneyland vacation they'd been begging for, it didn't matter that they weren't tall enough for the grown-up rides they'd been anticipating. They were content simply to be there, immersed in a world with its own aesthetic, currency, philosophy. They were happily immersed in theme.

When the girls reached middle school, Mrs. Klein began the process of differentiating them. "Francine's the smart one," their mother bleated at anyone who'd listen. "And Rebecca's fun." Statements like these had the net effect of offending all involved.

It was a false distinction. Though Bex performed "fun" in more obvious ways than Francine—makeup, invitations to parties, laughing with a suggestively open mouth—Francine was entirely content to stay inside and read. Her idea of fun was simply quieter, and solitary. And where Francine was book-smart, Bex possessed a gather-ye-rosebuds vivacity that gave her an air of worldliness and earned her the reputation of a heartbreaker long before Francine knew anything about love.

As the girls grew up, their bodies seemed to mold to suit their mother's conceptions of them. Bex stayed thin and conventionally attractive, shedding her freckles and doubling down on her laugh. Francine's weight fluctuated based on her academic calendar, ballooning before exams and other periods of heightened stress.

Despite their differences, Bex looked up to her sister. She could tell her parents valued Francine's gifts above hers. Mrs. Klein was too misanthropic to be a socialite, and Papa Klein was an absence, living in the family blind spot. Unfortunately for Bex, charisma was not a virtue in their house. She admired Francine's model behavior, her good grades and levelheadedness, and Francine in turn listened with a twinge of envy to her little sister's tales of parties crashed and boys kissed.

At sixteen, however, Francine found it difficult to model much of anything. Her mood was low enough to rival her father's. The Kleins had been living on the textbook royalties for years now, and possessed the desperate mien of people milking previous achievements with no mind toward accomplishing anything new. Depression descended plague-like through the house. And to make matters worse, Francine's public high school in Meadowdale had not recovered from the riot three years earlier over the murder of an unarmed black man, Lester Mitchell, by an unidentified white shooter. Relations between the black students, who comprised 70 percent of the class, and their white counterparts, were tense. Twin girls, Aida and Ida, who were bused in from less prosperous blocks than the Kleins', stalked Francine for eight months straight because they said she looked at them funny in gym class.

It was entirely possible that Francine had looked at them funny. She stared off into the middle distance for much of her first two years of high school, and particularly in gym. She sleepwalked through her early teens, passing her classes without effort or enthusiasm, spending long periods of time alone in her room after school. She avoided her mother; she avoided the twins; she avoided looking at herself in the mirror. She thought herself fat and ugly. Solitude suited her, but she had a gnawing feeling that there was something better on the other side.

There was. Fed up with Meadowdale, she petitioned her parents to use some of the textbook money to enroll her in a prep school half an hour south of the Klein house, where she thrived. Classes were capped at twelve students and the teachers all had advanced degrees. She had a sort-of fling with a clarinet prodigy. She might have felt guilty about the opportunities afforded her (and not, for example, Aida and Ida) had she not been having all that *fun*. For it was then, in her junior year, 1970, that Francine fell in love with Paris.

This was due in part to a very cute AP teacher with a master's in French lit, but could more likely be attributed to her sense that Paris was the anti-Dayton: sophisticated, blasé, cultured. She dreamed of it often. Paris—a whole city with a theme! The theme of Paris! She took to practicing new French faces in the mirror at home, each belonging to a heretofore unrealized soul she now found inhabited her: The Bemused Critic. The Judgmental Voyeur. The Neglected Mistress. She dressed in black and picked up smoking. Her newfound interest coincided beautifully with a time of hormone-induced angst and increasing disaffection with her parents, as Francine was able to disguise her frustration with her home life in learned quotations ("*L'enfer, c'est les autres*") instead of turning combative like her sister.

She dropped the act only for her grandmother. With Grandma Ruth, Francine could express in extremely unhip, un-French terms how much she loved the language and the culture, the guttural *R* and feminist existentialism, even the drab paintings of gleaners from the mid-nineteenth century, which moved her in some unnamable way. "One day," said Grandma Ruth, "you will go to Paris and send me a postcard." Francine nodded. "I will," she promised, "I will."

Francine's teacher in her senior year was a husky-voiced thirty-something named Joanne who had boundary issues. She seemed as though she'd been waiting for the seventies all her life. She wore knee socks and plaid miniskirts in a sexed-up approximation of the student uniform; years later she would be quietly dismissed for sleeping with two male students who couldn't keep a secret. Francine was in thrall to her. Joanne radiated knowingness, and prepped her protégé for an eventual trip to the City of Light. There were rules—but they were elegant, sensible rules! Don't Bring Wine to a Dinner Party. Don't Wear Sneakers in the Street. Buy Your Bread Fresh Every Day. Francine learned not to get chrysanthemums as gifts; they were considered morbid, used for decorating graves on All Saints' Day. There was so, so much to learn.

She excelled at French, and in her last months of high school was looking forward to majoring in it at Wellesley, far away from home where her mother, living with a man who could now be said to resemble a corpse with no exaggeration whatsoever, was beginning to unravel, lashing out and picking at her skin.

"Why do you have to go that far away?" her mother asked, her fingers trembling as they stroked a scab on her cheek. "Are you a *lesbian* now?"

"No," said Francine, through the collar of a black turtleneck. "They have a good French program."

"I don't believe there aren't any good programs between here and Massachusetts."

"It's one of the best in the country."

"What on earth do you think I'm going to do when you're gone?"

"You'll have Bex for two more years. And she's talked about Ohio State, right?"

"Rebecca is a silly girl. She's not serious. Not smart, like you."

Francine looked away. "I'm sorry."

"Promise me you'll buy some new clothes."

"What's wrong with my clothes?"

"Black. Only black. What are you, depressed or something?"

"Mom . . ."

"That's right. You aren't." She shivered as she peeled the scab. "You have no *right* to be depressed. Hear me? No right at all."

When Grandma Ruth died, Francine was the only one who seemed to care. She wept for a whole week. She'd never felt so alone. Meanwhile, her mother annexed the house next door and began discussing an illegal plan to build an addition that would join the two homes into one exceedingly long ranch. There were no speeches, no *in memoriams*. It fell to Francine to pen an obituary, which ran in the back of the *Dayton Daily News*.

> Ruth Klein, age 74, beloved grandmother, died in her home in Dayton
> on Tuesday, March 16, 1971, of natural causes. She is survived by her
> sister, Myrtle Klein, of Columbus, her son, David Klein, and his children,
> Francine and Rebecca Klein, also of Dayton.

"Too many commas," Mrs. Klein said, reading over Francine's shoulder. "It's hard to follow."

All told, having no point of comparison, Francine did not consider her childhood to be damaging until years later, when she began to study psychology in earnest, a career path determined (on top of everything else) by a random encounter with a copy of *Games People Play* that her mother forgot to reshelve in the den.

The summer after senior year was marked by two significant pieces of mail. First there was the roommate questionnaire. Wellesley College wanted to know what hours Francine kept; whether she preferred to study in her room or the library; whether she liked to play her music loud. She wasn't sure how to answer. How could she know her college routines and habits when she wasn't yet in college? How could she state who she was when she didn't even know? She had prepared herself for an East Coast education in French language and culture. She had not prepared herself for an education in how to live.

One question troubled her in particular. Was she a smoker? Strictly speaking, yes, she did smoke. But she hadn't always smoked. Only these past two years. She had been a nonsmoker many more years than she had been a smoker. She had smoked only as long as she had been interested in French, and even then, the smoking was only an accessory to the language. She didn't like the idea of herself as a smoker. She was a Francophile, so she smoked. And besides, she didn't want her mother to find the questionnaire and harangue her about cigarettes. (Mrs. Klein worried about airborne toxins damaging the surface of her paintings.) Francine checked NO. She was decidedly not a smoker.

The second piece of mail, which arrived one month later, was a letter from Mary Rooney, whom the college had paired with Francine on the basis of their questionnaires. It read,

Dear Fran (can I call you Fran?),
I'm so looking forward to living with you. I think college will
be great. My older sister went to Wellesley and she enjoyed herself

very much. I'm from Bala Cynwyd, in Pennsylvania. I like field
hockey but I'm not going to do it in college. There probably won't
be enough time. Here's a question: which one of us should bring
the stereo? I woud like a stereo in the room. I can bring mine
unless you were already going to bring yours.

Yours Sincerely,
Mary Rooney

The benign missive riled Francine. Maybe it was precollege
nerves, but she was irritated by Mary's note, particularly the assumption that Francine owned a stereo—which she did, but still.
Not everyone owned a stereo! What kind of person made such an
assumption? There were people, like her friend Ellie, who did not.
Francine wasn't able to bring her stereo, anyway, as she shared hers
with Bex, not because the Kleins couldn't afford two stereos, but
because one of Mrs. Klein's bizarre rules was: No Doubles.

In September of 1971 Francine moved to Massachusetts, having
made the private vow never to return home again—not until she
was her own person, independent, with her own life. She was immediately taken with New England, and the campus's perfect, Olm-
stedian distillation of the region. The lake, the glacial topography,
the conifers turning for autumn—she was smitten. She lived in
stately Cazenove Hall. Mary Rooney turned out to be a decent person (though Francine regretted lying about smoking, which became
an inconvenient secret to keep) and the camaraderie of her hallmates buoyed her through a rocky adjustment period. She made
friends with interesting stories, and from interesting places: a physics wiz from the Upper Peninsula; the defecting lesbian heir to a
retail empire; a poet with a summer home somewhere called Cape
Cod. The lack of men was not a problem, for the most part. Francine missed boys, the sight of them, their charming sort of idiocy,
but she was here to learn and become worldly, to be taken seriously.
Wellesley was the kind of place that made serious women out
of girls. And then there was Boston, the bus that took you from
campus to Harvard Square, dropping you smack in the middle of all

that history and brainpower, all that redbrick and iron-gated excellence.

Home tugged at her sleeve every now and then. Mrs. Klein insisted that her daughter double major because French was a "thin" subject. Francine chose psychology. "Well, I suppose two thin subjects are better than one," said her mother. Psych was less glamorous, but Francine had a knack for it. It would take a few years before she admitted to herself that she had a gift for the subject that she lacked in French, despite her enthusiasm for the latter. The *DSM* read like a road map to her parents' minds.

But her underclassmen years were leading toward one thing, one place, a place where she could *use* her education, a place where she could smoke in the open, in the streets: Paris. In the spring of her sophomore year she enrolled in a two-semester program that would take her there.

The apartment was in the 5th arrondissement, near the métro Censier–Daubenton, and on weekend mornings the chatter and fuss of the markets on the rue Mouffetard massaged her consciousness, and Francine woke to the mingled smells of fresh bread and garlic sausage, the sounds of salesmen peddling Honduran grapefruit and California lemons, pigeon eggs, rabbit, charcuterie. She lived with a friend from college, Linda Sussman, one-quarter Corsican and known at Wellesley as the MBWoC, or Most Beautiful Woman on Campus, who had managed, with a few tasteful photos posted across the Atlantic, to line up a boyfriend in Paris before she even set foot in Europe. Jean-Charles had blue eyes like Linda's. His father was an Egyptologist.

The apartment wasn't much, a galley kitchen and a common space with an alcove that made for a semiprivate second bedroom, but who cared? This was Paris. Every morning Jean-Charles and his friend Guillaume, a film student, brought baguettes over. Francine and Linda would be waiting with coffee, butter, and jam. These four, plus the two Pierres (le Blond et le Brun) and a recovering heroin addict named Cecile, comprised a *bande d'amis* who met for lunch at the Quatre Sergents. The Quatre Sergents crew communed across from the Lycée Henri-IV after morning classes. There were all sorts of juicy dynamics to navigate. Guillaume had dated Cecile, and helped her get clean, but now Cecile was interested in Pierre le Blond. Linda, with her philosophy minor and Connecticut nose, had caused Jean-Charles to leave *his* ex, who was Guillaume's sister. Nourished by this extremely French-seeming gossip (and Guillaume's occasional flirtations), Francine enjoyed every minute at the Quatre Sergents. There was a jukebox stocked with American music in the back, and every now and then Pierre le Brun would put on "Johnny B. Goode" and sing with a heavy accent. They convened so often at the Quatre S that the owners, M. and Mme. T——, regularly stopped by their table to ask if anyone wanted cigarettes. Francine always said she did, in part because each time M. T—— returned with a pack of Rothmans rouge for her, he'd set it down and say, with a wink, *"Rouge et mûr comme les tomates en Californie."*

If being American lent Francine a bit of exotic intrigue, it was nothing compared to the status boost she received from rooming with Linda Sussman. Linda was built for a see-and-be-seen city like Paris, a city of street-facing chairs. The Bande du 4S had assembled around her. Even Guillaume, whose sister was heartbroken when Jean-Charles dropped her for Linda, could not hold a grudge against her beauty.

On Saturday afternoons, Francine went to the movies. Linda was usually busy with Jean-Charles, or studying at the Bibliothèque Sainte-Geneviève (though it was impossible to imagine anyone as ruthlessly stunning as Linda Sussman hunched over something as anachronistic as a book), but Guillaume, who found easygoing Francine a welcome change from manipulative, addiction-prone Cecile, was usually happy to tag along. They'd open a copy of *Pariscope* and survey the listings. This was the year of Francine's cultural education. It was the year of Hitchcock, Antonioni, Godard, and Fellini. She watched only two contemporary films in all her time abroad.

One was *American Graffiti*, at Linda Sussman's homesick urging; the other, *Can Dialectics Break Bricks?*, at Guillaume's.

It was also a year of conventional education, albeit with a European-inflected air of intellect and theory that not even Wellesley, with all its rigor, could provide. For her thesis paper, Francine had chosen as her subject the phenomenologist Maurice Merleau-Ponty. Merleau-Ponty was something of a minor figure in philosophy, when one considered the grand sweep of the field, but Francine identified with his position. She was not exceedingly ambitious, like Guillaume (who longed to pioneer a new movement in cinema), nor did she command attention like Linda Sussman. Francine was simply smart, and smart enough to know what she wasn't capable of. She was never the standout in her Wellesley classes, never the Sartre. She was always the Merleau-Ponty—smart and dependable, contributing in discreet but important ways. And there was the added benefit of his field, phenomenology. Studying his work, Francine was in effect writing a psychology paper—it just happened to be in French.

On Armistice Day, the whole Bande du 4S took a train to Café König in Baden-Baden where, vindicated by history, they ordered croissants and spoke loudly in French before giddily fleeing the scene. They spent the night in Strasbourg at Guillaume's parents' place.

"*Donc*, Francine, tell me: What will you do with your life?" his mother said.

The question had an odd ring to it. Francine realized her mother had never asked her this before. "Well," she said, clearing her throat, "I think—I think I would like to study, and then practice, psychology."

Guillaume's mother looked puzzled, then muttered something to her son. "Ah!" she said suddenly. "*Psychologie! Bon.*" She nodded meaningfully. "Good. I think you will do this. I think you will be *magnifique*."

Francine slept with Guillaume twice that winter, but felt nothing for him beyond friendship, and was happy to feel nothing. She had no need for anything more. Cecile dumped Pierre le Blond, found heroin again, and then, with Guillaume's help, she quit. Nothing befell the Bande du 4S that friendship could not fix.

In the spring, as soon as it was warm enough to travel, Francine and Linda booked a trip to Austria. In her last days, Grandma Ruth had signed a check for $1,000, which she passed, with shaky hands, to Francine. Francine had cashed the check but was unable to find a purpose for the money worthy of her grandmother—until now.

A last-minute case of whooping cough kept Linda from going, but rather than invite Guillaume, Francine decided she'd go herself. Some time alone might be nice, she thought. Some time apart.

She was a young woman traveling the continent by herself, and she took a certain amount of pride in her navigation of the buses and trains and the airport. She made her way into the valley, found a place to stay, and soon she was breathing in what people must've meant when they said "mountain air."

She wasn't at peace for long.

Never in her life was she able to figure out how, 4,500 miles away, her mother was able to track her down at the bed-and-breakfast in Innsbruck, but somehow, Mrs. Klein found her. The housekeeper called Francine inside and passed her the telephone.

"Hello?"

"Francine! It's your mother."

"Mom?" She cringed at the hysterical voice.

"That's what I said. Listen. Are you there?"

"I'm here."

"Can you hear me?"

"I can."

"It's about your father."

"Is everything okay?"

"No, no, *no!* Everything is *not* okay! Your father is sick. It's awful, awful. You should have seen him. He couldn't swallow. Understand? He couldn't *swallow*. His face was like mush. His words came out funny. Francine, he's at the hospital now. You need to come home."

"Where's Bex?"

"She's here."

"Is Dad okay?"

"He'll be fine. We're bringing him home tomorrow. But it's not the same. No, it's not the same. You'll need to come home."

"Mom. I'm in Austria."

"All the more reason to get here right away."

"I can't come home. Not now."

"You went to France, you had your fun. Now it's time to come home. You have certain responsibilities. Your father couldn't *swallow*. His face was like *mush*."

The thought of returning to Dayton to take care of her father was inconceivable. Untenable. The provincialism! The narrow-mindedness! Her mother's painted harlequins! The empty house next door, Grandma Ruth's house, taken over, changed—no. It couldn't be. Not when there were two months left in the semester. And the summer. The summer in Paris!

"I'm sorry," she said. "I can't."

"Francine. Don't be a brat. Don't leave me here with him."

"You have Bex. That should be enough."

"I don't *want* your sister, I want *you*. Come *home*."

Francine made a quick mental calculation. She had enough money to finish out her term, assuming some help from her friends. "I'm sorry."

"Francine Klein, you *will* come home. I gave you *life*, I raised you myself, without anyone's help, I made sure you had *food to eat*, I enrolled you in that *school*—you will come home. Understand? You will come home. It's right that you should come back. It's—it's only *fair*."

The word gutted her. *Fair*. Tears wet her freckles. She had resolved not to return to Folsom Drive. Fair or not, she couldn't do it.

"No, Mother," she said. "I'm staying." Then she hung up the phone, turned around, and walked out through the front door to the porch where she'd been sitting. She pulled up her chair and took the last sip of the orange juice on the table before her. The mountains rose up with unqualified majesty behind the neat row of colorful buildings in the city center, close enough, it seemed, to touch. The peaks were draped with snow.

"*Noch eins?*"

She looked up. The housekeeper was standing in front of her, pointing at her glass. Francine must have seemed confused, dazed, because in the moment it took for her to realize herself and begin to formulate an answer, the housekeeper asked, in English, "Another?"

NINE

The tornado tore the roof off Concourse B.

Though it took only thirty hours for the maintenance crew to restore the airport to 80 percent functionality, to determine which gates to reopen and how, to cordon off the areas that needed cordoning, to make cosmetic repairs and achieve a standard of operation that the FAA could, under pressure from the major carriers, deem "safe," for an out-of-towner who hadn't heard the news, the shabbiness of the building—the boarded-up windows, the doors slapped with caution tape, the blacked-out light fixtures—was cause for concern. Anyone could tell it was a perilous rush job. A ramshackle portent. And unfortunately for Arthur, his children did not require further proof that St. Louis was a low-rent city abandoned by history and held together with staples and glue.

Confirmation bias, he thought, against his will. *Yes, Francine, I know.*

Friday. Sunset. Driving north through Overland on I-170, hurtling toward the airport like an extinction-hauling asteroid, Francine's Toyota Spero was drenched with light. For years Arthur had driven an orange Honda with a cratered hood, but after Francine died he sold it for cash and commandeered her car. It was filling with the same light presently conquering downtown, a light of mystifying post-storm intensity that warped parabolic around the Arch before catching, chromed, in the windblown debris. This, he'd thought, *this* was what the weekend was about. The luminous and not the broken. The light and not the wreckage. The dappled gold that filled his car and not the plywood bolted over the airport's row of blown-out windows.

But as the Spero pulled up to the Arrivals curb, a great pallid cloud now hoarding the sun, all the old anxieties returned.

Three days.

So much could go wrong.

There were temporary parking spaces at Arrivals. Arthur pulled into one, lowered his window, and idled. In his agitated mood he couldn't help but notice the pitiable state of his surroundings. The lipedemic, mashed-potato legs of obese travelers. The insecure pageantry in pilots' epauletted uniforms. He was flanked by two vehicles: a white van captained by a youth pastor and a blue pickup with truck nuts. Midwestern diptych.

His nerves brought the broth of his thoughts to a boil. He tugged upward on his seat belt, felt the strap choke his chest, briefly losing himself in the asphyxia.

On the radio, reports of a small bomb blast in Kashmir.

It wasn't all bad. The house was immaculate. He'd cleaned thoroughly. His hands still smelled of laboratory citrus. He was proud of the work he'd done, and was starting to like the idea of returning to Chouteau Place. Triumphant. He'd called Ulrike the previous day to reassure her of the efficacy of his plan, and the sincerity of his promise.

"I need the weekend," he'd said. "Friday through Monday. Then they're gone, and we'll be set. You and me."

"Are you certain about this?"

"Sure I am, sure."

"Because I am late to tell the fellowship committee."

"Tell them—tell them no! Tell them you're staying put, right here. You're gonna be a star at Danforth, that's obvious."

"I do not have one friend in this city."

"Friends? Who has *friends*?"

"Arthur—"

"It's gonna be great."

"If I stay, you realize I will stay forever."

"Like I said. For the foreseeable future."

"For all of the future, Arthur. This is where my life will be."

"Of course! I mean, you can't see what you can't see—"

"It is that kind of language which makes me pause!"

"I'm saying, by definition, you can plan for the future as much as you want, but you can't *predict* it."

"But you are planning on us."

"Yes."

"We will live together."

"Yes."

"And you are certain about this."

"Yes . . . inasmuch as I can be about something as unpredictable as the future."

"Arthur!"

"Okay, okay. Look. What is it you want in life?"

"To do my work. My research. I want to be a professor with tenure."

"And how does one accomplish that goal?"

"I write a book."

"Exactly. And what do you need to write a book?"

"Time. Space."

"Perfect. So. I'm happy to say you've been accepted."

"Accepted?"

"To the Arthur Alter Scholarship Retreat for Limber Historians."

"Arthur . . ."

"Room and board included. Sexual favors not required but highly recommended."

There was a long pause.

"Okay. I will tell them no."

"Good."

"Arthur?"

"Yes?"

"I like you very much."

"You're not terrible either. Okay, gotta go. Talk soon."

The future was bright and gilded and plush. He summoned the feeling of Ulrike's thighs on his, her small, round ass a cushion in his lap.

Arthur purpled. He scrambled with the seat-belt buckle and released the strap, gasping for air.

Travelers were beginning to dribble out from the airport, grouping by family on the curb. What was the plural, he wondered, the noun of assembly? Herd? Swarm? *Murder.* That was it. Had to be. A murder of families on the curb. Huddled en masse, tottering five deep toward stationary cars.

"This is the first major attack since the coalition government—"

A jewel of salty sweat stung Arthur in the eye.

"The militants opened indiscriminate fire—"

"Leave me alone!" he shouted, striking the steering wheel with his palm. A honk farted through the lot.

Among the murder of families, which was beginning to thin, Arthur identified a lone figure by the airport's stuttering doors. He was pacing, alternately petting one arm of his cable-knit cardigan and fingering the zipper on his khaki weekend bag. Expensive gear, but Arthur recognized the body underneath. Its legs, and their overburdened walk, gave him away.

Ethan.

All that could be said about Ethan was that it might've been worse. Arthur had colleagues with shit kids, real upstart asshole sons who'd waited for the first signs of senescence—forgetfulness, new drug regimens, cryogenically frozen political affiliations—before returning home with a bouquet of brochures, armed with an accountant friend's advice on what to do with the house. The house in which their fathers lived. Sure, these colleagues of Arthur's were a little watery, their thoughts a little stale, but they didn't deserve betrayal. Eviction. Not from their sons. Not like that.

Ethan was different. Ethan would never forsake him. The kid was too compliant. Even now, Arthur thought of his son as he was at ten years old, a meek little ballplayer in Franklin Park, afraid to swing at Arthur's underhanded lobs for fear that the vibrations in the bat would sting his hands. Arthur and Francine had called him the Potted Plant. He was that still, that unobtrusive. Still and unobtrusive was no father's dream, but it was preferable to oedipal vengeance.

Arthur might have turned into a shit son himself had his father's heart not exploded on the eve of his forty-ninth birthday.

Ben Alter didn't drink himself to death, but the liquor surely helped. So did the failure. He had the gene for it. Homozygous FF. Doubled. There was no point in dressing it up: Ben Alter's had been a cash-strapped life spent in other people's mouths. Arthur couldn't imagine it, those daily descents into the hot, gummy gapes of his patients, scraping rot, installing caps and crowns. Demeaning work. Demeaning but, in theory, lucrative. No one *likes* dentistry. They like money. But Benjamin Gurion Alter could not even make that work. Could not acquaint himself with profit. There were troubles in his house, money troubles, and Arthur was certain that this, too, rushed his father down the moving walkway in the airport of his life.

For many years Arthur feared death in general and his father's in particular. Was convinced he'd go the same way. One sharp pouncing pain. Sudden. Wham. Laid out by some inherited myopathy, an aneurysmal rupture, an atherosclerotic blast. He'd survived forty-six, and forty-seven, forty-eight . . . and as he awoke on the morning of his forty-ninth birthday from uneasy dreams and found himself unchanged, *alive*, he realized that he'd been given the gift of more life—and the curse of not knowing what to do with it. He'd never been afraid of the finitude, the end of consciousness, the interminable nothingness. No, what Arthur feared most was a messy death; a death that left things unresolved. His father's death. Paperwork. Property. Unfinished business. A death that echoes one's failures in life. With bureaucratic consequences, and disorder.

A debtor's death.

The crowd on the curb dispersed and Arthur saw his daughter, brooding beside Ethan in a military field jacket, rusted-copper curls falling to her shoulders. She looked like her mother, but without the womanly heft. She looked carved out. Still, the mere fact of Maggie, his combative, sanctimonious daughter, here in St. Louis was promising. She would not be easy like her brother. But her presence meant that Arthur had a chance.

"The government is closely monitoring the situation—"

He offed the radio, honked his horn.

Ethan waved. Arthur waved back in acknowledgment. As his children walked toward him, he opened the driver-side door, bent to shield himself behind it, and spat on the pavement. One last purging of the venom.

"Kids," he said, standing to greet them.

Ethan bounded toward him, his arms outstretched. Arthur gave him a begrudging hug and took in a nose full of cologne. It was never comfortable, holding a grown man in your arms.

"Good to see you, Dad."

"You too, kiddo."

His daughter tossed her oversize duffel into the trunk. If Ethan was a potted plant, Maggie was a dandelion, a cunning weed tearing through the garden. A pain, to be sure—but you had to admire her fervor.

"Maggie," he said.

"Driving Mom's car, I see."

"Welcome home."

She muttered something and slid into the back of the car.

Okay, he thought. *She's still punishing me. Fair enough. Good to know.* He stepped into the driver's seat.

"All right now," he said, revving the engine of the Spero. "Who's hungry?"

Arthur's devotion to Piggy's Smokehouse, a barbecue dive in Midtown St. Louis, rivaled, in sheer religiosity, any time-honored culinary tradition he could think of. The Passover seder plate. Catholics and their wafers. Yes, when Arthur imagined roping his children back into his life, he pictured it beginning at Piggy's, the three of them around a picnic table laughing hot, piquant laughs, their tongues alight with barbecue tang.

Piggy's did barbecue the right way, which is to say the Memphis way and not, crucially, the St. Louis way, which dispatched with the dry rub and slow smoking that made the whole endeavor worthwhile in the first place. The restaurant was a sanctuary for Arthur, a place of refuge and escape, an off-campus counterpart to the African Studies Library. (Francine, the only semi-observant Jew in the family, had in her Conservative upbringing missed the chance to develop a taste for pork. She loathed the smell, and never once stepped foot inside the place. Arthur felt differently. He was a Jew in temperament but not practice, who would've deemed himself agnostic were it not for the incontrovertible fact that he'd gestated in a Jewish womb.) Piggy's opened in 1996, a few months ahead of the Alters' move to St. Louis. But it had been hungrily accepted by the city, and so vintage was its charm that for years Arthur believed the place preceded him by decades. When eventually he realized that it didn't, that its history in the city could be tracked alongside his, he came to think of Piggy's and its development—the opening of second and third locations, the menu's gradual inclusion of combination plates and Frito pies—as a mirror for his family's trajectory. Moving to St. Louis, raising his children. Seeing them through college and into adulthood. In bringing Ethan and Maggie there now, he hoped they would remember the many afternoons spent under its wood beams; that the pork and the corn and the slaw in their waxed-paper-lined baskets would invoke the unbridled potential of grade school, familial warmth, the vulnerability of youth.

But when they stepped into the unassuming restaurant, its walls adorned with logo merch, Arthur wasn't met with the reaction that he'd hoped for. Maggie exhaled through her teeth, the hiss of pressurized air brakes popping open their valves.

"Piggy's?" she said. "Really?"

"What's wrong?"

Maggie's eyebrows arched. "You're kidding, right?"

"I have no idea what you mean," he said. "Come on. Let's grab a table."

His son sat beside him, his daughter across. Above the picnic-style table hung a hollow plastic piggy bank, spinning lazily, its tether winding and unwinding in the breeze of a ceiling fan.

Ethan took it upon himself to hail a waiter. He craned his neck, one languid hand extended like Adam's on the Sistine Chapel ceiling. Arthur, momentarily distracted by the enervated, fey quality of the gesture, observed his son and freestyle theorized that his mannerisms must be biologically linked in some grand unified way with those of other homosexuals around the world.

He set the theory aside. "How was the flight?"

"Ethan upgraded to first class," Maggie said, addressing the ceiling fan.

"You didn't sit together?"

"It was a free upgrade." Ethan blushed. "The airline offered. I had the miles from when I was—it's a perk of traveling so much for work. I was entitled to an upgrade."

"'Entitled' is a good word," Maggie said.

"Hey," said Arthur. "Be good."

Be good was one of his canonical imperatives. It meant a thousand things, *calm down* and *sit still* and *shut up* among them. What Moses accomplished with ten commandments, Arthur crushed with one. A solitary rule, all-encompassing and impenetrable. It didn't merely implore you to be good. It forced you to wonder what "good" actually meant—and how you'd failed to be it.

"Was there a storm or something?" Ethan asked, one hand still hanging in the air. "The airport was a mess."

"Big one."

"Mm."

"Tornado."

"Oh."

"Yeah."

". . . Yeah."

A waiter appeared and saved them. Arthur, relieved, ordered

ribs with potato salad and green beans. Ethan nodded and said, "Same." Maggie asked for water.

"We're putting in our food order too," Arthur said.

"I know." She looked at the waiter. "I'll stick with water."

"You're not hungry?" Arthur asked. "You look like a stick."

"Dad . . . ," Ethan said.

Maggie's cheeks flushed. "I'm a vegetarian."

The waiter excused himself.

Arthur fought a scowl. "Since when?"

"Since ninth grade."

Piggy's had been instrumental in her decision to give up meat almost a decade earlier. As a girl, on mandatory outings there with Arthur, she'd listen as he griped about his marriage and attempted to betrayal-bond until the waiter came to take his ruined basket. After one particularly bitter trip, she'd returned from Piggy's to find her mother with a bandage on her finger. "What's that from?" Maggie asked. "Stupid me. I jammed it in a door," Francine said. But Maggie believed, and in a way never ceased to believe, that Arthur's comments at the smokehouse that day had somehow been the cause of her mother's injury. That by some metaphysical force—Maggie was ten years old then, and the world was nothing to her if not a jumble of such forces; what made airplanes fly? Why did tennis balls eventually stop rolling?—her father's words had actually damaged her mother's body.

She came to associate petty cruelty with the smell of burning meat. It made her physically ill. When she met her first vegetarian, the costume designer for her high school's production of *Rent*, an abridged version from which all references to AIDS had been gracelessly removed, she realized there existed an ideological defense against the consumption of meat, and by extension father-daughter time. She'd found her excuse. Shortly thereafter she told him that she could no longer go to the smokehouse. That Arthur had forgotten this fact was another instance of the way his actions rippled through her life while he floated up above it, unaware.

"I guess I'm not surprised," she said, "that you'd forget something like that. Which, clearly, you have."

"Forget what? That you were a vegetarian? I thought it was a teenage thing. I thought maybe you'd given that up."

"*Given that up?*"

Immediately, Arthur knew he'd stepped into a minefield. She was slipping into her teenage self—rotten, bellicose, unsparing.

"It was actually a pretty important decision for me. In terms of my identity. And personhood. But like I said, not surprised. You're forgetful. Right? You forgot my birthday *constantly*. Like, whoops, Dad forgot, ha-ha, what a forgetful absentminded-professor type."

"I know your birthday."

"Oh yeah?"

Arthur deftly changed course. "But what we're talking about here is something else. Don't forget that I've known you longer than even *you've* known you. My humble apologies if I thought your abstinence from meat might be a passing thing. If I thought that teenagers go through phases. That you might have changed your diet."

"It was an important part of my identity!" she shouted. "*Is* important!"

Ethan shielded his face from the verbal shrapnel. Civility: time of death, 7:43 p.m., CST.

It bothered him that this was how things were: Maggie, who professed to hate Arthur and took every opportunity she could to provoke him, received, paradoxically, all of his attention. Whereas Ethan let his father have his way, never fought, never made a nuisance of himself—and Arthur rewarded this behavior by ignoring him.

He watched his father and his sister trade insults, pushing their frustration back and forth across the table. He was disappointed in his father for missing the point, for harping on the vegetarian thing, the politics of identity. The fact was, Maggie didn't look well. Hadn't looked well since the funeral. It didn't take a therapist to make the next few associative leaps. Ethan of all people knew the weird ways grief could rattle your life, the control it took away from you; and what better way to reclaim that control than by the strict regulation of one's diet? But Maggie was prickly, and quick to lash out—traits she'd inherited from their father—and Arthur, in his aggressive pose, couldn't see past her defenses.

He thought he should intervene. But he didn't want to stick up for his sister if it meant pissing off his father. On the flight over, tempted by the SkyMall in his seat-back pouch, Ethan had decided to ask his father for a loan. A bailout, until he was on his feet again. Their relationship wasn't ideal, but he hoped that Arthur, like a government staffed with too many ex-bankers to be impartial, would rescue him with a stimulus package.

"I hate to break it to you, Maggie," Arthur was saying, leaning forward on his elbows, "but you are not your beliefs. Your positions. Your *stances*."

"Here we go."

"There's no such thing as a feminist. Did you know that? No such thing as a Zionist either. No environmentalists. No Communists or anarchists. How about that? See, there are *isms* but not *ists*. People aren't ideas, Maggie. People aren't positions. People are people. Wants, urges, actions. That's people. Flawed. Selfish. Ducking blows as they come." He was having fun now. "All this identity crap, and I see it every day on campus, this assertion of preference and belief—it's a teenage thing. An adolescent phase. 'I am this but not that.' 'I like this but not that.' The choose-your-own-toppings mentality. It's all marketing. You realize that, don't you? It's a convenient way to get you to buy more CDs."

"*CDs?!* Do you hear yourself?"

"I'm sorry"—he wasn't—"but it's true."

Maggie ignited with anger. There were countless reasons to dislike her father—he was an emotional cheapskate; he'd betrayed her mother; his cynicism had tainted her life like a drop of pee in a swimming pool—but the worst of it was how he'd managed, despite his low level of parental involvement, to shape her life. When she rebelled, she rebelled against *him*. She had made herself his opposite. He was the mold around which she formed. Or the form around which she molded? Her mother, who knew a thing or two about Gestalt psychology, would've had the answer.

"So, hypothetically," she said, "if one were to, I don't know, *philander*, that wouldn't make one a *philanderer*, would it? Because identity is bullshit, right? We're all just urges, right? Hm. Yeah, I see your point. That all sounds very smart, and very convenient."

In the reflection in the window behind his daughter, Arthur saw the tension in his face. Sweat pooling at his hairline. A distended, porky vein down his forehead. Not an hour into the weekend and she'd already tripped him up.

He opened his mouth, not knowing what might come out, when the waiter returned and slid a basket of dark, delicious, unkosher meat on the gingham tablecloth before him.

TEN

Drinking, Francine Alter once told her son, is not something that Jews do. She said this back in 1997 because Ethan was suddenly a teenager and just as suddenly there were parties where before there were none—parties in basements, parties in garages, parties stocked with skunked beer and sake (sake: it was the one libation midwestern academics always had but never drank), and directives always went down smoother in the guise of social commentary. But Ethan was thirty-one, his mother almost two years' gone, and he was sweating in the dark before the hallway liquor cabinet.

He snatched a dusty fifth of Polish potato vodka from the bottom shelf and took a swig. He'd survived Piggy's the same way he'd survived his childhood: with his head down. Pretending to be somewhere else. His father and his sister hadn't torn each other apart, not yet—that was a warm-up, the hors d'oeuvre, the teaser-trailer to their mutual antipathy—and both were now asleep upstairs. But he couldn't avoid them all weekend, couldn't ignore the present circumstances. The fact of being home.

Shortly after receiving his father's letter he'd dedicated himself to the mission of closure. If only he could speak with Charlie, if only they could see each other as they were—if only he could get an apology out of him, or at least an explanation—then surely, surely, Ethan would be able to move on. It was this lack of closure, he'd decided, that was keeping him from real relationships, real intimacy. After sophomore year he'd entered into a period of physical and emotional celibacy. He was nearly over Charlie before that night in the botanical gardens, before Charlie reached out and touched him. The touch had dragged him back into the fray. He still felt phantom fingers on his ear. He'd never let himself feel for anyone like he felt for Charlie. Shawn had always suspected Ethan of cheating. At the time Ethan chalked it up to Shawn's flirtatiousness, projected back at him. But the well-groomed blond was right. Ethan's heart was always somewhere else. And then, in 2012, a chance encounter had done it again. Charlie was always appearing when least convenient, pulling Ethan back to pain, to hurt, to love.

Francine was diagnosed with breast cancer that December, and Ethan had flown home to see her. A vast, flocculent cloud darkened and devitalized the city, mimicking the family mood like weather does in memories. One night while his family slept, insomniac and lonely, Ethan commandeered the car and drove, somewhat aimlessly, to the Carnivora Club.

The gay scene in St. Louis endured in the Grove, a business district in Forest Park Southeast at the far end of Manchester Avenue. There was something inescapably Missourian—unpretentious, sensible, blue-collar—about the clubs there, which operated in the Venn diagram overlap of Americana and kink. Which is to say that you could order a superb bacon double cheeseburger in the Grove, but a leather-clad waiter would serve it to you in a dog bowl.

Carnivora, a lone gay bar by the botanical gardens, stood apart, drooping below the scene like the heavier testicle. It was a haven for stragglers too old or too tired to keep up with the Grove's fickle crowds, the drag queen dramas, the spiteful rivalries between club owners. Carnivora was quiet. Low-key. It sat at a subtle corner where two one-way streets crossed in a highway-bounded residential neighborhood. A tin KING OF BEERS sign dangled over the entrance. Only a blinking neon fixture, four cursive words in the window, gave the place away: LA CAGE AUX CARNIVORES.

Ethan pulled up to the bar. He was tired, physically and existentially kaput, burdened by visions of the months to come: the tense conversations, the medical jargon, the total impotent uncertainty. He needed a change of scenery. He needed a drink.

He stepped inside to find the Carnivora Club empty. Two stools were missing seat cushions. *Fried Green Tomatoes* glowed on unsynchronized televisions mounted above the bar on either side of a poster hung in tribute to partying and Mayan eschatology both: THIS WAY, it read, TO THE APOCALYPSE.

Ethan lowered himself onto a stool. The bartender was a talkative bear happy for the company. "I have two dogs," he said, unprompted, in a voice at once gruff and elastic. "Total fucking assholes. Cute, though. You just want to eat them up. Don't get me wrong, they're great, but sometimes you feel like—" And he made a strangling gesture with his hands. Ethan mustered a nod. It was hell being home.

There was no draft, only splashy drink specials and bottled beer. Carnivora's signature cocktail was the Blue (Collar) Hawaii, a local take on the tiki-bar staple, which called for twice the rum and Blue Raspberry Kool-Aid in place of curaçao. Ethan ordered one. He raised the glass to his mouth, sweetness zipping down his throat. He downed it and ordered a second. The bartender hummed "Barbeque Bess."

"Men's room?" Ethan asked.

"Down that hallway," the bear said and nodded. "Mind yourself back there."

Ethan slid off his seat. On the screens above him, Kathy Bates was losing her mind in a parking lot.

He proceeded down the hall, sweeping his teeth with his tongue, tasting the sugar. The corridor was longer than it looked, growing darker toward the end. Ethan became aware of a muted groan, emanating (it seemed) from behind the door of the men's room.

Perhaps it was the alcohol, or maybe the insomnia, or else it was the news of Francine's diagnosis, but Ethan—honestly, what possessed him?—opened the door.

What he saw, in the restroom's pale green light:

A dribbling sink. A housefly looping through the air. And a

wide-necked joe in a Blues jersey groaning on the toilet, one hand gripping the sink to his left, the other pressed flat against the wall. It took a moment for Ethan to register the other man, the second man, the man on his knees with his back to Ethan, kneeling with his head between the hockey fan's legs. A pang of recognition stunned Ethan where he stood: printed on the back of the second man's jacket, flying through the aperture of a giant letter A, was a cawing all-American bald eagle. The man turned, and at the first glimpse of those green eyes, Ethan fled the men's room. He threw some wrinkled bills on the bar and drove home, blowing past a series of stop signs. The next morning, he called Teddy back in New York and dumped him.

Five years after Charlie planted renewed hope in him with a touch to the ear, Ethan was making peace with the thought that it had been a drunken mistake, that he had read too far into it. Charlie was one of those straight guys who experimented, and Ethan had been his laboratory. That's what he believed, until the scene at Carnivora. He wanted nothing more than to show up at Charlie's house the next day and ask for—*demand*—an explanation. But he was needed at his mother's side.

Now, home again for the first time since the funeral and more than a little tipsy, Ethan felt prepared. This time would be different. This time he'd go through with it.

Ethan swigged the vodka.

And again.

He steadied himself on the liquor cabinet and sunk to the floor. He sat with his back against it, facing his mother's former office. DR. FRANCINE ALTER | COUPLES & FAMILY COUNSELING. This was the place where Ethan had first overheard the words *dysthymic depression, panic disorder,* and *persistent anxiety* as a boy and realized—with accumulating panic and anxiety—that they applied to him. He'd come of age in this hallway, eavesdropping on his mother's patients. You could hear them despite the soundproofing, if you leaned in close. He learned about boundaries from the couple who could not spend one moment apart. He learned about betrayal from the woman who would not stop cheating on her husband, and he learned about forgiveness, then denial, from that same husband, who refused to give up on the marriage. He learned a great deal from one couple in particular, the Pfeffers, who had been seeing Francine for years. They'd taught Ethan inadvertent object lessons in compromise, as when they were divided on the matter of more children; in grief, when Gerry Pfeffer suffered a fatal stroke; and in the horrors of high-functioning depression, when Lauren was left to run her house by herself.

Ethan stared at the nameplate. FRANCINE ALTER. The words weren't really there, he thought, drowsily. They were absences, laser-cut into— or out of—the metal. Divots. Dimples. COUPLES & FAMILY. The letters were illusions, depressions defined by what had been removed.

"Can I get some?"

Ethan startled and looked up. Maggie stood above him, eyeing the vodka.

"Sure," he said. "It's awful."

Maggie bent to accept the bottle and took a conservative sip. "Ew. Blech. Not good."

"I told you."

"'Polish Potato Vodka'?"

Ethan stared into the middle distance. "Why not? A tribute to our ancestors."

She sat beside him and sniffed the rim. "Are we Polish?"

Ethan took the bottle back. "I don't know. Probably."

"Thereabouts."

"Satellite states."

"Right."

"Wherever persecution complexes come from."

"Yeah, yeah." She motioned for the bottle. "Weird to be here, right?"

He nodded.

Maggie sipped and winced. "It's not like I remember somehow. You can tell Mom's not around. It's too clean, but . . . not in a good way, you know?"

"Fake clean."

"The plants are dead and it smells like Windex."

"It's uncanny. I think Dad moved some stuff around. I can't place it . . ."

"Oh, he definitely did."

"And it's quiet."

"It *is*, isn't it? Although I don't think of Mom as the biggest talker."

"It wasn't her," said Ethan. "It was all her patients. All the people she brought into the house. There were always people around."

"Yeah. I miss that."

"The talk."

Maggie took another sip.

"Maybe slow down," Ethan said. "Empty stomach and all?"

She hugged the bottle to her chest. "Don't worry about my stomach. It's not your concern. Okay?"

"Okay."

Maggie arched her back. "Do you think Mom was good at her job?"

"Hm." Ethan exhaled loudly through his nose. "Does it matter?"

"I guess not," she said. "But I hope she was."

"She knew how to handle Dad. That's not nothing."

"And she was smart. She was, wasn't she?"

"Yeah. But, again—does it matter?"

"I want to remember her as someone who was good at what she did. As someone who was smart. Now that she's gone I feel like she's up for grabs or something. It's on us to remember her correctly. Like, if we don't, who will? I want to get her right. Because however we choose to remember, that's how it's going to be. That burden is ours. I don't want to get it wrong or sell her short. Or have it be relational, like, 'this was what Mom meant *to me*.' I want to remember her *as she was*. But I'm also worried about, you know, deifying her. There are so many ways to be wrong about someone."

"You worry too much," Ethan said.

"Pot, kettle."

"Yeah, yeah, okay."

"You never told me why you quit," she said.

"Quit what?"

"Your job."

"Right. That." Ethan shook his head. "It wasn't for me. I didn't want that responsibility. Half the time they brought me on to justify a decision they'd already made. I was just the excuse."

"I always suspected you thought you were too good for it."

"That's not it, Maggie. That's not it at all."

She picked at the label on the bottle. "I think this is the first time we've done this."

"Done what?"

"Hang out. As adults. You know."

"I guess that's true."

"I think Dad had a way of making us . . . single-minded. I'd say 'independent' but that seems like giving too much credit. There was no effort to *bring us together,* as far as I can remember."

"We aren't close in age."

"What I mean to say is that I don't think we were taught how to deal with other people. Including each other."

"You can't blame everything on him."

"But he *is* responsible."

"How?"

"He just is," she burped.

Ethan laughed. "I'm cutting you off."

Maggie lowered the bottle, half-empty, to a coaster of moonlight on the floor between them. They sat awhile, the vodka tickling their stomachs. From upstairs, the scratchy sound of Arthur's snoring could be heard, texturing the silence, while Ethan and Maggie stared at their mother's name in brass.

"I want to steal you for the day."

Saturday morning. Ethan sat at the kitchen island with his father. Between them, a plate of chocolate Donettes and a carton of grapefruit juice, impulse buys that Arthur had brought back from the Circle K on Delmar with the urgency and nutritional cognizance of a Paleolithic hunter-gatherer.

Ethan, head pounding from the vodka, said, "Okay." He would have to find Charlie tomorrow.

He looked at his half-eaten Donette and cursed his chronic acquiescence. What was it about his father that provoked such slavish obedience? Why couldn't he stand up for himself?

He took a deep, restorative breath. Time alone with his father might be a good thing. It would give Ethan a chance to bring up the tricky matter of money. The loan. It was a sensitive subject, given his mother's inheritance, but what would Arthur do, deny him? His eldest child? His only son?

Ethan knew what he needed from his father. What his father wanted with him was another matter. But Ethan was okay, for the time being, with simply being wanted. He downed his glass of grapefruit juice, imagining it coursing through his body, a purifying drink to wash away the stress, the nausea, the mild hangover, and met his father in the car.

The University of Missouri–St. Louis, or UMSL (*UM-sull*) and Danforth were locked in a sibling rivalry, in that one sibling was unaware of the existence of a rivalry at all. Danforth, like a flashy, ambitious older child—established more than a century earlier than its public counterpart—boasted a $7 billion endowment, a top-ten medical school, and a deliberate ignorance of regional competition. The med school, and the undergrad pre-med program, were the institution's proudest achievements: the alumni magazine frequently bragged about the university's medical facilities, the "dizzying array" of laparoscopic, endovascular, and remote-controlled technologies, the faculty's achievements in the field of incisionless surgery, their ability to pull patients' appendixes out through their mouths. This robotic upper hand was funded by the students, who, lacking Ethan and Maggie's faculty-parent "discounts," paid $60K per year and received little help from the university's paltry aid program. (Though the lack of economic diversity among students was an acknowledged failure of Danforth's, the university had at least solved the problem of racial diversity, increasingly admitting the wealthy children of Nigerian aristocrats in the place of African Americans more likely to apply for financial aid. "As long as they're black," whispered one trustee over a hot mic during an infamous State of the University address in 2013.)

Meanwhile, UMSL was $8 million in the hole. The university had recently consolidated the College of Fine Arts, the Center for Media Studies, and their entrepreneurship MBA into the centralized Institute for Business Arts. Danforth was packed with international heirs and east-coasters; UMSL, a public institution, mostly served Missourians. But despite these differences the schools were only six miles apart, a fifteen-minute drive in Francine's Spero, separated by the little towns of Wellston, Hillsdale, Beverly Hills, and Normandy.

"What are we doing here?" Ethan asked as his father pulled the car into the parking lot of UMSL's Dedbroke Performing Arts Center.

"You'll see."

Ethan stepped out of the car and followed his father inside. The center's lobby was shabbily decorated with approximations of "abstract" and "modern" paintings on the walls. Pigeon shit Pollocked the glass windows. In the center of the lobby Ethan registered a cardboard standee, a two-dimensional woman in a lilac gown and slippers, her cardboard legs pressed together, arms arcing over her head.

Her dimensions were uncanny. She stood around four and a half feet high, not life-sized but not any other recognizable scale either. She smiled blankly at Ethan. "What are we . . . ," he began to ask again, but a silver-haired usher with plantar fasciitis appeared behind him and, limping, pushed them across the lobby, through the auditorium doors. "You're late," she scolded. "You almost *missed it.*"

Ethan dropped into the scruffy fabric of an auditorium chair. More than half of the semi-tiered seats around him were empty.

"Hey," he said. "I need to ask you for a favor."

"Huh?" Arthur snorted, the spiked sound sticking Ethan in the ribs.

"This is hard."

"Okay . . ."

"What I wanted to ask you was . . ."

Arthur raised an eyebrow.

"Was . . ."

The prospect of putting his desperation into words was crippling. He hated begging, hated telegraphing his needs, and it was never easy admitting failure to one's father.

"Have you—did you . . . Have you noticed anything weird about Maggie?" He bailed. "Does she look okay to you?"

His father hushed him. "It's starting."

All at once, the murmuring voices around them thinned to a whisper. The tentative squeaks of a tuning orchestra flared throughout the performance hall. Somewhere in the darkening room, Ethan heard the nasal whine of an oboe.

Maggie woke at noon to church bells.

Or, wait, no—it wasn't the sound that woke her but the silence around it. The way the rusty chime rang unclouded through Chouteau Place. It was Saturday, the bells wouldn't truly go berserk until tomorrow, but they still rang on the half hour, and their clean, defiant sound startled Maggie out of bed. Ridgewood had its churches, too, Irish and Italian and Gottscheer Catholic, but their bells were one factor in a larger system, an ethno-ambient collage of catcalls, Puerto Rican dembow riddims, and Chinese-delivery motorbikes. The resulting soundscape was so constant and so rich that Maggie had become suspicious of anything else. She'd forgotten the oppressive silence of Midwestern suburbs, and yes, she meant oppressive in *that way*—like the pyramids (potentially built by her ancestors) in Egypt, this kind of majesty came at a cost. This kind of peace meant unrest somewhere else. Someone had to pay for it. Someone somewhere had to suffer for this neighborhood to stay quiet enough that the wind in the trees was the sound of paper money, rustling.

The house was quiet too. No sign of Ethan or her father. Maggie stomped downstairs, her feet thudding against the beige carpet-runner. A yellow legal pad on the kitchen table read OUT W/ ETHAN in Arthur's negligent scrawl.

Alone in the house, the whole day stretching out before her, Maggie set about redistributing her family's wealth.

She scoured the house for items of interest, things of value sentimental and objective. She made space in her duffel bag for her beloved stuffed elephant, Susan B., which Arthur had placed at the foot of her bed (sentimental), along with the tortoiseshell barrette (sentimental) that she'd worn daily for two years straight in preschool. She swiped a pair of gold cufflinks (objective) that she'd never seen her father wear. She nabbed cash from his sock drawer. She wrapped four crystal-stemmed wineglasses in a pillowcase from the linen closet and stashed those in her backpack—one pair for drinking, one pair to pawn.

Sorting things, reassigning them—it was the rare occasion when Maggie felt that she controlled her life. That she could shape her destiny. Her mother's money, the inheritance, was completely out of her hands. Undeserved and unasked for. What was Maggie supposed to do, *enjoy* it? Live it up beneath the fiscal ghost lights of her mother's life? Literally profit off the worst thing to ever happen to her? And who's to say the money would have made life any better? It had practically ruined her brother!

Maggie didn't like moochers and leeches, the freeloader types from college whose parents underwrote their bad plays and bought studio time for their alt-folk acts. But she was also skeptical of anyone with a really good job. Anyone who made really good money at a really good job had blood on his hands. You didn't make good money without exploiting someone. Somewhere in the corporate structure, someone was losing, and losing big. The poor. The environment. Maggie wanted no part of it. Which is why she had to steal, or redistribute, every now and then. It was a confusing set of principles she'd arrived at—but perhaps no more confusing and muddled than the actual economy, of which she could not make heads or tails.

She continued to redistribute. The grand prize, the thing she had come for, was a Tiffany cocktail watch that had belonged to her mother. It was a square, diamond-studded piece on a black satin strap, roman numerals bordering the blank face in white gold. Super showy as far as Maggie was concerned, much more in Bex's domain than her mother's, but its value was sentimental too. In her rush to live monkishly, to possess as little as she could, Maggie had forgotten to bring a token of her mother with her to New York. And the token that she wanted was the watch.

For a time, while Maggie was in high school and for reasons that weren't entirely clear to her, her mother befriended, or was befriended by, the wife of the manager of the St. Louis Cardinals. Maggie wasn't sure how this had come about—she only knew that the manager's daughter was a classmate of hers, and the worst kind of social demagogue—but all of a sudden Francine was being whisked away to the city's most upscale restaurants: Tony's Italian, Al's steakhouse, Morton's steakhouse, Fleming's steakhouse.

The manager's wife and her friends were five to ten years older than Francine, platinum blonde, extremely white, politically conservative. Maggie suspected, and could only hope, that her mother got an anthropological kick out of dining with them—that Francine joined their clique in the name of science. Or else she liked the free steak, which was almost always comped, the manager's wife dismissing Francine's plastic with a look of *Are you kidding me?*

Either way, these were not her mother's people.

Sometime in the course of this new friendship, which lasted for about ten months in the spring of 2006, the manager's wife hosted a fund-raiser at the Chase Park Plaza hotel. The cause was ALS, the cost per plate was $300, and the players' wives, many of them models, spent the cocktail hour working the room, mingling with donors and laughing gracefully with their mouths closed.

Francine dragged Arthur along. He wore a brown suit.

"What do you think it cost to host this here?" he asked. "Answer in research grants."

"Shh," she said. "And besides. You have to spend it to make it." When Arthur excused himself to the men's room, she sneaked away and bought a $100 raffle ticket.

After a speech from the manager's wife and a harrowing short film on motor neuron disease, the shortstop's wife, a Dutch dancer whom the shortstop had allegedly fallen for on a post–World Series bender in Amsterdam, approached the podium and listed off some alphanumeric characters that matched the sequence on Francine's ticket stub. It took a moment for her to realize what had happened.

Maggie's memory of that night was clear: Her mother coming through the kitchen door, face flushed joyful red, her sequined dress catching and releasing frenzied light. A glass case rested in her palm. She removed the top to show Maggie the watch.

"Isn't it beautiful?"

"I guess," said Maggie, then sixteen. "I mean, it's a little . . . much. Right?"

"Tell me about it," Arthur groaned.

But Francine wasn't listening. She stared at the watch, the expensive-looking but altogether-unlike-her object.

"Are you crying?" Maggie asked. Little crystal tears welled in her mother's eyes.

"You have to understand," she said in a fragile voice. "I never win anything."

Maggie had never heard her mother speak this way before. She'd never heard her talk in terms of victory and defeat—nor was Francine prone to admissions of self-doubt. Maggie had instinctively wanted to defend her, but how could she defend her to her? Francine never won? But she was perfect and good! What could it mean that a woman like her mother, beautiful and wise and cunning, never felt as though she won? And what did it say about Maggie, who worked tirelessly to emulate her?

It tore her up, even now.

But where was it? Not in Francine's modest jewelry drawer, not under her parents' bed, not among the scattered pens and spotted seashell paperweights on her work desk. Maggie stomped around the house, searching in vain. She thought to look in the last place she'd expect. But the house had lots of last places. Too large for a four-person family, much less a family of three, the house was comprised almost entirely of last places.

She tried the basement, her first last place. But the watch was not among the slumping beanbag chairs, at the oxidized feet of the Ping-Pong table, or behind the rowing machine Arthur salvaged from the Dumpster outside her middle school. It was not in the unfinished laundry room, where a black burn stained the wall behind the washing machine. The watch was not in her second, third, or fourth last places either.

Her fifth last place was the dining room. She was digging through a handsome chest of drawers, riffling through inherited silverware, when she opened her thumb on a monogrammed dinner knife and spun around in pain. There, hanging on the wall before her, was a message from her father.

ELEVEN

With Arthur in Zimbabwe, Francine devised a syllabus of indulgence. Free from his meticulous accounting, his obsessive bookkeeping, and his tightwad inquisitions ("I was just in the shower—there are two soaps. Did you buy more soap? Why do we have two soaps?"), she took a much-needed sabbatical from austerity. She saw movies. She bought a down jacket. She went to the Museum of Fine Arts and brought home a glossy Thomas Hart Benton print from the gift shop, which she framed and hung in the living room above the accent chair she'd also purchased in his absence. It wasn't a radical program. But Arthur, whose genius lay in imposing his will on those closest to him, was deficient in the consumer psychology that gave life in America purpose. There weren't many things he didn't consider to be indulgences.

Solitude was the one luxury for which Francine lacked the requisite emotional, and material, currency. She missed Arthur—she did—and there was also the matter of rent, which she couldn't cover on her grad school stipend alone.

She tried advertising the second bedroom, which she and Arthur had been using as a study, to the greater Kenmore area at large. For one interminable weekend her apartment swarmed with all manner of vexatious punks, marathoners, Irish Catholics, Sox fanatics, preppies, Fort Point artists, and Harvard Square grand masters. There was something wrong with each of them. Too outrageous, too intense, untrustworthy. A retired woman in her sixties asked where she could store her porcelain owl figurines. An admittedly handsome Southie boy suggested with non-rhotic confidence that he share Francine's bed in an effort to save space. Just when she was resigned to paying rent herself and eating out of Goya cans all year, she met a candidate she deemed, in the flattering light of her desperation, a safe bet.

The safe bet had a heartland smile, wide-set eyes, and guarantors. Marla Bloch was a psych student like Francine, though two years behind her in the program. They had Ohio in common. Marla hailed from Cincinnati, and was curiously unashamed of her home state. She openly admitted to her bafflement at New England winters, Bostonians' poor manners, and graduate study in general. She vocalized the thoughts that Francine never dared to say, lest her veneer of East Coast sophistication crack. Things like "This reading is dense!" or "It's so nice to meet another Ohioan!" or "It's hard to spell 'amygdala'!" She wasn't wrong in her feelings—their readings *were* dense, Marla's midwestern manners *were* appreciated, and that little almond of nuclei was truly an orthographic puzzler—but these were things Francine had learned not to admit aloud. Marla Bloch didn't mind. She was a truth teller, a bluntly unselfconscious girl of a type Francine recognized, warmly, from home.

Marla wrote a blank check for utilities and the two women shook on it.

Whereas Arthur considered even the North End to be a tourist trap, Marla, upon move-in, taped a list to the fridge, an actual list, of the top ten things she wanted to do and see in the city while she earned her degree. Francine snickered when she saw it.

"Oh my god, I'm sorry," she said, catching herself. "I don't know why I did that."

"You laughed." Marla looked confused.

"No, no, I'm sorry," Francine said. "It looks like a great list. Let's pick something to do."

"Why did you laugh, though?"

"I didn't mean to, I promise. I'm thinking what my boyfriend would say."

"What would he say?"

Francine suppressed a swell of cynicism. "Nothing. He would've thought it was a great idea. Come on. Let's go to the Old State House. I've actually never been."

With earnest, chipper Marla at her side, Francine discovered Boston. Her new roommate walked unembarrassed with a map out in front of her, pausing to stop locals for directions. Unlike Arthur she had no reservations about entry fees at historic churches, museums, and other landmarks. And whenever she leaned too close to a painting or stepped inside a church mid-Mass, she was quick to laugh at herself in a manner that suggested only mock embarrassment. Francine suspected that beneath it lay an abundance of artless self-esteem.

Marla was a talker. But she didn't talk, as Francine's mother did, as though she wanted to murder the silence before it got her first. She talked to pass the time. Nothing revelatory, whatever crossed her mind. And what crossed her mind more than anything, Francine discovered, was sex. She claimed to be "hung up" on a high school boyfriend from "a million years ago." She talked about how much "fun" they used to have "in bed," harping on the "bigness" of his "thing" and the feelings it provoked in her. Marla's combination of frankness and puerility confounded Francine at every turn. In Francine's undergrad years at Wellesley, sex had been political. Gynocentric. And Arthur was more interested in doing it, efficiently, than discussing it. But then here was bushy-tailed Marla Bloch, whose limited vocabulary of euphemisms did not prevent her from expounding on the subject day in, day out.

Francine would have liked to forget about sex completely in her boyfriend's absence. To devote herself to scholarship and celibacy. But Marla wanted to talk. Wanted to "chat" about "boys." More than once, after sharing a bottle of cold duck, Francine went to bed thinking that she'd have to watch herself around this girl.

Meanwhile, Arthur left her piece by piece.

She began to forget. She lost his mouth first, so that when she tried to picture him, the lower half of his face appeared smudged out by a pencil eraser. His eyes turned brown in her remembering, not hazel, which was what they were—canny, high-strung hazel. It was not until she forgot the particulars of his nose, rounding his into the mere *idea* of a nose, a stock nose, that she realized his ears—round or pointed? Lobes attached or free-hanging?—had slipped quietly from her mind days earlier.

And yet. In Arthur's absence, her mental image of him cloudy, a dim facsimile, Francine grew increasingly fond of him. Longed for him. She *liked* the man in her mind, the blurred approximation. He was even better than she remembered.

After finals, Marla threw a party. She was the only graduate student in Francine's program guileless enough to do it. "I want it to be wild," she said, "like they were at Ohio State." She flirted with a few themes before settling on the one that tickled her the most, and brought Francine along to xerox the invitations.

You Are Cordially Invited
To Marla Bloch's First Annual
Freudian "Slip" Party
Lingerie/Underwear Only
No Shirt, No Shoes, No Pants, No Problem
Friends & Lovers Welcome

"Marla, this is ridiculous," Francine said. "No one is going to come to a—a *lingerie* party."

"I'm sorry, but you're wrong."

"You don't think the concept is a little . . . immature? I'm twenty-nine years old. David? From our subsection? Is *forty*."

"You're wrong. We're giving people exactly what they want."

"I think he has kids."

Marla tweaked one of Francine's curls. "Fran," she whispered meaningfully. "Sweet, innocent Fran. Listen to me. We're girls. And we're giving other girls, and boys, permission to see each other. Each other's *bodies*. Trust me. It'll be a blast."

"We're not in high school anymore."

"People will come."

"We're not even in college."

"Francine Klein. We are having this party. Never—and I mean *never*"—and here Marla arched her back—"underestimate the appeal of lifting taboos in a controlled environment."

One week later, the Kenmore Square apartment accommodated its first social gathering since Arthur Alter attached his name to the lease.

Half an hour before the party, Francine drank alone, sequestered in her room, having dressed, or undressed, into a conservative nightgown that could safely double as legitimate pajama-wear if the party went bust. At nine o'clock only a few nervous first years from her program sat on the living room couch, throw pillows resting on their groins. "Don't lose faith in me," Marla told her through the bedroom door, behind which Francine was pretending to read. "Don't lose faith. And don't you *dare* go to bed, unless you're bringing someone in there with you." Sure enough, by eleven the living room was full of PhD candidates, some well into their thirties, mingling in their bras and briefs, inventing reasons to touch one another on the thigh and shoulder.

When Francine stepped out of her room, having gathered from the swelling noise that a party was in fact taking place, Marla, considerably drunk in a satin kimono, shouted, "Francine Klein, everybody!" A smattering of confused applause rose and quickly drained from the room.

The party was all skin and id. Repressed wishes materialized throughout the small apartment. Overdressed Jungians gown-and-gloved to Prince. A first year and his TA had become entangled on the couch, her nipples and his erection straining confidently against the glosses of fabric that contained them. Sex-deprived Francine stirred with a contact high. The sensation of her thighs grazing one another beneath her nightgown was enough to flush her cheeks a telling pink.

"This is your apartment?"

A stranger was leaning on her refrigerator. He was draped in a bedsheet tied toga-style at the left shoulder. The bottom hem hung halfway down his calf, where it abruptly conceded to a pair of black dress socks.

"Do I know you?" she said, ducking into the fridge for a beer.

"I'm a friend of Marla's." He nodded toward the living room, where a kid with a farmer's tan was inspecting the fabric of her kimono.

"Marla, right. The great facilitator. Don't tell me you're from—"

"Cincinnati."

"Dayton."

"You're kidding."

"Do all Ohioans here know each other?"

"All us expats? Sure. I was going to say, we haven't seen you at the meetings."

"Ha. Don't think I got that invite."

"Consider yourself invited. We gather Sundays on the deck of the USS *Constitution* and play euchre." He tapped his can against Francine's. "I'm Dave."

"Francine."

"Messner."

"Klein."

Dave Messner resembled at least three different boys from Beth Abraham Synagogue in Dayton. He was large of ear and wide of forehead. The lower face a tribute to nostrility. He was twenty-eight and already male-pattern balding, an easy Type III on the Hamilton-Norwood scale. But when he smiled, as he smiled now, his features softened into something gentler.

Messner was in finance. He said it could be stressful, at times, but that he enjoyed the intellectual stimulation. Francine heard *stimulation.*

"For now," he explained, "I'm at the Boston branch of a boutique brokerage firm . . . Ha. Try saying that three times fast."

"Boston, boutique, broker," she slurred. "Blah."

"Can I get you another?"

"Oh, no," she said, shaking her can. "I'm—" But she found it empty.

"Drank that pretty fast for a member of the tribe."

Francine blushed.

"I'm sorry! Sorry. Joking. Truly. Here, let me make it up to you." Messner fetched a beer from behind her and attempted to open it with his teeth. Foam shot up his nose and across his face. Francine laughed.

"Oh, this is funny, huh?"

"A little."

"I hereby rescind my apology."

She laughed again, and wiped his face with a dishcloth. "Apology or not. You are forgiven."

"Many thanks." He smiled.

"Well all right, then."

They surveyed the rowdy apartment. A quartet of ABDs in briefs had written names on index cards and affixed them to their sweaty foreheads: B. F. Skinner, Wilhelm Wundt, two Erik Eriksons.

"You probably have to keep an eye on things," Messner said, "and I might not get another chance. I want to ask: Can I call you?"

"Call me?"

"To talk sometime."

"But I'm here, now."

"I know. But it's your party. You might have to rush off somewhere—"

"In this tiny apartment?"

"—and take care of something. I don't know. Still . . . can I? Call you?"

Good question. According to the terms of her arrangement with Arthur, she was, technically, single until his return. Informally separated for the duration of his stay abroad. Free to explore for a

limited time. But did she *want* to? Arthur, out there in the bush—
she envisioned a scene collaged from *National Geographic* and *The
Gods Must Be Crazy*—certainly wasn't getting any. Should she?

"I think you can. Yes. I think you probably can."

He uncapped the pen dangling from a string taped to the fridge,
the pen with which Marla had written QUINCY MARKET and SWAN
BOATS and OLD NORTH CHURCH, and took down Francine's number on
his palm. "I'll call," he said.

"I'm sure you will."

Outside Boston was ideally dark, the Citgo sign in its third black-
out year, stars overhead like neurons firing.

By early June their calls had become routine. By the end of the
month they were, in Messner's words, "seeing one another." He
took her on dates. This alone was a revelation. Dates he paid for. At
restaurants. He was a selfless gentleman, everything Arthur was not:
communicative, civilized, interested in her studies. Willing to treat
himself, and her. He possessed the humble demeanor of a boy who'd
been bullied in high school and the confidence of a man who'd tri-
umphed anyway. He quickly committed himself to Francine, attended to her every need, read and expressed concern over each
micro-expression manifesting on her face. He said he cared only for
her, and his work, in that order. "This is the happiest I've ever been,"
he confessed, "going to the office in the morning and seeing you at
night." He was a bighearted, serious man. Seriousness: that's what
he and Arthur had in common. But where Messner's seriousness
bred success in the form of reliable American currency, Arthur's
brand of agitated sobriety made him something of an absurd figure.
An underground man, raving at the sky.

She wasn't sure how Arthur fit into all of this. Messner was ac-
celerating the course of their relationship, and Francine didn't know
what it meant. She was single, after all, but only temporarily. Was
temporary singlehood really singlehood? Was freedom still freedom if it came tagged with an expiration date? She talked to Arthur,

semi-regularly, on the phone, and they wrote letters. But the calls were always awkward—the pressure to make the most of their limited connection crippled conversation—and the letters took weeks to arrive.

"You and Davey are adorable," Marla told her one evening after Francine returned alone from dinner with Messner, her belly warm with angel hair and scallops. "Does he know about your boy abroad?"

"Were you waiting up for me?"

"Does he?"

Francine sighed. "No. And, Marla, I'd appreciate if you didn't say anything."

"Ooh, I'd never." She smiled. "Our secret."

"Good."

"One thing, though. Has he . . ."

"Has he what?"

"Okay. He hasn't."

"Hasn't *what?*"

"If you don't know what I'm getting at, he hasn't." Her lips curled into a Cheshire grin. "Davey's a nice boy," she said. "But he has his preferences."

It wasn't long before Francine found out. On a bright summer day in June, the indisputable daylight exhibiting itself in flares across the rippling Charles, at his request Francine bound Messner, gagged him with a rubber ball, and applied gentle pressure to his throat while dripping hot paraffin candle wax on the stockbroker's shorn chest.

When Arthur first left, the quality of Francine's work, as well as her overall satisfaction with life—for an academically minded young person like herself, the two were inextricably linked—had shot up so fast that she woke each morning in a kind of electric delirium. Feverish, frantic. All this free time! She could study as late as she wanted, eat and sleep according to her schedule. No more nursing

Arthur's ego back to health after a perceived slight at work. No more trips to the Army/Navy for used socks, two dollars for as many pairs as you could carry in your hands. She made friends and apprenticed herself to a dynamic young professor who wore jeans and whose class was dedicated to dismantling *On Human Nature* piece by piece.

But since meeting Messner, her grades had dipped. He laid claim to her evenings, halving her study time. Soon she was performing at the same sub-satisfactory level that she had when Arthur was around.

The young professor asked to see her one afternoon after class.

"Are you all right?" he asked. "You seem . . . distracted." He looked Francine up and down and nodded. "Mm. Distracted."

"I'm fine," she said. "I've been busier than usual."

"Boy trouble?"

"Um . . ."

"Remember," he said, putting his hand on her wrist. "You have so, so much potential. You deserve someone great."

"Okay."

He looked her in the eyes. "Hey," he said. "Never settle."

Her mentor's unexpected lechery aside—she knew that when a man says "never settle," he means "never settle for anyone but me"—Francine felt that on some level he was right. She *was* distracted. Messner had a hold on her. Was this the cost of romantic entanglement? A dulling of one's ambition, a hold put on potential? Marla, too, was right: Messner was a nice boy. Too nice, Francine thought. He bullied her with his niceness, sending gifts, surprising her at work. He gave her unsolicited financial advice, and always during foreplay, imbuing the proceedings with a weird, transactional feel.

He was the kind of guy who couldn't stand for silence. Like if they were walking around Franklin Park and she was quietly admiring the scenery—she'd always had a thing for calm, green places, where social custom called for silence—he'd turn to her and say, "Is everything okay? Is everything all right?" He needed constant affirmations. And he took offense if Francine ever objected: "Sorry for caring," he'd say. "Sorry I'm trying to be a good boyfriend." He used the word *boyfriend* every chance he got.

In August, Francine's father died. Amid the myriad complications that ensued—the two trips back to Folsom Drive, the wrangling of her mother's moods, Arthur's patchy sympathy call, the apologetic bailing on the lab where she'd been working that summer—she told Messner that she'd have to take some time apart.

"What?" he said, over the phone. "Why? I'm coming over."

"Don't. Listen. Something's happened." She shook her head and told him about her father.

"Francine. Wow. Thank you for telling me. It's good to know you trust me. I'm coming over."

"Dave—"

He was there twenty minutes later.

"Don't you have work?" she asked him.

"I took off."

"I didn't think that was allowed."

"This is more important. I'm your boyfriend. I'm going to help you through this—this—*tragedy*."

"Dave, you're not—look, it's not just my dad, okay? I've been meaning to talk to you about us."

"Death makes people crazy."

"Okay . . ."

"Don't worry. Don't worry." He got up and began to pace. "I'm going to help you. You need a level-headed person around."

"I want to deal with this myself."

"You don't know what you're saying. Lie down."

"I know what I'm saying."

"How are you feeling?"

"I'm fine."

"Water?"

"No."

"I'll run out and get you tissues. And tea. Do you drink tea? What kind of tea do you like?"

"Dave. Dave. It was two weeks ago."

He blinked in disbelief. "Two weeks? . . . *Two weeks?!* Why didn't you tell me sooner?"

"I've been busy. Things have been a little *hectic*, as you can imagine." She was fighting to control her breath. "And I need some time alone. To think."

"Alone time is the last thing you need. You need support. The presence of loved ones."

"Don't tell me what I need, please."

"But I—"

"Please. Go. I'll call you in a few weeks."

"What you need and what you want may well be different—"

"*Go.*" With her index finger she reminded him where the door was.

"All right," he said, backing away. He palmed the doorknob. "One thing: Is there any money?"

"I'm sorry?"

"Did he leave you any money? Answer the question. This is important. I know it's blunt but it's important."

"Please leave."

"Tell me."

"Leave!"

"*I have some information.*"

She exhaled loudly. "What information."

Messner took his hand off the knob. "Listen. You can kick me out but I've got this tip. And I want to help you. I want to share it. If there's money involved, you need to hear this. Can I stay?"

"Five minutes."

Messner hurriedly explained that a friend of a colleague knew for a fact that big things were due from the presently undervalued Z——— Group, a conglomerate with subsidiary companies in everything from microprocessors to consumer foodstuffs, and that if she let him, Messner would invest the money for her, rounding out the primary investment with some stable, long-term stocks. He was doing the same with his money. "This is life-changing information. Deus ex machina stuff. You'll be thanking me for this in fifteen, twenty years," he said. "Trust me. Don't put it in a shoebox under your bed."

"Are you done?"

"Yes."

Francine huffed. "There is *some* money."

Messner's eyes widened. "I knew it."

"It's not much. A small amount. Most of it is with my mother."

"It won't be small for long."

"Answer me something, Dave."

"Okay."

"And be honest."

"Always."

Francine exhaled. "Are you good at your job?"

Messner smiled. "The best."

"And you know what you're talking about?"

"I do."

"And the money stays in my name, under my watch?"

"Fran. Fran. Yes. All of the above. Trust me."

"Okay. Okay. Come by tomorrow and we'll talk. But I need some time right now. I still think we should take a break."

"Whatever you say." He smiled. "But let me know if you change your mind."

Guilt metastasizes. Mutates. Travels. After placing her financial future in Messner's capable hands, guilt sailed through Francine's blood vessels and took distant, lumpen forms: guilt about not spending time with Marla, guilt about how much she ate. Guilt about not doing coursework, guilt about doing coursework instead of other things that needed doing. Guilt about guilt, guilt for feeling guilty in the first place. She came to believe that her initial guilt, the guilt from which these other guilts grew, had to do with the fact that she could not be the kind of person who did not feel guilt, the kind of pleasure seeker who regretted nothing. She did not consider the guilt that Messner had planted in her in exchange for helping with her father's money. She never allowed herself to believe that his generous advice had been a deliberate ploy to guilt her into seeing him again. Because the longer her father's money was under his care, and the more it appreciated (slowly, but surely) in value, the more she felt she owed him. She was indebted to him. Beholden. Which resulted in more guilt, and more time at his side. By the time she drove Marla's Ford Vengeance to pick up Arthur from the airport on a frigid, slush-gray December afternoon, there was nothing in her life she did not feel guilty about.

When Francine saw Arthur outside the airport, standing above the snow-trimmed curb in the fog of his warm breath, she was struck by a guilt more powerful, and more tender, than any she'd ever felt with Messner. Seeing Arthur in person, through the frosty window of her car, she remembered, with affection, Arthur's determination, his passion, the way he charged at life headfirst and wore his faults for all to see. He was everything that gentle, insidiously caring Messner was not. She loved this deranged man waiting in the cold.

She beckoned him into the car. He met her lips with a cold kiss.

"You're freezing," she said.

Arthur nodded. "Yeah."

She was nervous about their reunion, and attributed his flat affect to the weather, surely different from the climate he'd become accustomed to in Zimbabwe. Or maybe his frigidity was karmic retribution for her dating Messner. In fairness, she'd been trying to leave him all autumn. But every time she told him that they needed to sit down and talk, some opportunity would present itself to Messner—tickets to a show in New York, a reservation at a fashionable restaurant—and Francine would have to postpone the conversation and continue, for the time being, to endure him. To accommodate his courtesies and kinks.

She told herself that she would drop him first thing tomorrow.

As they drove through wintry Boston, Francine tried to stoke conversation. "Your last call was a little patchy," she said. "What exactly happened over there? I didn't expect you back this soon. I'm excited to see you! But I didn't expect you."

Arthur stared through the passenger-side window.

"By the way, I have this subletter," she said as they arrived, leading him up the stairs to the apartment. "She's been in the second bedroom. She'll be out by the end of the week, but needs a few more days to find a new place and move."

"Okay."

Something was wrong. Arthur hated strangers. Why wasn't he arguing with her? What had happened to him?

Francine opened the door and stepped into a space that felt, immediately, hostile. Marla met her eyes from the couch and gasped, loudly. Messner was pacing through the living room.

"What are you doing here?" Francine asked.

"You told me you were leaving town for the weekend," Messner said.

"I needed time—"

"And who is *that*."

Arthur stepped forward and out of the fog that had enveloped him since landing in Boston. "Who am I? Who are *you*?"

"Ooh," said Marla. "Mexican standoff."

"I'm her friend," said Messner, pointing at Marla, "and *her* boyfriend." His finger fell on Francine.

"I don't think so."

"You don't think so?"

Arthur gave Francine a long, understanding look before turning back to Messner.

"No, I don't," he said, in the voice of the man she'd fallen in love with. "Because *I'm* her fiancé."

Messner threw up his hands. "*Fiancé?!*"

Francine was stunned. "It's—um—"

"I think you should be going now," said Arthur.

"This is bullshit!" cursed Messner. "Bullshit! You didn't tell me you were engaged!"

"Well—"

"She is."

"Hold on, hold on, hold on," said Messner. "Where was he this whole time?"

"He was away," said Francine meekly. "Africa. Zimbabwe."

"And what the fuck was he doing there?"

She met his bloodshot stare. "Helping people."

"I can't believe this. I can't fucking believe this." He turned to Marla. "Did you know?"

"Um . . ."

"You did! Holy shit, you did! I'm the last to know. I guess that makes me an idiot, right? A real goddamn idiot!"

"You're not an idiot," said Francine. "If I can explain . . ."

"There's nothing to explain. You're a liar. A fucking liar and a terrible person. Understand? Terrible!"

"Wow," said Marla. "Most people live and die and never get to see stuff like this."

"I'm sorry you feel that way," said Francine.

"I don't believe it. I don't."

"Believe it," Arthur growled.

"I want to hear it from her." Messner flared his nostrils. "Are you going to marry this asshole?"

Marla drummed on her thighs.

Arthur looked longingly at Francine.

She inhaled. Exhaled. Steadied herself. And with convincing gravity, she said, "I am."

Not once in the course of their initially fictive—and subsequently real—engagement, nor marriage, did Arthur ask her about Messner. Who he was, and what had transpired between him and Francine. He simply did not want to know. This, to Francine, was the most charitable thing he had ever done. To not ask questions. To let it go. He had given her the greatest gift a partner can give, and the most difficult: a conditionless second chance, no questions asked.

That first night in bed, after Messner had stormed out forever,

Arthur wept and told her everything. The Moyos, Rafter, Jamroll, all of it. The sleeping sickness. The tsetse flies. When he finished, Francine, who by now was also weeping—for her partner's failure, yes, but predominantly for the town that bore the brunt of his ambition and would pay for it for years to come, and the comparative meagerness of her suffering in his absence—wiped her eyes and calmly led him to the bathroom. She bathed him in the coffin-wide tub, kneeling over the porcelain rim, scrubbing him with a hand cloth as his tears salted the bathwater. She told him it would be all right. That he had done his best. And, grateful for his silence on the Messner question, assured him that the flies were surprise variables. That there was no way to predict their arrival. That man could not control the course of nature. *It's not your fault, Arthur,* she told him, even if she didn't entirely believe it herself. *It's not your fault.*

After his bath, Francine said that she had a surprise for him. She dried Arthur off and laid him on the bed. She wrapped a necktie around his eyes and knotted it tight at the back.

When the first drop of hot wax landed on his fleecy chest, he yipped.

TWELVE

They drove in masculine silence: tense, dumb, lonely. Out the driver's-side window, three abutting cemeteries shared unincorporated, golf-green land, hidden from the road behind overgrowth, utility poles, pointless signage (↔), downed circuits. Missouri gets rural so fast, you don't even have to leave the suburbs, Ethan thought, staring straight ahead in observance of the first rule of male silence: look away.

Arthur caved first.

"Good show."

Ethan nodded. "Mmm."

"It was . . . elegant."

"Uh-huh."

Silence is a breeding ground for sadness, where memory never fails to turn up, but all Ethan could think about was the spectacle he'd just witnessed. The last few hours. The parties, the sorcerer, the birds, the death plummet. Through his window, a row of double-mortgaged ranches flowed down a hill.

"So . . . ?" said Arthur. "What did you think?"

"What did I *think?*"

"Yes."

"Of the University of Missouri–St. Louis production of *Swan Lake?*"

"Yes."

Ethan shook his head in disbelief. "I . . . I don't think anything. I don't know. What *was* that?"

"I agree it was a little over-the-top."

"No, I mean . . . Dad. Why did we do that?"

Arthur cleared his throat. "I thought it might be fun."

"The ballet?"

"Mm-hmm."

"Is that a thing you do now? A hobby you picked up?"

"No."

"Then why did we spend two and a half hours in that auditorium?"

"For you."

"For *me?*"

"That's right."

"Why?"

"I'm taking an interest. In you. This is me taking an interest."

"In me?" he asked. "But what does the ballet have to do with—" And suddenly it dawned on him.

And Ethan laughed.

It had no point of origin, the laugh. No catapult. But it shot bottom up through his body, rattling every organ, strumming every vein.

Arthur stiffened. "What? What's funny?"

Ethan tried to answer but the laugh was a closed loop. All feedback. Nurturing itself, choking out speech.

"What is it?"

He tried to answer but he couldn't, consumed now in a spasmodic full-body laugh, a laugh that does not touch language, a laugh untethered from its origin, acousmatic, solipsistic, immoderate, uncivilized.

"What's funny!" Arthur barked.

What's funny? What's *funny?* What's funny was this: though Arthur shared building space with the gender studies department, and by now had surely wrapped his head around the differences between sex and gender, beauty standards as social constructs, and

the normative phantasms that coerce people into mutually disagree-
able intercourse, for all his understanding of queer theory, Ethan
realized in a fit of sublime laughter, his father did not understand
queer people. His father did not understand *him*. All at once Arthur's reasoning revealed itself:

Gay → *Ballet*

and struck him as ill judged, reductive, and so uncharacteristi-
cally simple that he could only laugh.

Ethan had never expressed even the slightest interest in dance.
Not ever. *Swan Lake*. At UMSL! It was too absurd to be believed.
Tears flowed freely from his eyes. That his father would attempt to
bond with him *at the ballet* was not merely a gross misjudgment of
Ethan's character. It pointed to a larger fallibility, a gap in Arthur's
armor, a design defect, and this, too—the years spent cowering beneath someone this obviously flawed, so beyond wrong about his
son in particular and people as a species—caused Ethan to shake
with laughter.

"Ethan!"

But he was beyond conversation. He was somewhere else. Arthur's knuckles whitened on the wheel.

Boston, 1994. Late summer. The sun warming the undersides of
clouds, a honeyed glow over everything. Yawkey Way garnished
with awnings. The wind sweeping wrappers and peanut shells, slipping the confusion of bodies, carrying the scalpers' murmur (*Tickets, tickets*) and the slurs of unrepentant Massholes. Hot dogs turning
over in water. A flood of red jackets and caps to match the banners
flying along the park's brick facade above arched and gaping green
gates. Fenway Park.

He knew that a tenth birthday was special but he hadn't imagined
it like this. A big day, the tickets ordered in advance, the unexpected
physical contact between father and son. The touch: Arthur holding

Ethan's hand in his, dark and covered in wild hairs, as he led him into the stadium.

"We're in the nosebleeds," Arthur said.

The outing had been his father's idea. Arthur had always followed baseball, but in the weeks leading up to game day his passing interest boiled over into something resembling religious fervor. At dinner, he stopped complaining about his work on the Big Dig—the endless negotiations with the city, corrupt contractors, abuses of the budget—holding forth instead about the ways the Red Sox became more lovable with each losing season, the appeal of a team cursed to fail. "With the Sox, it's not the other team you're up against," he lectured. "It's your own disappointment. You watch season after season, knowing they're not going to make it—but you watch. And when you lose, what you feel is not the pain of being bested. It's the pain of knowing better. The pain of having tricked yourself once again into dumb, blind faith. Ethan, you'll see this firsthand at the game. It's not us versus them. It's the individual fan at war with himself. A *city* at war with itself. If we had any sense we'd make Bill Buckner our mascot. Our state bird! Boston is a pair of legs and the ball of victory keeps rolling through. And isn't that enough to make the game worth watching? Isn't the self more compelling than a conventional adversary, the whole us-versus-them barbarity you see in other sports?"

Francine translated. "He's excited to take you out," she said. "Ten years old. It's a big one. Double digits."

Arthur was prone to periodic bouts of enthusiasm, manic highs followed by long stretches of gloom. But this was different. For once, he was looking to *share* his excitement. And he had zeroed in on Ethan, steering him into the vortex of his ardor. Maybe, Ethan thought, his father wasn't indifferent to parenthood after all. Maybe he was waiting on this birthday, double digits, to begin.

"I'm going to let you in on a secret," Arthur said when the day arrived at last.

A secret! Ethan beamed.

"The markup on food and beverages at the park is criminal. A beer will run you four bucks more at Fenway than it will at a bar across the street."

"Why?"

"Because the park sets their own prices. It's like a sovereign state."

"Mom said I should get a Fenway Frank."

Arthur shook his head. "I'm sure she did. But that's playing into the stadium's hands. And fortunately for you, your father isn't one to be jerked around."

He packed two brown paper bags with bagels, apple slices, Cape Cod potato chips, and, for Ethan, a juice box. Ethan marveled at his father's ingenuity.

"Grab your winter coat," Arthur said.

"Why? It's hot out."

"Do it."

Ethan fetched his coat from the hall closet and returned to the kitchen.

"Put it on."

The down jacket puffed him out, enfolding him in his body heat. Arthur zipped him up halfway and stuck the packed paper bags inside the coat. "They never suspect the kid." Arthur grinned.

They found their seats in the right-field bleachers. They were far from the action—miles, it seemed, from home plate—but Ethan preferred it that way, tucked into a distant corner of the park where there was less competition for Arthur's attention. They had a better view of the checkered outfield than they did the diamond. A sliver of the Citgo sign rose from behind the blank emerald face of the Green Monster.

"Get our dinner out," Arthur said. Ethan shed his jacket and passed his father one of the bags, a jolt of complicity lighting him up inside. They'd broken a rule, sneaked food into the park, and Ethan made a private vow to take it to his grave.

Arthur took a bite out of his bagel. "What we should do is put you in Little League," he said, chewing. "Put you in a jersey. Put you in the batter's box. All eyes on you. The pressure. The thrill. That's what we should do. You watch the game today, you see if you like it. I can train you. I can help you. You'll see."

Nothing sounded less appealing to Ethan than that degree of pressure—or thrill, for that matter—but if it kept his father like this, excitable, interested, he would readily sign up. He speared his juice box with the straw and took a drag on it.

The innings stacked up, one after the other. "What you're seeing in baseball is what you're seeing in the country at large," Arthur said. "The decline of the American male. I'm not passing judgment one way or another—I'm saying, it's the historical moment we happen to occupy. We think of the sport as a national pastime but that's changing. The makeup of the teams is changing. Not that immigration is anything new. Your great-grandparents were immigrants, of course. But we live in the world of NAFTA now and you don't need to look any farther than Fenway to see it. The Dominican Republic in particular is churning out some interesting prospects. It's big business down there. Kids dropping out of school at twelve, thirteen, fourteen—a little bit older than you—hoping to make it big in the States. The MLB has a rookie academy down there. We're not seeing much from Japan, interestingly, though they've had baseball since the 1800s. I won't speculate on why that is but for all its civility there's still a strong bodily component to the game and my theory is that in many cases the Japanese aren't physically large enough to compete at this level."

He paid little attention to the content of his father's disquisitions but enjoyed the fact of their happening. It excited him to see his father excited, and to think he had some role in it, the birthday an occasion to shell out for tickets.

But he also noticed, with the clear eyes of a child who spends most of his time alone, that none of the other men in their section, not even the fathers with young sons, were holding forth like Arthur was. They didn't talk—they yelled. They hurled heckles and cheers in the direction of the diamond, or else they shouted down the aisle for beer. Arthur did this, too, but awkwardly and without conviction. For his part, Ethan stayed quiet, clapping when his father did. It was more dignified, somehow, to make noise with your hands. He was working his way up to a vocal cheer.

In the bottom of the fifth, a ball went flying over the outfield, hanging in the air above his father's head. "Dad—*Dad!*" Ethan sputtered, tugging on Arthur's arm with his right hand and pointing at the sky with his left. The ball hung in the air at its peak and then fell with a *thwack* into the ready glove of the right fielder. Arthur laughed. "Don't mistake a pop-up for a home run," he said. "That's a life lesson you can use."

Arthur stood during the seventh-inning stretch. "Get up," he told Ethan. "This is where we get our blood flowing again." A couple slid past them down the aisle, part of a larger migration of spectators toward the restrooms in the bowels of the park. A man behind them said, "Hold my beer a minute."

The names of corporate sponsors were booming over the stadium speakers when Ethan felt a wetness on the back of his head, something tamping down his hair and trickling, cold, down the back of his neck. He brought his fingers to the wet spot, the whorl from which his hair grew clockwise.

"Dad?" he said.

Arthur looked down. "Jesus," he said, "what did you . . ."

Ethan followed his father's eyes to the man standing behind him: tall, blue-eyed, broad shouldered, in a tight T-shirt that hugged his arms as he stretched them. He stood beside a freckled boy about Ethan's age. The boy had a plastic cup of beer in his hands, filled nearly to the brim.

Arthur bent to meet the freckled boy at eye level. "Did you do this?" he asked, pointing to Ethan.

The boy shook his head.

"Did you spill beer on him?" Arthur said again. "It's okay if you did. But you have to come clean and apologize."

The blue-eyed man looked down at Arthur. "Are you talking to my kid?"

"He spilled on my son."

"Don't talk to my kid."

"He needs to apologize. Look at him. His hair's all wet." Arthur patted Ethan's head. "It's running down his shirt."

"Fuck off," said the man.

"Dad . . . ," said Ethan.

"Hey," called a woman two seats to Ethan's left. "What's going on?"

"This pervert's talking to my kid," the man in the T-shirt said.

"Pervert!" the woman said to Arthur.

"I'm not a pervert. I'm looking for *your* son to apologize to *mine*. For spilling *your* beer on him."

"Fuck off, pervert," said the man.

Arthur shook Ethan by the neck. "Apologize," he said to the boy.

Ethan tensed. "It's fine, Dad."

"Listen to your kid," the man said, sneering at Ethan.

Ethan scrambled for a place to look, somewhere he could divert his gaze until the humiliation had ended. He met the eyes of the freckled boy, whose mouth was screwed up in disgust.

"I want an apology."

"You're a pervert."

"And you're a goon."

"Come again?"

"You're a goon!"

"You wanna take this outside?"

"We are outside."

The man spat and rolled up his sleeves. "Let's go."

"I'm not going anywhere."

The man cocked his arm and lurched forward. Arthur flinched, his hands raised in front of his face. He froze in place, then looked down at Ethan, his son's face flushed red.

The man laughed. "Guess we know what the big guy's made of."

"Okay. *Okay*. We're leaving."

He pushed Ethan down the aisle, trailing behind him.

"Smart move," the man called after them. "Faggot."

Ethan cringed, his breath catching in his throat.

Arthur was silent on the T back home. When Francine greeted

them at the door, and asked, "Back so soon?" he pushed past her and disappeared down the hall. He slammed the bedroom door behind him.

"What happened?" Francine asked, but the tears were already falling down Ethan's face. Somehow he knew that this was it, there would be no more baseball games, no more outings at all.

Until now.

Twenty-one years later, in a station wagon rolling through the suburban Midwest, Ethan wiped his eyes. He took a long, slow breath. "Dad," he said, his voice laced not with fear but love, and pity.

Arthur's cheeks flushed impatient red.

"You did good," Ethan said. The words surprised him as much as they surprised his father. "You did good."

THIRTEEN

M aggie went to Forest Park to clear her head. Same route she always took, ever since her golf-ball-mongering days, cutting through Danforth past construction cranes and the Seidel Library, a Starbucks, and a student center. Her bandaged thumb hung at her side. Wind cooed through gothic archways. The sun was somewhere else. The quads had emptied for spring break, leaving only nervous test-preppers behind, future doctors and lawyers with standardized exams still to come. Corners of the campus were haunted by spectral pre-meds, MCAT answers tucked under their breath.

She could not imagine why her father had hung the photographs. Four of them, framed, in a row on the dining room wall. She could not, for the life of her, imagine why.

Each image portrayed a foreign landscape, a terra incognita, the beige dirt tufted with ochre grass. Tree-covered hills in the far background.

All four pictures centered on two figures, posing before a cylindrical concrete structure. There was Arthur: young, raffish, Jewfro'd, hair sprouting from the neckline of his collared T-shirt. And there was a little boy, black, thin, wide smile, a canoe-shaped depression down the center of his torso.

Four photos, four poses.

1. Arthur kneeling, with his hand around the boy
2. Arthur with the boy on his shoulders

3. The boy and Arthur back-to-back

4. The boy in Arthur's lap

In the pictures, her father was smiling wider than she'd ever seen him smile before. He was touching the boy, and being touched. Arthur, who balked at the most obligatory of embraces. Arthur, around whose body was a force field, even to his children. And the boy. He looked happy, posing with Arthur like he was his friend. His older brother. His father.

Maggie and Arthur had been at each other's throats since she was old enough to speak. But it wasn't until the end of her freshman year, when Francine told her about his time abroad, that she began to fear him. What she might have inherited. What she might become. If her father had once been like her—determined, ambitiously philanthropic—did that mean she would one day be like him? Her good intentions weaponized against the people she was trying to help? It was a chilling thought. She expended tremendous effort trying to put it out of her mind. And now she was confronting Arthur's missteps—his crimes—face-to-face. He *wanted* her to see them. She suspected they'd been hung for her benefit—not Ethan's, *hers*—but why? The images portrayed a happy man, a blameless man, a loving man in the prime of his young life. But Maggie knew the truth. Knew how things had turned out over there. This was the Before picture. Did *he* know that *she* knew what came After? Maggie had never asked him about his time abroad, for fear that he would confirm her mother's story, or worse—that he would say in no uncertain terms that it was his mistake that had led to all this death. Her head hurt. She couldn't parse her father's hypocrisy. But what was the purpose of the photos? What did he want from her?

Maggie shook her head and pressed on.

Forest Park was a thirteen-hundred-acre civic center with a sledding hill, art museum, fountains, zoo, and skating rink, plus a state history museum less concerned with the Missouri Compromise than the World's Fair, which was once held—proudly, still, to some people, 111 years later—on its grounds. She walked the outskirts of the golf course sweating confusion and stress before climbing the hill to the art museum. Across from the museum entrance, at the center of a small pavilion, stood a bronze statue of Louis IX on horseback, the *Apotheosis of St. Louis*, overlooking the fountained basin below. Standing there at the top of Art Hill, above picnickers and paddleboaters, reeling from the sight of the photographs in her dining room, Maggie felt that she herself was reaching some kind of upside-down apotheosis—and that a reckoning was close at hand.

She turned to face the bronze horse. And, whoa, she thought she recognized the person standing by its side.

"Dee?"

"Maggie . . . ?"

"Hey!"

Dee Hall had gone to middle school with Maggie. They hadn't been especially close. Dee's father was the school principal, and by sixth grade Maggie was already wary of authority figures, even if the figure in question belonged to a historically wronged minority, as Principal Hall, the school's only black administrator, did. That her father wielded such great influence over the students' lives made Dee, to Maggie's mind, unapproachable.

"What are you doing in St. Louis?" Dee asked, stopping short of a hug. She tugged the leash of the beagle at her foot that was trying to wander away.

"Just visiting. Ooh, puppy." Maggie crouched, stroked its ears, and sprung back up.

Dee had gone to Stanford on a tennis scholarship, a full ride that more than validated the long hours Principal Hall spent feeding her balls, critiquing her topspin, returning her serves. Arthur had taken a brief, passionate interest in Dee after seeing her hit in Shaw Park. For one month in 2006 he spoke only of Dee, her powerful backhand, her excellent form, expressing these opinions loudly in front of the daughter who'd never fascinated him in quite the same way.

The other thing about Principal Hall was that his wife died while Dee and Maggie were in seventh grade. Breast cancer. Like

Francine—though at the time Maggie didn't understand what breast cancer even was, or that years later she would become one of its proxy victims. Now, she felt, she could forgive Dee for being such a tennis talent, and besides, they were bonded by their losses—wasn't that the key to Kevin Kismet's algorithm?—and Maggie rushed to make sure Dee knew it.

"I haven't seen you in so long," Maggie said. "Maybe not even since my mom? . . . Died?" She didn't feel great using Francine for conversation fodder, but was too relieved to find a fellow sufferer to mind.

"Oh, right. I heard about that," Dee said, with less sympathy than Maggie had hoped for. She tucked a twist behind her ear and said, "I'm sorry that happened to you."

"Yeah, thanks . . . I mean, you know, I remember what happened. With your mom. I thought—yeah. Anyways. I understand. She used to give me piano lessons."

"Mm-hmm." Dee's beagle yapped.

"Yeah! But I, I quit. After a while. Not because of her, though." Maggie stretched her digits. "Clunky fingers."

Dee nodded, and looked out on the park. A toddler waddled across the grass at the top of the hill. Its father followed close behind, mimicking a monster in pursuit.

"What are you up to lately?" Maggie asked.

"Living here. Moved back a few months ago."

"Oh, bummer."

"It was my choice."

"Yeah?"

Dee rested her right hand on her hip. "I went to school out west but I came back."

"Why's that?"

"I felt obligated after what happened."

"Mm. For sure." Maggie paused. "Sorry, after what happened?"

"The riots."

"Right."

"The protests?"

"No, yeah, sure, I know. It's still going on, then?"

Dee cocked her head.

"I'm in New York myself," Maggie said. "Queens, but also kind of Brooklyn? Right on the border."

"Okay."

"I don't have a *job* job right now, but I help out in the neighborhood. People who don't speak English that well. Running errands and that kind of thing." Maggie wanted to be Dee's friend. To have a friend, period. Someone in St. Louis who could save her from her family. Someone to talk to.

"Hey," she said. "You could visit! New York!" Maggie put a little Broadway gloss on it, twinkling her fingers.

"There's a lot of work to do here."

"Sure, right."

"Listen, I should—"

"You look great, by the way."

"Thank you."

"Still playing tennis?"

"Sorry?"

"I said, 'Still playing tennis.'"

Dee sighed. "No. No, I was injured." She said something about her rotator cuff. "It was pretty bad. But it gave me some perspective."

"Hey," said Maggie, feeling Dee's attention slipping. "So if I didn't say it back then, back in school, let me say it now—I'm sorry. For your loss. Your mom. Because I get it. Unfortunately, now, I get it."

Dee scowled. "It's a little late for that."

"What? What are you talking about?"

Dee huffed. "Maggie. Do you remember, when my mom was diagnosed, I got into awareness raising for a while."

"Sure, sure."

"I made T-shirts and hats, and sold them—"

"During Free Block, right. I remember your little stand. Lots of pink."

"Yes. Pink hats, all that stuff. The proceeds went to cancer research."

"Right."

"Do you remember what you said to me?"

Maggie shook her head.

"You said—shit, Maggie, really? You came up to my booth, and you said, 'Do you know where those T-shirts come from?'"

"Okay . . ."

"And you said, 'China. *Made in China* means *Made in Sweatshops.* Some little kid stitched that under slave conditions.' You hassled me in front of everyone. For selling T-shirts. For promoting breast cancer awareness! While my mom was sick. I was like—are you kidding?"

"Well, I—okay! I mean, it's true! But okay, sorry."

Dee shook her head. "You were super shitty then, you know."

"I said I'm sorry."

"I told my dad about it. You know what he said?"

"Principal Hall?"

"He said, 'Don't worry, honey. She's an Alter.'"

"Meaning . . ."

"Meaning you and everyone in your family are incurably self-involved."

"Wow. Okay."

The beagle snarled.

"You were always on a crusade, Maggie. And it was never right. That was always your problem. You were never upset about the right things."

"This is really, really mean," she muttered.

"'Made in Sweatshops.' God, Maggie. A few miles north of here, everything is falling apart. The grand jury letting that cop off the hook—people are upset. *I'm* upset. And you. You don't even know what's going on. You don't have a fucking clue."

"Yes I do!"

Dee flicked her wrist. "Come on, Sampras," she said, tugging on the beagle's leash. "We're going." And she disappeared behind the statue.

Maggie needed a hit of affirmation. A quick salve to rub on the burn. She fished through her pocket, removed her phone, and pulled up her text thread with Emma.

SAT, MAR 28, 6:24 PM

Coming tn?

En route

Yay!!

SAT, MAR 28, 10:32 PM

Get home ok?

Maggie?

SAT, MAR 28, 11:46 PM

Pls call back

SUN, MAR 29, 12:03 AM

Is everything ok

MAGS

TUES, MAR 31, 2:29 PM

???

She pressed the Call icon and raised the device to her ear.

"Hello?"

"Emma, hey! It's me. Maggie. I mean, you knew that, obviously. So . . . yeah. Hi."

"Hi."

"What's up?"

"Not much."

"How's New York? I'm in St. Louis right now. Do you remember Dee? Dee Hall?"

"Um, yeah. Sure. Hold on." Cackling, ambient fuzz while Emma futzed with the phone. "Principal Hall was her dad."

"Yeah! Right! I just saw her, actually."

"Okay."

"I should've asked if she remembered you!"

"I guess."

"Mm-hmm."

"Yeah."

"So . . . what else is going on?"

Emma scoffed. "Seriously, Maggie?"

"What?"

"Jesus Christ. I was worried about you."

"Huh?"

"You have no idea. It's like—after you passed out at my apartment I completely freaked. But when you came to, you said you were fine, and that you'd text me when the cab dropped you off at home."

"Oh! Sorry. Yeah, I forgot."

"Why didn't you text back? Or call? I kept trying to reach you. It's been *weeks*."

"Yeah, I forgot. My bad. Hey, can I ask you something?"

"*What*."

"Am I likable?"

"Excuse me?"

"Am I likable. Yes or no?"

"What are you—I don't—Maggie, that's a weird thing to ask right now. I'm kind of pissed at you, to be honest."

"Right, but that aside, can you answer the question?"

"Fine. Fine. Yes, sure."

"Yes what."

"Yes, I like you."

"I know *you* like me. But what I'm saying is, am I *likable*. Not only to friends but to the general public. Do I have qualities that make me a likable person."

"You're acting ridiculous. You're acting like a child."

"Am not!"

"'Am not.' Do you hear yourself? You sound like a kid throwing a tantrum."

"I do not throw tantrums."

Emma snorted. "That's practically all you do."

Maggie huffed. "You know what, Emma? Your whole 'nice girl' thing? It's an act. I know you had everyone fooled when we were kids, but I never believed it. Not me. No one's that perfect! I knew it. I know who you are."

"Maggie?"

"What."

"Don't call me anymore. Okay? I don't want to see you for a while."

"What th—" Maggie said, but Emma had already hung up. "This day is such bullshit," she muttered, and shoved her phone back in her pocket. She thought of texting Mikey, but decided that if she was such a *terrible person* that all she did was *alienate people* and *piss them off*, then she better not. *Yeah*, she thought, *better to* be alone *if I'm going to be* such a nuisance *to other people.*

She stormed down Art Hill. Couples lay on the grass, nose to nose, admiring one another. Young parents with infant children traded turns napping in the sun. A Labrador took off running and dove straight into the basin at the bottom of the hill, disturbing the path of a paddleboat.

She kicked a pebble. Why was everyone so difficult? And why was Maggie inclined to feel generous and loving to people that she hardly knew, downtrodden or otherwise, while it was basically impossible, by comparison, to maintain positive relationships with the people already in her life? She had an easier time with the denizens of Ridgewood than her actual friends and family. Mrs. Wong, whom Maggie had assisted with her W-2. The Polish baby. And the boys! Bruno and Alex, who saw her like a sister. A mother. A mentor. An example.

She had reached the bottom of the hill. She stood at the edge of the basin, looking out on the weak fountains spaced far apart within it. Maggie turned around. The sight of the grand museum, with its columns in front and wide stone wings, reminded Maggie of the National Gallery in London, and of the first and only overseas vacation that the Alters had ever taken as a family. (Modest trips were annually made, at Arthur's insistence, to national parks, famous canyons and geysers, and tourist-friendly caverns throughout the contiguous United States; Maggie recalled her father chewing out a crystal-hawking hippie in Sedona who'd followed him into a restaurant, insisting that Arthur's chakras were discolored.) But London, in the first year of the new millennium, had been an exception. Arthur booked a hotel in Belgravia and secured theater tickets to a long-running farce. The meaning of the trip, Maggie later guessed, because every anomaly in a family's routine has a meaning, a reason, was a house fire Arthur had caused the previous fall while doing laundry. His incompetence and neglect with regard to household chores had almost bankrupted the family, or worse. Surely, Maggie reasoned, he had to be repenting for *something*—transatlantic flights weren't cheap. They left in the spring of 2001. She was eleven years old.

The Alters slept on the plane and landed in the morning, heading first to the hotel for breakfast and check-in, then immediately to the National Gallery in an attempt to push past the jet lag and adjust to the local time. Each member of the family went in search of their own pleasures: Francine to the impressionists, Ethan to the Titians, Arthur to the Turners. Maggie spent her time in a hall of devotional paintings, transfixed by the gory depictions of Christ. The Alters' exhaustion made them all delirious, defenseless, leaving the art to have its way with them. It was the best day they had in London, each Alter in a different room, humbled before their respective conceptions of genius, with the knowledge that an hour or two later they would reconvene at the museum café and share what they'd seen. Separation and reunion—they needed both. Not simply because their lives were better for the balance, the ability to be individuals and a unit also, but because knowledge of the eventual coming-together freed up their time apart, and because the coming-together was only bearable if they knew they would be able to separate again.

"You can see Theseus's ship way off in the distance," Ethan said later, at the café. He shook his head in awe. "And the sky is so *blue*. I just—yeah." He blew air through his lips.

Francine smiled. "When you were little, you know, you used to love Greek myths."

"I did?"

"Oh, absolutely. You practically begged me to read them to you!
Night after night. Always the same book—I think it's still at home.
D'Aulaires'."

"And you ran around the house in a bedsheet for a week," said
Arthur, frowning at the menu. "What's an 'Americano'?"

"Hm," said Ethan. "I used to like myths." He considered this. At
sixteen years old, nothing interested Ethan more than himself, the
iterations of personality that preceded this one. "Hm. I like that. I
like that I used to like that."

"I want a regular coffee," Arthur grumbled.

"Maggie?" Francine said. "Are you okay? You seem quiet."

Maggie frowned. "Did the Jews kill Jesus?"

Arthur snorted.

"Maggie!" Francine said. "Where did you hear that?"

She had heard it at school, months earlier, but the thought hadn't
struck her until she'd seen an altarpiece depicting the crucifixion
that morning. Jesus, gaunt and pale, almost skeletal, wounds weeping blood, surrounded by betrayers and admirers. She knew that
Jesus had been crucified, but the word meant little to her until she
saw the nails depicted, driven through his hands and feet, and felt a
phantom pain where her stigmata would've been.

"Did they?" she asked again. "Did *we*?"

"No," said Francine. "We didn't. The Romans did. Pontius
Pilate."

Arthur laughed. "Yeah, it was the Romans. But we ratted him
out. So, you know. We're not killers, but we're cowards."

"Don't say that," Francine scolded. She turned to Maggie. "The
story that the Jews are responsible has been used to justify a lot of
anti-Semitism."

Maggie's stomach knotted. "I feel . . . not good," she said.

"Jewish guilt," said Arthur.

"What's that?" asked Maggie.

"It's what makes us Jewish," said Arthur.

"*Arthur.*" Francine punched his arm. "That is *not* what makes us Jewish."

"What's Catholic guilt?" asked Maggie.

"Where did you hear that?" said Francine.

Arthur rolled his eyes. "Catholic guilt is a knockoff. They stole it from us. Everybody's gotta have guilt now. It's not enough for the Jews to keep it for themselves! No, no, *everybody's* gotta have their version. *Everybody's* gotta feel bad in their special way."

"Catholic guilt comes from disappointing God," said Ethan. "Jewish guilt is when you disappoint your parents."

The rest of the trip was a letdown. Arthur tortured the family the whole time, trying to squeeze every productive minute out of the day. Museums, Tower Bridge, Hyde Park. Fights outside the V&A. "It wouldn't kill us," said Francine, "to take a nap." But the notion of sleeping away the expensive vacation was untenable. It rained.

On their last drizzly night in London, while her family tried to hail a cab from the farce, Maggie let go of her mother's hand and wandered toward the streaked, neon windows of a strange store-front. She approached and put her hand on the wet glass. She stood face-to-face with a mannequin head, bathing in red light. The head was covered in a black rubber mask. The nose extended forward into a snout. Two ears poked out from the top. The mouth was zippered shut.

"Maggie!" Francine called after her. "Come back!" She scurried toward her daughter and took her hand, pulling her back to where Arthur and Ethan stood. "You scared me," Francine said. "Don't run off like that. And that place isn't for kids."

"They sell married masks," said Maggie.

"What?"

"Married masks. Like the ones those people wore when Daddy set the house on fire."

"I didn't *set it on fire,*" Arthur said.

"Which people?"

Maggie stuck out her tongue and panted.

Francine blushed. "Oh! Oh, Maggie . . . yes, well . . . not all married people wear those."

"They don't?"

Ethan laughed.

"No, honey," Francine said. "Not all." She turned to Arthur, but he had wandered into the street, rain insinuating itself into his corduroy blazer as he chased down a hackney like a maniac.

Ulrike Blau languished in a paddleboat. Hers was the craft that had swerved to avoid the Labrador who'd plunged into the basin.

"Whoa! Look out!" her co-passenger said as displaced water sprinkled their faces.

"Thank you," she said, "but I am fine."

She sat beside Greg Mod, a graduate student in the history department. He wasn't one of her advisees, but Mod had sought her out with a question about his thesis anyway. He said he was free only on Saturdays, and when she explained that her office was locked on weekends, he'd suggested meeting at the park. But his question, it turned out, was administrative in nature and easily answered. "Great," he said. "Well, now that we've taken care of that. Seems weird to turn around and go home, right? On such a nice day. Do you want to rent one of those boats?" Ulrike, wary of upsetting him—she'd heard many stories about disgruntled American students, the power they wielded over faculty; the petitions; the protests—accepted.

"This is fun," said Mod as the Lab swam past. "Don't you think?"

"Yes."

"Hey, how'd you end up at Danforth, anyway?" Mod was a dedicated student of European history with a Habsburg jaw. His eyebrows were always raised, or he'd been born with them too high on his face. His limited range of expression typically modulated between Surprise and Interest. Ulrike wasn't sure, but she thought they were presently hovering somewhere around Interest.

"Well, Greg"—she pronounced it *grayg*, with a long *a*, eliciting Surprise—"I have been looking for a long time for a place to settle in. For a place to work."

"And that's here?"

"It could be."

"Oh, that's great. Great news."

"Do you think so?"

"Well, I thought—I mean—it would be great to spend more time with you. To learn from you, I mean. You're brilliant, you know." Mod turned, staring off at Art Hill. At that angle he was not entirely unhandsome. "Anyhow, I'm glad you'll be sticking around."

"Why is that?"

"Well, like I said, you're brilliant, and a good lecturer. 'The Politics of Leisure in Fourteenth-Century Court Life' was a showstopper, and I know showstoppers. Did I tell you I'm from Branson? Branson, Missouri. Whole family is. I know a good show when I see one."

"Thank you."

"I'm sure the grad students all have crushes on you."

"I am sure they do not."

"Don't be modest! I know at least one who does."

"Who?"

Mod blushed and pedaled faster, turning the little plastic boat.

Ulrike was surprised at Mod's forwardness. Compliments were scarce in her relationship with Arthur, and she enjoyed the attention. She wasn't particularly attracted to Greg, but for two years now she'd felt seen by Arthur exclusively. She'd seen herself through his eyes. It was refreshing—flattering, even—to be admired by someone else.

"I appreciate it, Greg. But I'm sorry. My type is more . . . older."

"Huh." Mod scratched his large chin. "Why's that?"

"You will not want to know."

Mod stopped pedaling and looked her in the eyes. He put his hand on the plastic divider between their bucket seats. "I want to know."

Ulrike hesitated. "It involves a long and finally destructive affair with the father of my childhood friend."

"Go on."

She thought of Arthur, his possessiveness, his pettiness. "Men do not like when I tell this story. They are . . ." She searched for the word. "Intimidated by it. You do not want me to go on."

"I do."

"You do not."

"Please."

"Are you certain?"

His brows bent back toward Interest. "Yes. Very much."

That evening, Arthur served baked salmon in the dining room. Maggie spent the meal staring at the photographs, her eyes panning back and forth between the young, cheery pictures of her father mounted on the wall and the sagging, red-faced man chewing loudly to her left. Time had had its way with him. Time, laced with whatever insidious chemicals leached from his glands, had changed him. She sat transfixed by the thirty-three-year gulf between the photos and her father's chair. Was anyone else seeing this? If the gulf bothered Ethan at all, he was doing a good job concealing it.

"Where were you guys this afternoon?" Maggie asked.

"We went to a show," said Arthur.

"A *show*?"

"*Swan Lake.*"

Maggie turned to Ethan and mouthed, *Ballet?* He smiled and shrugged.

"What are you teaching these days, Dad?" he asked.

"'Engineering' Social Change," he said. "And a special topics course for seniors."

"Only two?"

"Only two."

"Is that normal? I feel like you used to have a much bigger load."

"The department is going through a transition." Arthur cracked his knuckles. "It's allowed me to pursue other areas of interest."

"Like what?"

"It's not so much what I'm doing with the time, but that I have it in the first place."

Maggie tried to make eye contact with her brother, and draw his gaze to the wall behind him. But Ethan was chewing, looking up from his plate only to nod at Arthur, leaving Maggie in the gawky position of making faces at no one.

"Last year they had me teach this one," Arthur continued. He chewed as he spoke, little flecks of salmon strobing as he opened and closed his mouth. "Technical Writing for Non-Native English Speakers." He snorted. "Who has the patience?"

"Maggie," Ethan said. "Weren't you doing something like that? Not technical writing, obviously, but, you know. Working with 'non-native speakers'?"

"I . . . uh . . . ," she said. Was no one going to address the photographs?

"Weren't you?" asked Ethan.

"Yeah," she managed to say.

"Well," said Arthur, "Good for you." He addressed Maggie directly. "I mean it. Someone's gotta help those people."

Ethan nodded. "Agreed."

"You don't like salmon?" Arthur asked.

"Vegetarian," Maggie muttered.

"Fish isn't meat."

"Then what is it?"

"What about you?" said Arthur, turning to his son. "How's work?"

Maggie coughed.

"It's . . . good," Ethan said. "You know. The same."

"They should promote you. It's about time. Shouldn't they?" He looked at Maggie.

"Um . . . yeah," she smirked. "I hear he's doing *spectacularly*. I think he should definitely ask for a promotion. He's totally earned it."

"I don't know," said Ethan. "I'm pretty comfortable where I am right now."

"Nonsense!" Arthur said. "It's decided. Ethan, as soon as you get home, you march right into your supervisor's office and ask—no, *demand*—some kind of promotion. A raise. You should always take what you've earned." He forked the fish into his mouth. "That's a lesson I've always taught the both of you."

FOURTEEN

For the self-conscious and put-upon, weddings are doomed affairs. In this sense Francine and Arthur's nuptials were a matter of fate. Everything that transpired, the bride told herself later, would have probably happened one way or the other.

Initially she'd envisioned a small reception, surviving parents and a couple of friends, tasteful—where champagne flutes would clink and fizz throughout a low-lit ballroom. Toasts and dancing, a little jazz trio. Double bass, piano, drums.

It was a matter of scale. She could not afford the kind of large, extravagant wedding that gave Arthur palpitations, but if you kept it small, and spent wisely, you could treat a select group of treasured persons to a special night. To this end she made an appointment at the Copley Plaza Hotel. *Yes*, she thought, walking through the gilded entryway they called Peacock Alley, beneath Empire chandeliers and coffered ceilings, grazing a cold marble column with her fingers—*this feels right*. This could be tastefully done.

She asked about the rates. The hotel gave her a quote.

Discounting the money that Messner had invested on her behalf, Francine could afford a Copley Plaza wedding for exactly two guests: Arthur, and herself.

"You're going to have to adjust your expectations," he told her when she returned to their apartment that evening.

"I know," she said, wiping her eyes. "I know. I was stupid for thinking I could have all that."

"Hey," he cooed. "I didn't say 'stupid.'"

"The ballroom and the music and—I can't believe I thought it would work."

"Obviously we'd never in a million years have a wedding like that. But I understand where you're coming from."

"Do you?"

"Absolutely. You're not wrong to want it. But, you know. We also live in the world."

She shrugged his hand off her shoulder.

"Call your mother," he said. "Maybe she'll help."

"I don't want her help."

"I'd call mine, but—"

"But she doesn't have the resources." Francine sighed. "I know."

Arthur's father had died years earlier, while Arthur was in college. His mother lived alone back in Sharon ever since, toiling behind a desk for the town treasurer. The loss seemed far away now, but he tried to put himself in the mind of his fiancée, whose grief for her father was not even a year old. The empathy didn't come easily. Their situations weren't comparable. Unlike Arthur's mother, Mrs. Klein had a financial cushion—the calculus textbook still sold reliably—that he imagined made her loneliness tolerable.

"It's the only thing I admire about my mother," he conceded. "She supports herself. You don't see that too often among widows. Excepting the underprivileged, who have no other choice . . ."

"She's an inspiration to us all."

"Do I detect a little bitterness there?"

"Well, your implication, the *subtext*, is that *my* mother isn't supporting herself. That she's not worthy of your respect."

"Sometimes I forget I'm marrying a shrink. Look. Not everything has a subtext. Sometimes there's only . . . text. I've seen your class notes, you know, lying around the apartment. '*Possible framework: hermeneutics of suspicion?*' Sometimes I wonder if we'd get along better if you read me at the surface level. If you weren't always in such a critical mood."

"I'm not a 'shrink.' And I know what you're getting at. You're saying that your mother, who does not approve of our marriage, by the way—"

"What? She approves!"

"She gave me the most half-assed congratulations, Arthur. And only after *I* called *her*. I basically had to beg for it."

"It's not that she doesn't approve of you. It's that she doesn't understand why we—why anyone—would get married. She and my father had a hard time. She assumes everyone will be as miserable as she was."

"She *wants* everyone to be as miserable as she was."

"Francine."

"I'm telling you, she doesn't like me."

"She doesn't like anyone," he said.

"Including you!"

"Including me."

They looked at each other and laughed.

"Ridiculous," he said.

"Absolutely."

"Call your mother. See what she says."

"All right," she said, shaking her head. "I will."

Francine's mother was happy to pay. For everything. Absolutely, no problem—provided the wedding was in Dayton. Francine said she'd think about it.

"What is there to think about?" Arthur paced their bedroom, massaging his temples. "She's offering to pay for it!"

"I don't want to go back there. This day is supposed to be about us, and she's going to make it about herself. Trust me. She's never done anything that wasn't in her own self-interest."

"Francine . . ."

"You watch. She's going to overtake this thing. She'll plan it all herself. Half of Dayton will be there."

"Who cares who shows up? Or where it is? She's offering to *pay for and plan the wedding!*"

"But it's supposed to be *our* day."

"Is it? Every day thereafter will be our day. No, no. This isn't about us. It's about getting through the day without anyone from your family inflicting bodily harm on me and mine. And vice versa. Consider it. Consider leaving it all to your mother."

The relief of delegating the planning had not entirely occurred to her before. Francine was mired in her thesis on the foundations of Merleau-Ponty's ethical theory. She didn't have time to orchestrate a wedding, especially on short notice. The mock engagement, and the real one, had happened in quick succession, and there was an undeniable momentum propelling them forward. She felt that if she didn't capitalize on it, the momentum would dissipate, and Arthur would drag his feet forever. Still, she harbored hope for a tasteful ceremony, a relaxing party, and at its end, a painless escape into a life that would be, at last, hers.

She looked at Arthur. Sweat gathered at his temples.

Sometimes she thought he was two different people. One was desperate, and petty, unable to hide his desperation or his pettiness because it was written on his face, apparent in his sweat, obvious in the quantity and stink of it. And one man, the other man, was generous and thoughtful, a man who'd gone away to do some good, a man who'd visited the cockpit during a recent flight back from vacation in San Francisco, and asked to be notified by secret code when the plane was roughly over Ohio. When the stewardess came by some time later to ask (strangely, Francine had thought) if Arthur wanted anything to eat (even though the food service hadn't started), and winked, he nodded knowingly, unbuckled his belt, and took a knee right there in the aisle, thousands of feet above her birthplace, to ask Francine to marry him. The gesture paid tribute to her origins without actually touching them. It acknowledged where she'd come from without making her go back. The plane's trajectory, flying over Ohio and toward Boston, seemed to nod at the past while pointing, with aerodynamic efficiency, toward the future. *I know who you are*, he seemed to suggest, *and I know who you want to be*. She'd said yes almost instantly.

Where was that man now?

She called her sister for a second opinion.

Bex said, "Mom's not to be trusted."

"That's what I thought."

"Then again," she said, "if your hands are tied, your hands are tied."

Mrs. Klein was all too thrilled to organize the wedding. She invited first, second, and third cousins, hordes of her group and association women. In order to accommodate this cast of hundreds, the reception venue was set at the Marriott in Midtown Dayton, which shared a parking lot with the headquarters of the National Cash Register Company and a red-sauce Italian restaurant. She drew up Victorian-style invitations in mauve and turquoise, Francine's least favorite colors. Francine couldn't tell whether it was an act of aggression or a demonstration of her mother's poor taste.

"Here's something fun," she said over the phone. "What if you and Arthur were at separate tables?"

"What? Separate tables? Why?"

"I'm sure Arthur wants to spend time with his family."

"He doesn't. Besides, hardly anyone from his side is coming."

"And you'll want to spend time with yours!"

"It's our *wedding*. We *have* to sit together."

"Okay, okay."

"Is that a promise?" Francine asked.

"A promise to what?"

"A promise to seat my husband and me at the same table *at our wedding*."

"All right, all right."

"I want you to say it."

"Say what?"

"That you'll seat us together."

"Fine."

"I don't want a 'fine,' or an 'okay,' or an 'all right.' I want you to say you'll put us at the same table. My god."

"It's whatever you want."

Francine slammed the phone down in anger.

She flew out exactly once to help make some key decisions. Home wasn't all that different from how she remembered it. Her father was gone, true, but he'd spent most of Francine's life in his room. The absence was nothing new. The real pain came from seeing the For Sale sign outside Grandma Ruth's house next door. "I can't sell the place," Mrs. Klein complained. "And the city says I can't turn it into an addition either." She shook her head. "That woman," she said, "finds ways to undermine me even now."

Francine went with her mother to see the caterer. A blue University of Dayton pennant was tacked to the wall behind his desk. "We have grilled salmon, salad, asparagus, and a bread basket for each table." He looked up at the Klein women. "Sound okay?"

"We need a side dish," Francine said. "People will be hungry."

"I don't think so." Her mother shook her head. "We have the bread."

"Bread is not a side dish."

"Bread is a starch. It's filling."

"Maybe a rice pilaf?"

"Fran, rice and bread are the same—they're in the same category. I don't want two of the same thing. I'm not paying extra for another starchy, filling food."

"I hardly think a rice pilaf is going to run you over budget."

"Don't shout at me! Not here!"

"I'm not shouting!"

"Yes you are! You are now!"

"Jesus fucking Christ . . ."

"*Don't curse!*"

"This is my wedding. I don't want hungry guests at *my wedding*."

"It is absolutely *not* your wedding! Check the receipts, Francine! Look whose name is there! Look whose name!"

"Do you need a minute?" the caterer asked.

Francine was mortified, but her mother wouldn't budge. It seemed the only say she would have over her wedding was the groom.

The next morning, Mrs. Klein asked Francine when she wanted to go to the Bridal Boutique.

"No," Francine said. "I'm not getting my dress there."

"What's wrong with the Bridal Boutique? Debbie Simchowitz got her dress there. You remember Debbie."

"Vaguely."

"She plays in the Cincinnati Symphony. Second violin. She was always talented."

"Good for Debbie."

"Though her father is a major donor to the arts, so who knows. Anyway, what's wrong with the Bridal Boutique?"

"It's tacky."

"Do you think Debbie Simchowitz is tacky?"

"Yes."

Mrs. Klein gasped.

"Look, Mom," Francine said. "I already have a dress."

"You do?"

She didn't. "Yeah. Back east. I have a . . . I have a fitting later this week."

"Fine," her mother huffed. "Have it your way."

The day after she landed in Boston, Francine scheduled an appointment at a family-run bridal shop on the garden level of a Victorian brownstone in the Back Bay. The shop was a mess, a basement jammed with hanging gowns and raw fabrics stacked in piles. A tri-paneled mirror faced her from across the room.

A woman with a thick bundle of graying hair teetered out from behind a rack of gowns. "Here for a dress?"

Francine nodded.

"Where's the rest of you?"

"The rest of me?"

"Yeah. Your mother, your sister, your friend, whatever."

"Oh." Francine folded her arms and pat herself down, like she might have someone tucked inside a jacket pocket. "No," she said a moment later. "It's just me."

The woman raised her eyebrows. "You came alone? Well. All right. Might as well get started, then."

Francine settled on a modest but fashionable dress with puffy, Princess Di sleeves that gathered at the elbows, a long train that buttoned into a bustle in back, and a plunging neckline to which she requested some extra lace be sewn so as not to scandalize the midwestern guests. She chose a bodice with seed pearls and a long veil that hung over the V-shaped dip the dress took in back. Francine returned for two fittings before finally getting it right.

"I can wrap it up, unless you want to wear it out of the store," the woman said. "Ha-ha."

"No," said Francine, "that's all right. I'd like it shipped to Dayton. Dayton, Ohio, please."

There was no rehearsal dinner. In retrospect this seemed like a mistake, though Francine wondered whether it was even possible to rehearse a catastrophe, to practice chaos with an eye toward refining it. Either way, it took a great deal of convincing to get Arthur's mother out to the Midwest in the first place. She was certainly not going to help pay for a dinner designed to feed numerous Kleins and hardly any Alters.

It was probably for the best. There were enough complications already. The dress arrived without a slip, and when Francine called the shop in Boston to complain, the woman said, "You brides are hysterical." She rushed with her mother to Elder-Beerman and bought one just before it closed.

The night before the ceremony, Mrs. Klein approached her daughter. "How would you feel," she said, her lipstick curling into a clownish smile, "about a limousine?"

"Excuse me?"

"How would you like a limousine to escort you and Arthur from the synagogue to the hotel?"

"What? Absolutely not."

"I thought it could be nice."

"I thought we didn't have a budget for pilaf."

"This would be my wedding gift to you. A limousine!"

"No."

"Why on earth not?"

"Because if you knew me, Mom, if you knew me *at all*, you would know that I hate being the center of attention. A limo is not 'me.' It's not me at all."

"Fine," she hissed. "Have it your way. Good luck tomorrow." And she left Francine alone in her childhood bedroom.

Bex knocked on her door a few minutes later.

"Everything okay?"

Francine blew her nose. "Tell me I'm doing the right thing."

"The right thing?"

"Tell me I'm marrying the right person."

Bex crossed her arms and nodded, her lips pursed. She had recently been dumped in spectacular fashion by a fabulously wealthy art dealer and avowed sex addict, with whom she was still infatuated. "I don't think there are 'right people.'"

Francine sobbed.

"Okay, okay! Yes. You're doing the right thing. Arthur's a smart guy, right? Someone that smart would know better than to treat you badly."

They were married on a Sunday morning in March. After they signed the ketubah, their guests assembled in the sanctuary. At 10:31 a.m., with the minute hand on its optimistic upswing, Arthur's mother huffed down the aisle to take her seat. She was followed by Arthur, who ascended the bima, digging a nervous fingernail into his thigh. Mrs. Klein walked chin-first past the many people she'd assembled by the sheer virtue of her connectedness. Rick Pietsch, an old roommate of Arthur's now in the pharmaceutical business, walked beside Bex, the two of them comprising the wedding party.

And then there was Francine. She wore a pearl necklace and

pearl earrings with tiny diamond accents. On her arm, in place of her father, was Uncle Ron, her mother's brother. She hardly noticed he was there and, in later years, would recall walking down the aisle alone.

Beside Arthur stood Reverend Kaplan. The battle over Kaplan had played out months earlier. Kaplan was a certified rabbi, but he didn't preside over ceremonies or deliver sermons. He was Beth Abraham's religious director. Years earlier he'd taught Francine her bat mitzvah portion. His house smelled like warm bread, and indeed at every lesson Kaplan's wife served Francine a small plate of crunchy Mandelbrot and a cup of tea. Kaplan talked to her in kind, pure tones, as if he'd never heard a critical word spoken in his life—as if he didn't know voices could do that. But he wasn't naive. Kaplan was a man of deep, profound experience. His son, Len, had cerebral palsy and was largely confined to a hospital bed right off the kitchen. Len was mentally all there but his body was thin and crooked like a bare tree branch. At the end of Francine's lessons, Kaplan would say, "Wonderful job today. Would you like to visit Len? He's looking forward to seeing you." This, from day one. On her first lesson: "Len's looking forward to meeting you." She felt important. Like she could make a difference for the boy. And Kaplan's face was all sincerity. In Francine went, through the kitchen to the white bed with brown end panels, where Len, lying with his arms splayed and his neck bent at an angle, would smile at her and nod his head up and down, with purpose. "He's so happy to see you," Reverend Kaplan translated. In his house, Francine mattered.

When she learned that Beth Abraham had recently ousted its senior rabbi for being "too intellectual," and in his place installed someone more "relatable"—one Rabbi Krantz, who sported a dyed-black comb-over and possessed the cognitive abilities of a fish—she lobbied for Kaplan in his place. It had been a long, drawn-out argument over telephone wires stretching halfway across the country. Francine wanted someone she knew to perform the ceremony, someone who wasn't reputed to be a moron. Her mother argued that Kaplan didn't perform weddings, *it just wasn't done*, and she didn't want talk about the weird role reversal jangling around the tight-knit Jewish community in Dayton. Ultimately, Francine prevailed. "As long as Krantz is on the bima," her mother said. "I don't want to rile the congregants. Besides. As you know, I like Krantz quite a bit. But Kaplan, too, is very good."

The service itself was swift and personal. Kaplan shared some words about Francine, and said that any man to marry her should count himself among the most fortunate on earth. (For a moment she wondered why she wasn't marrying Kaplan.) They exchanged rings. Arthur's hands were soaking wet. The sweat lubricated his fingers, and the ring slipped right on.

All Arthur had to say now was the one sentence of Hebrew he'd been asked to memorize from a transliteration. *Harei at m'kudeshet li b'tabaat zo k'dat Moshe v'yisrael.* One sentence. *By this ring you are consecrated to me as my wife, in accordance with the laws of Moses and the people of Israel.* A handful of syllables. A pail of consonants and vowels. She looked at him expectantly.

"Ha . . ." He cleared his throat. "*Ha—har . . .*"

Kaplan tried to get him started. "*Harei at m'kudeshet . . .*"

"*Ha . . .*"

"*Harei at . . .*"

"*Harei . . . Har . . .*"

Arthur looked up, helpless. He shook his head at Francine. She stared at the floor, mortified. Then she made the mistake of looking out at the sanctuary, where she saw one of her mother's eyebrows raised high above the other.

"*Harei at m'kudeshet li b'tabaat zo k'dat Moshe v'Yisrael,*" Kaplan whispered. Arthur muttered something close enough.

"*Harei atah m'kudash li b'tabaat zo k'dat Moshe v'Yisrael,*" Francine said in turn.

And with that, in the mosh of mangled Hebrew, they were married. When the new couple stepped out of the synagogue, past throngs of strangers, Francine was stunned to find, parked at the curb of the temple, a white limousine. Beside it, her mother stood laughing.

———

The hotel was a blocky, Soviet-looking complex. The ballroom was packed with people Francine had never met and was sure she would never see again. Mrs. Klein commandeered the newlyweds and dragged them around the hall, introducing them to her friends and relations.

Lunch was served. (There was an indignity in this, the meal and the hour, lunch instead of dinner, naked daylight and not magic, permissive dark.) The food wasn't particularly good, but Francine busied herself with eating, stuffing her mouth to keep from lashing out at her mother, who was ruining the most important day of her life, and her husband—the husband she had defended a literal seat at the table for—who was presently munching a stalk of asparagus with a terrified look on his face.

Then, all at once, Arthur's mother was standing with a half-empty glass of water in one hand, a soupspoon in the other. Chatter thinned. People stopped eating, their forks suspended in the space between plate and mouth. Francine's cheeks went hot. *What are you doing?* She tried to compel his mother to sit down with her mind. *Sit,* she thought. *SIT!*

"As the mother of the groom," she said, tugging on the *oo* in *groom* with sinister relish, "I want to congratulate these two young people on their wedding. What a lovely service, wasn't it?"

There was unmistakable sarcasm in her voice. Was this on purpose, or how she talked?

"I'm proud of these two."

Okay. Maybe she's just being nice.

"However . . ."

No!

"However, I find it odd that they're getting married. After all, they already live together. I mean, why buy the cow?"

Whispers slithered through the room. Fourth cousins dropped their forks. Mrs. Klein had not let on to the more conservative faction of the Dayton contingent—people Francine didn't even want at her wedding in the first place!—about the newlyweds' prior cohabitation. Someone coughed. A napkin fell softly to the floor.

Francine excused herself. She walked briskly to the women's room and leaned over the sink. Her shoulders heaved. She whimpered. She knew now what Arthur meant about getting the day over with. The wedding was not about the two of them. It was about her mother, and her mother's people. *If I have children*, she thought, already four weeks pregnant with Ethan (though no one, not even Francine, knew it), *if I have children, I will not dominate their lives. I will give them the opportunity to make their way in the world, for better or for worse.* She looked up at herself in the mirror. The color had left her face, her lashes clumpy with mascara.

The door swung open, and Bex entered. "Oh, Franny," she said, embracing her sister.

"It's all wrong," Francine cried. "It wasn't supposed to be like this. I knew Mom would make it difficult but I couldn't have imagined . . ." She hiccupped between sobs. "Why anyone would . . . and that speech . . . so *embarrassing* . . ."

"It'll be okay," Bex cooed, rubbing Francine's back. "Everything is going to be fine. It's one day. One day in the course of your whole life."

Arthur barged in. "I know I'm not supposed to be here," he said, pausing in the doorway. "But you're wanted in the ballroom. The mothers are having it out, and we need all the help we can get."

FIFTEEN

On Sunday morning, in sync with the bells, Maggie woke to find her father at the foot of her bed.

"What . . . what time is it?" she asked, dropping her head back on her pillow.

"I want to apologize."

"For . . ."

"Piggy's. I shouldn't have taken you there. I should've been more thoughtful. I should've been better."

Maggie yawned and wiped some morning crud from her lips.

"Let's spend the day together," he said. "Father-daughter."

She spoke into the pillow. "What time is it?"

But she knew: it was six a.m. Maggie's father possessed an internal alarm that rang at five thirty in the morning, every morning, and by six he was showered and dressed and probably waking his children to deliver news that could have easily waited another few hours. In Ridgewood, Maggie had been in the habit of sleeping until the men began work on the pit outside her window at nine. But here was Arthur, a petty tyrant of the morning, slinging propositions at her while the sun was still low in the sky. She didn't know how to respond. It was an ambush.

Maggie sat up and blinked herself awake. Arthur was already dressed in his weekend wear: a white, sweat-wicking collared T-shirt and brown pants. Not denim, not khaki, just *pants*, woven from an indeterminate material and sold at stores known only to fathers.

"What did you want to do?" Maggie asked through a film of throat-clog. "I was going to visit Mom."

"Later. There'll be time later. I need you today. Please."

"All right. Let me get dressed."

He left and closed the door behind him. She rose from bed, stretching. She felt the sleep draining from her body, but it was replaced by a nervous, skittish feeling that rose up from her stomach. Sundays were, for Maggie, one long witching hour. An open portal through which demons came, interminable stretches when the ghosts of her grief piled on top of her boilerplate anxiety. Sundays in St. Louis were especially rough. The city hushed, and nothing tempted her monsters like silence. She shuddered at the thought of the empty day before her, and steeled herself for whatever Arthur had planned.

On her way to the bathroom, she ran into Ethan in the hall.

"We need to talk about the photos."

"What photos?"

"In the dining room. On the wall?"

"Oh, those. From that trip he took, right? To Zambia?"

"Zimbabwe. Did Mom never tell you?"

Ethan shrugged.

"Oh, god. Well, there's a story there. I'll explain later."

"I thought they were kind of nice."

"*Nice?* Not, I don't know, self-indulgent? Egotistic? Megalo*maniacal?* Admit that they're bizarre, at least. Dad looking all white savior."

"He looks happy."

"He does look happy."

"I've never seen him that happy."

Maggie nodded. "Same."

"Well, I think it's nice."

"Am I insane? I feel like an insane person. Did he brainwash you or something? At the ballet?"

"He's a human being," Ethan said. "I think he's making an effort this time. Didn't you say this time was different? Wasn't that why we came?"

"Sure, right," she said. "This time is different."

Maggie was skeptical. She had to be. To lower her guard was to make herself vulnerable to whatever scheme he was running. And there was definitely scheming going on. Something was up—and so it was with great wariness that she lowered herself, two hours later, into the passenger seat of her mother's old car.

"You get breakfast?" he asked.

"Yeah."

"Eat enough? This is going to be an excursion."

"Where are we going, anyway?"

"You'll see."

She held still while her father backed the car out of the driveway, her nerves creeping up with every silent second.

"Dad? Can I ask you about the, um, new addition? To the dining room?"

"Of course. I'm glad you noticed," he said.

"You are?"

"Absolutely. I've always meant to tell you about my time in Africa."

Maggie blinked. "You have?"

"It's something that I think would interest you."

She felt her pulse at her neck, in her wrists. "Tell me."

Arthur scratched his head. "When I was young," he said, "I wanted nothing else except to be a good person. It's funny, you know, we have that in common, even if you don't realize it. One thing you'll learn as you get older is that empathy gets harder to drum up. That muscle atrophies. You have a family, you'll understand. You start to look out for yourself, your personal unit, and soon enough you forget how to look out for anyone else. But back then I was young and I wanted to do something with my life. I wanted to be a person of consequence. That's who I was. Your mother and I were dating at that point. Dating but not married. I was working at an engineering firm where I came up with a, a, building material, you could call it, that wasn't going to be implemented in the States." He lowered the sun visor. "I'd been reading up on

Zimbabwe. A friend of mine from work had family there. And I thought, 'That's a place I can go. That's a place where I can help.' I thought I might build things with this material. It was cheap to produce and the standards there were much lower. In rural areas you didn't need contracts, patents, all of that. They let you build. So I did. Outhouses. It's not a sexy cause, I know that, but it's a necessary one, and I wasn't afraid of the work. Sanitation. It's the unacknowledged bedrock of civilization. I got a grant. Maybe you've seen my proposal. There's one in the African Studies Library on campus. A little bound book. We used to have some at home but they were lost in the fire." He shook his head. "Anyway, I was there for about a year. Safe, inexpensive, sanitary outhouses. That was the idea. It was an eye-opening experience to say the least. I can tell you, I've never felt more purpose in my life. Growing up, I didn't have all the advantages that you did. My father worked hard, but he drank, and though he wasn't a mean drunk, he wasn't exactly the model of a responsible parent. We didn't have money to throw around. I got a chip on my shoulder about this, even in college. Especially in college. What I'm trying to say is that I thought I knew what struggle looked like. What poverty looked like. But until I went to Zimbabwe I had no idea. I've never understood how anyone can spend money so conspicuously once you've seen how other people live. Even if you haven't seen them, you know those people are out there. Everyone knows. Now you have the internet. I'd witnessed it first-hand. There was no coming back from that. I know this sounds strange but I was thinking of you the whole time I was there. Not *you*, you weren't born yet—but I was thinking about my children. How I'd want them to learn from my example. How I'd want them to be proud of me. I wanted to raise my kids to be good people and I wanted to have done some good myself. I can't stand hypocrisy. You and me, Maggie, we're not all that different."

The whole time Arthur was talking, Maggie had been bracing herself for the turn. The part when things went awry. But Arthur had slowed the car to a stop, and was looking at her expectantly. As though that was where the story ended.

"Who's the boy," she said.

"Sorry?"

"In the photos. Who's the boy with you."

Arthur nodded solemnly. "Ah. Yes. There was this boy, he lived near the outpost where I worked. He used to come around some-times. We couldn't communicate, not verbally, but we passed the time together. Great kid. He'd come around and watch me work. We developed a, a, *friendship*, you could say. A colleague of mine took those pictures of us. On an old film camera. I had to get them digi-tized. I think they bring a little life into the house. Am I wrong?"

I think they bring a little life into the house.

Maggie trembled. "Yes."

Arthur cut the engine. "What?"

"Yes. You're wrong. I don't think they bring life into the house. I think—I think they have the opposite effect."

"What are you talking about?"

"I know what happened over there."

He tensed. "You know what, exactly?"

"I know about the flies, Dad. I know about the sleeping sickness."

Her words hung in the air. Arthur coughed. "Does Ethan?"

"No. But he deserves to. I don't know how you can live with yourself. Honestly. To do what you did. To facilitate a *plague*—regardless of your intentions—and walk away, unpunished . . ."

"Unpunished?" he erupted. "*Unpunished?* Who said anything about unpunished? Did it ever occur to you that I've been punishing myself ever since?"

"It's not the same thing!"

"I know it's not! I know, dammit! I've been waiting to be pun-ished all my life! Every morning I wake up—" He clapped his hands together. "Nope, still here. Still feeling awful. Fucking awful. But I can tell you one thing. When that day comes—when that other shoe finally drops—it won't be you who does the sentencing. Hold anything you want against me, Maggie, anything I've done to you, but for god's sake don't judge me for that. It's not your place. You weren't there."

Maggie was pinned to her seat. She'd seen him yell before but never like this, with such lacerating self-awareness.

"Let's go inside," he said, shaking his head, "and try not to spoil the morning."

Maggie looked out her window. She'd been so consumed in his story that she hadn't even noticed where he'd taken her.

The Future Pet No-Kill Shelter for Animals was located in the Hill, an Italian enclave rich with bakeries, and churches, and fire hydrants painted like *il tricolore*. On the corner of Wilson and Marconi sat St. Ambrose Roman Catholic church in all its brick and terra-cotta glory. A mile south was Sublette Park, once home to the Social Evil Hospital, where nineteenth-century prostitutes were given medical treatment and taught life skills.

Maggie knew the neighborhood well. The shelter, which provided a home for more than four hundred homeless strays (plus low-cost spay-neuter programs and a pet-food pantry), had been her extracurricular stomping ground in middle school. Ever since she was young she'd had a soft spot for animals, and dogs especially. (Cats were too self-involved, prickly, and judgmental—too human— to return the love that made caring for animals worthwhile. On top of that they were too smart, and Maggie, the child of a university professor, did not place a great deal of value on raw intelligence.) But dogs were her Achilles' pet, capable of dissolving all her angst with the flick of their dumb, furry tails.

For years she'd been a regular volunteer at the no-kill, feeding, handling, and socializing with the homeless pups every Sunday afternoon. But between her college workload and her growing interest in human suffering, she'd found it difficult to keep up her visits. She missed it. Her contact with animals in college had been restricted to the fraternity-funded petting zoo that came to campus during finals as a stress reliever. In Ridgewood she had only Flower, the Nakaharas' miserable Lab, resigned to his cramped little corner.

She followed her father into the no-kill. His admission of guilt, or at least of guilty feelings, put her in a complicated position. How could she shame someone who had already shamed himself?

Arthur's self-hatred robbed her of the fun of hating him. Where had this man been all her life? And what were they doing at the shelter?

They approached the front desk. A wire-haired woman in a turtleneck apologized for the state of the place as a dusting of ceiling plaster fell from overhead.

Maggie sighed. Severely underfunded, the no-kill competed for public grants and private donations with two other shelters within fifteen miles. A few years earlier, one of the other shelters, which euthanized unadopted strays, sent a libelous mailing to local residents, slamming Future Pet for laundering money. When there wasn't any money to launder! *God,* Maggie thought, recalling the incident. *What some people will do to kill a dog.*

"My name is Arthur Alter. I called ahead. I spoke to a Suzanne?"

"That's me."

"Well, hi." He flashed a creepy smile. "I believe you said my daughter and I might be able to help out around here today?"

"That's right."

"Let us know how we can be of use."

She reached into a drawer and removed two brushes, which she placed on the desk in front of her. They were combination brushes, with pins on one side and bristles on the other.

"We have a limited range of tasks for first-time volunteers," Suzanne said. "We like to start out simple. You'll take these back to the kennels and work your way down the hall, one by one. We have a lot of shedders, and we want them looking cute and clean and ready to be whisked away to a forever home." She smiled and two coins of light settled on her round red cheeks.

"I'm not a first-time volunteer," Maggie said. "I used to work here."

"You did?" The woman looked confused. "That's funny. I don't recognize you."

"Worked, volunteered, whatever. It was a while ago. Anyway, I know where the kennels are." She turned to Arthur. "Let's go."

"Lead the way," he said.

They walked through a narrow corridor to the fluorescent hallway where the dogs were kept. On either side of the hall were individual kennels with cinder-block walls and barred doors. When Maggie had started volunteering there in high school and asked about the prison-like conditions, she was told that the atmosphere, in addition to being cost-effective, actually encouraged adoptions. "If we make the dogs look too comfortable, no one will take them home," her supervisor told her. "Guilt is a powerful force in a place like this."

Maggie let herself into the kennel of a yellow Lab. It was a cramped little cell. She could almost touch the walls on both sides if she stuck her arms out. Arthur stepped into the kennel next to hers. She couldn't see him through the cinder block but the wall didn't reach the ceiling. She crouched beside the lab and nuzzled it. The dog licked her face and panted stupidly, happily. *Remain skeptical!* she thought.

"Dad," she said, her voice carrying over the wall. "Do you remember Céline Default?"

"Guy Default's kid?"

"That's her."

The student children of Danforth faculty formed an awkward coalition. They all knew each other, all nursed the same insecurity regarding the merits of their intelligence, and rarely interacted in public lest anybody think they were admitted on nepotistic grounds. Céline was double legacy, if "legacy" connotes a parent employed by the third school to call itself the Harvard of the Midwest. Independently wealthy, Guy and Mathilde Default nonetheless both taught full-time in the French department, he theory, she language. "Did you know," asked Maggie, "that her dad wrote a book?"

"Well," said Arthur, from his kennel. "I assume he has."

"Not an academic book. I mean, a novel."

"A novel?"

"Self-published."

"He *didn't*."

"He did. Yeah. During his and Céline's mom's separation. It's super awkward. It's this thinly veiled account of his affair." The Lab panted, its hot breath on Maggie's neck.

"Oh."

"Yeah. It made Mathilde out to be this shrill monster. And of course the Guy character was totally put-upon, shouldering the family's burden, mourning his youth. Mopey-middle-aged-man stuff. There are two—*two*—scenes in which he stares at his naked body in the mirror and, you know. *Evaluates* himself."

"Meaning . . ."

"He examines his penis," Maggie said. She lowered herself to the floor of the cell and began brushing the dog's pale yellow coat.

"Oh."

"Size as metaphor—"

"I get it."

"Yeah."

"So . . ."

"So what?"

"What's your point?"

"I don't know. Just occurred to me."

She knew she should stop talking but she couldn't. "It's like, is infidelity a prerequisite for tenure?" He didn't answer her. "You know?"

There was a long pause. She could hear, over the wall that separated them, the scratchy, repetitive sound of Arthur brushing his animal. "I'm not tenured," he said finally.

"Right," she said, beating back a sudden swell of pity. As combative as she was, as much as she wanted to keep her father in check, she did not feel at home in cruelty.

She stood on the crate and peered over the cinder-block wall. Arthur was on his knees before a brown pit bull with a streak of white down its chest.

"Um, Dad?"

"Yeah?"

"Bristles."

"Hm?"

"Flip the brush. You're on the pins side."

"Ah." He turned the brush in his hand. "Bristles."

After leaving the shelter, and despite her father's request that she join him for lunch—*not* at Piggy's, he assured with an apologetic laugh—Maggie asked that he drop her at the Missouri Botanical Garden.

The gardens were her mother's place. Francine had loved it there. She used to visit every Sunday morning in the spring, bringing Maggie with her only once or twice per season. More often than not she insisted on going alone, and when she returned she radiated calm— a warm, peaceful emission with a half-life of an hour or however long it took Arthur to find something new to stew about. Now, stepping out into the greenery, Maggie wished she'd taken her father up on lunch. She felt light-headed, stirred by memory and low blood sugar both.

The grounds were divided into sub-gardens, the most impressive among them drawing inspiration from international horticulture. Francine adored the Chinese garden with its plum trees, peonies, and lotuses; the red-bricked Victorian District with its hedge maze; the curt alpine dwarf shrubs and forbs of the Bavarian garden; the Japanese garden's four understated islands. That her favorite place in the whole city was so cosmopolitan, so un–St. Louis, only bolstered Maggie's conviction that her mom had been unhappy in her life there. That she had left the Midwest at eighteen only to be drawn against her will back to it. That she had forgone a lifetime of fresh seafood and career prestige in Boston for a city utterly familiar to her in the worst way.

Most of all her mother loved the Climatron, a massive greenhouse encased by a lattice-shell geodesic dome. Maggie was no great fan of the place herself. The honeycombed bulge of deltoid panes rose up from the green earth like a—well, like a cyst, a giant manmade cyst, a technotumefaction held in place by a network of aluminum tubing. It looked like the eighties as imagined by the sixties.

Holistic circles, amniotic encasements, gesturing toward a unified future. But the sixties had been wrong, and now the retrofuturistic structure seemed to indicate a time that never was, inhabited by people who never were. Inside the dome was no better. It was humid underneath the panes, a makeshift rainforest thick with Amazonian dampness. Ferns, and other green things, filled the space, the only nonconforming colors coming courtesy of the four Chihuly sculptures planted throughout, glass stems and bulbs compensating for the disappointing experience of unadorned nature. It was like being inside a theme park. Maggie wished she understood why the Climatron appealed to her mother, but the reasoning was gone, gone along with the billion facts and memories and preferences Francine spent half a life collecting.

Before she died, she'd asked to be cremated, but never specified where she wanted to be scattered. For a few days after the funeral her remains were kept in a small black box that Arthur had placed for the time being on the desk in her home office. He couldn't bear to look at it. Maggie, frustrated with his inaction, took it upon herself to disseminate the remains. One evening she covertly transferred them into a cigar box that she sealed with Scotch tape and slipped inside her backpack before sneaking it into the gardens.

She considered the Victorian District, the xeriscaped Ottoman garden, the Butterfly House. She considered the Climatron.

It had to be the Climatron.

But as it turned out, dispersing a person's remains inside a popular glass attraction was not as easy as Maggie had hoped. She needed to find a private corner apart from visitors and watchful garden staff, which proved impossible, as there were (obviously!) no corners in the dome. She stalked the circumference. There was nowhere she could stand undetected.

An overhead voice announced that it was almost closing time. Maggie removed the cigar box from her backpack. Coming upon a quiet stretch, she stepped off the gravel path and sat on a smooth, wet rock, placing the backpack on the ground in front of her. Behind her, a three-foot waterfall pushed clean, clear water down a stream that ran through the middle of the dome. Maggie looked left, then right, maneuvered the cigar box behind her, and let its contents tip into the stream.

Her father was furious. "The botanical fucking *gardens*?" he'd shouted. "What kind of resting place is that!" But Maggie's conscience wasn't troubled. If there was one piece of wisdom, one tired adage that she heard in the weeks after her mother's death, it was this: *There's no wrong way to grieve.* In other words, grief was a stage on which one could perform all of one's basest impulses and indulge one's selfishness, repercussion-free, especially when said impulse pertained directly to the grief. Maggie told him that she'd spread the ashes all throughout the park, as her mother would have wanted. The dome, she'd decided, would be her secret. She wanted the specific location of her mother's final resting place to be knowledge she alone possessed, and why not? She had loved her mother the most.

Now, entering the Climatron almost two years later, sweating upon entry into the mock rainforest and surrounded by the sounds of trickling water, leafy rustlings, and piped-in birdcall MP3s, Maggie felt a strangeness coming over her. It rose up from within, seized control of her body, like her blood had changed course, reversed direction as she passed through the motion-sensing doors of the dome. Was it the humidity? Something else? A fly buzzed her ear. Was Maggie projecting or did she feel her mother's presence in this place, flowing with the water, rustling with the leaves? God, it's hot in here, she thought. It's all too much. A lot to take in. *Bzzzz.* Wow. God. It's all so much sometimes. Like how does everyone manage it? The day to day? Hey, young lady, watch out. They're plants. Really, really, humid. Someone talking. Overhead. Mom? No. Automated. The Missouri Botanical Garden welcomes you. *Bzzzzzz.* Welcome to the Missouri Botanical Garden—

SIXTEEN

As he pressed the buzzer beside BUGBEE at the address he had found online, Ethan was struck by the feeling that he was not ringing a doorbell at a Central West End apartment, but begging admittance to the next stage of his life. His future, gate-kept by his past. The almost-immediate click of the door unlocking before him only heightened this impression. It was as though his fate were waiting for him. Climbing the stairs, he steeled himself for whatever, whoever, awaited him on the fourth floor. The young man he'd known in college would not have lived in this neighborhood—had once railed against this neighborhood—but then again, the young man he'd known in college thrashed his heart. Ethan decided it was an auspicious sign. Proof that change, however slight, was possible.

The man in the doorway was both Charlie and not. Like some-one had stuffed Charlie in a barrel and rolled it down a hill for a decade. His forehead was still his forehead, wide like a projection screen, only now a little weathered, a little wrinkled. A faint cowlick still adorned the front fringe of his short hair if you knew where to look for it. And his eyes. Those were unmistakable, if a bit paler than Ethan remembered, as though the intervening years had di-luted their color—in Ethan's memory, the color of green tea leaves—with a few drops of milk. How to resolve the boy with the man, when he'd loved the boy for his boyishness? Ethan had been robbed of the chance to age slowly with him, to witness and adapt to his changes. If nostalgia was history without its teeth, seeing Charlie now was all teeth and no history.

"Ethan?"

"Charlie."

"Oh, shit."

Charlie froze for two interminable seconds before stepping forward and embracing him, a brief hug consummated by three back pats in quick succession. On the third, he released him. "From Danforth."

"That's right."

Charlie looked down the hall in both directions. "Here, why don't you—come in."

Ethan followed Charlie into the apartment. He was so startled by Charlie's invitation (and the hug, the hug!) that he almost failed to notice the dorm-like quality of the apartment, the bare beige walls and IKEA furniture.

"Can I get you something? Cup of coffee?"

It was not yet noon, though Ethan had surreptitiously sipped a paper-bagged beer on the walk over. "I'm okay, thanks."

He hadn't come for coffee. He'd come for closure, an explanation, an apology: those two words, *I'm sorry*, the code that would spring the padlock on his life. But now, having been welcomed into Charlie's place, Ethan wondered whether he hadn't been ambitious enough. An apology was the *least* he could ask for. What if, in talking with Ethan, Charlie remembered what it was that drew them together in the first place? What if Ethan allowed himself to hope for something beyond closure—to hope, instead, for its opposite?

Charlie sat on a gray polyester couch and motioned for Ethan to take the white plastic shell chair by the kitchen island. "Ethan. Ethan . . . Alter, right? Man. It's been what, ten years?" He squinted, searching Ethan's eyes.

"Closer to eight."

"Right. Eight, right." A moment of silence passed between them. "So what have you been up to?"

Ethan stuttered through the necessary exposition. New York,

good health, between jobs. His hands trembled on his lap. It felt like someone else was speaking for him. He hated his words as he heard them aloud. He hated the sound of his life.

"Yeah," said Charlie. "It's tough out there." Ethan took note of how he crossed his legs, one knee stacked on top of the other.

"So you stuck around St. Louis?"

"I took off for Texas, actually. I was a physics major, if you re-member." *I remember.* "Family all at Anheuser-Busch." *How could I forget?* "I felt bad leaving town, leaving my brothers behind, but my dad kept pushing me. He had ideas about me, about what I could become. I wound up at the Johnson Space Center in Houston."

"Oh, wow. Doing what exactly?"

"Flight control. Do you know anything about telemetry?"

Ethan shook his head. Charlie described the mission operations control room, where he sat in front of a console, monitoring the status of spacecraft and satellites, "kind of like in the movies." He spoke in the private language of acronyms, MDMs and FCRs and FIWs. "I was there long enough to get my training in. I was good at my job and the money was good too," he said. "But six or seven months after we graduated, everything fell apart."

Ethan nodded. "The financial crisis."

"Right. That too. But no—in November, they bought Anheuser-Busch."

Over the next few minutes, Ethan learned that "they" referred to InBev, a Brazilian-Belgian brewing conglomerate, which took control of Anheuser-Busch in 2008. The $52 billion acquisition granted In-Bev access to the United States' vast distribution network, creating the largest brewing company in history. In the recession year that followed, however, sales of Bud Light and Budweiser plummeted. "Their top two brands were in crisis," Charlie explained. "But in-stead of fixing anything, they let people go. Long-time, die-hard peo-ple, it didn't matter. And guess who felt it most." He described a period of panic at the St. Louis headquarters, a reign of terror as legacy employees like his brothers suddenly found their key cards obsolete, their personal effects boxed and left for pickup at the front desk. "It felt wrong to be in Houston with all this shit going down. My dad wanted me to stay down there, but then he got sick."

"Oh, Charlie—I'm so sorry."

He looked at his feet and shrugged. "That's okay. It was quick, at least. By then I had already decided to move back. My mom was all alone, my brothers were out of work. I didn't have a choice."

"So what are you doing here?"

"I got a job at Boeing. They love Danforth grads, it turns out."

"That worked out well."

"It's all right. It feels like a demotion, being so . . . earthbound. What's important is, I see my mom every couple days."

"That's really great of you."

"It's just what you have to do."

"I'm surprised you live so close to campus," Ethan said.

"I like being near the school." Charlie smiled out of the corner of his mouth. "It has its perks."

"Absolutely," Ethan said, emboldened. He felt like he was back in Charlie's room in Wrighton again, able to say anything. "You probably didn't hear—I guess I don't know how you would've—but my mom died. Breast cancer. About two years back."

"I'm sorry to hear that."

"Yeah. It happened fast. Kind of took us all by surprise."

"Oh, shit."

"Yeah."

And then it all came tumbling out: Arthur's affair, Francine's decline, the time spent shut inside of his apartment. Francine's inheritance, the reckless spending. The debt. The feeling that he had been a prisoner all his adult life: of his body, of his class. The past twenty-three months sprayed out of him like so much keg-pressurized beer. He grew dizzy, light-headed, as he recited the litany of his troubles. "I don't know," he sputtered into his lap as he finished. "I don't know what I'm doing. But I can't tell you how much of a relief it is to tell someone."

Ethan looked up. Charlie looked like he might say something, his lips searching for a shape, but then his mouth shut. He was still for a moment, and then said, "I'm sorry about your mom."

It was a simple, tired sentiment, but hearing it from Charlie warmed him inside.

"Thanks," he said.

Charlie nodded. "What brings you to St. Louis?"

"My dad. He asked us back. Well, that's the official reason. You have to understand, Charlie—I came back for you."

"Me?"

"You. You're the reason, Charlie. I wanted to see you, I had to talk to you. I've been thinking a lot about the last time we spoke."

"When was that?"

"Senior Week, the Botanic Gardens . . ."

Charlie shrugged.

Ethan's earlobe burned. "You said you wanted to get out of St. Louis?"

"I was drinking a lot back then."

"Come on. You must remember."

"It wasn't a great time for me."

A door slammed shut behind him. Charlie stood. "Hey," he said.

All at once the mood in the apartment changed. A young woman in a pink, form-fitting dress shuffled into Ethan's sight line, trailed by the boggy smell of low-grade weed. She paused in the entryway.

"I slept at Maddie's," she said.

"Don't you have class today?" Charlie asked.

"In an hour. Who's this?"

"This is Ethan," Charlie told her. "We were roommates in college."

"Hey."

Ethan traced Charlie's gaze to her freckled cleavage. His stomach sank.

"Hi," he said.

She nodded and disappeared down the hall. A moment later, the sound of water rushing through pipes surrounded Ethan, followed by shower-patter.

Ethan turned back to Charlie. "Hallmate," he said.

"What?"

"You told her we were roommates. We were hallmates. We never shared a room."

"Right," said Charlie. He took a few steps toward Ethan, leaning over him. "So, listen—what are you doing here? How did you find me?"

"I wanted to see you."

"Okay, but *why*."

"I was—I was *hoping*—" Ethan sputtered. What *was* he doing there? "I was hoping to talk about what happened."

"What happened."

"In Pittsburgh."

"Listen, man," Charlie whispered, "I don't know what the fuck you're talking about."

The girl was humming in the shower. "Who is she?"

"Who?"

"*Her.*" Ethan nodded down the hallway.

"Lindsay? She's a girl. No one."

"Does she live here? Is she with you?"

"That's not your business."

"She's a child."

"She's twenty-one."

"We need to talk, Charlie. About us."

Charlie said, quietly, "Go."

"Why are you doing this?"

"You can't knock on my door after ten years—some kid from college or whatever—and make these accusations—"

"I'm not accusing you of anything. I'm—I'm asking you to acknowledge what happened."

"I don't know what you're talking about."

Ethan shut his eyes, took a long breath through his nose, and opened them again. "I saw you."

"What's that?"

"Carnivora. Three years ago. I saw you. In the men's room—"

"Get the fuck out of my apartment."

"NO!"

The force of Ethan's voice stunned Charlie. He froze where he stood.

"Babe?" called the girl from the bathroom.

"You don't get to do this!" Ethan said. "You don't get to deny me this. You can kick me out but you can't tell me it didn't happen!" He was on his feet, though he didn't remember getting up. Standing, sweating, pointing a rigid finger at Charlie. "You idiot! Don't you see I'm trying to help you? You're a—liar! Your life is a lie, and you think that only hurts you but it doesn't! My god. After all this time . . . Why can't you admit it? Admit to what you are? God, Charlie. You fucking idiot. *Can't you see I'm trying to help you?*"

As soon as he finished the question, he knew these were the last words he'd ever speak to Charlie. His fellow man came at him. A burst of static popped in Ethan's brain. His vision blurred. Lights fireworked around him. His long-sought-after closure came moments later, as he found himself in the hall outside the apartment, a door slamming in his face. He tasted iron. There was shouting on the other side of the door. A bead of blood fell from his nose, staining the carpet.

He stumbled downstairs and into the sushi restaurant next door. He approached the hostess and asked if he could use the restroom. She recoiled. "Oh my god, what happened to your face?"

"The restrooms, please."

"They're for customers but—they're in the back. Jesus Christ. You look like an exception if I've ever seen one."

In the restroom, Ethan surveyed the damages. The pain at the center of his face was extraordinary. His nose had been knocked into a strange shape. It was purple, and crooked down the middle. The bridge veered off like something that had changed its mind. Blood clogged his nose. He'd never felt anything like it before. Never even broken a bone. His most significant injury before this had been self-inflicted—wasn't that always the case—when he'd gotten carpal tunnel in his teens. He'd always distanced himself from conflict, kept to the fringes of the fray. And yet here he was with an unceasing, atonal pain across the bridge of his nose. It took all of his resolve not to focus on the knot that throbbed below his eyes, scarcely out of view.

He brought his finger tentatively toward it, recoiling at the touch.

Ethan turned under the flickering light, observing his nose at every angle. It was an unsightly, even nauseating rupture. It might turn someone's stomach, someone who hadn't expected to see it, someone who expected something aquiline and clean in its place. But Ethan, taking a moment to adjust, thought he kind of liked it. Kind of liked the look of the afflicted.

Why didn't he feel worse? The pain, and the rush of confrontation, drowned out his anger. He didn't have the bandwidth for sadness either. He felt *relieved*. Unburdened. Buzzing with energy. It seemed to Ethan, composing himself in the restroom, that the lethargy he'd grown so accustomed to in New York was lifting. His heart beat faster than it had in years. Nose inflamed, blood electric, he stepped out of the restroom, out of the restaurant, and into the stunning daylight.

According to the Climatron guard in the neon-lime safety vest, Maggie had been out almost two whole minutes. A worryingly long faint. The guard had been standing nearby, said he'd heard her body crumple. "No other sound like it," he added, with the grizzly wisdom of a man who'd lived, who'd *really seen things*, his nicotine-stained moustache curling into a smile. A veteran, probably. Maggie, sitting up, tried to guess his age and align it with a war from history. Korea? Vietnam? She was too mixed-up to say.

"You should eat something," he told her. "Protein. And water. Lots of water, okay?"

Maggie nodded.

The guard escorted her out of the dome and directed her toward the on-site Cafe Flora, where, at his insistence, she ordered two sausage links, three strips of bacon, breakfast potatoes, and two eggs over easy. "That'll do the trick," he said, before returning to his post.

When the food arrived, she stared at her plate. Reflected there, in the greasy glisten of the bacon, the quivering, watery eggs, the sizzling hash, and the fat sausage, was everything she stood in opposition to: factory farming, the consumption of animal flesh, consumption in general . . . She tried to remember when everything changed. When food lost its appeal for her. When she'd stopped looking forward to meals and started skipping them, ballooning with dread when she had to share them with others, the inevitable inquisition—*Aren't you hungry? Not gonna finish that?*—a thousand pairs of eyes on her. The awareness of her body. The real estate that these thoughts occupied in her mind, and the energy she expended driving them away. And the shame of it. The shame of not wanting to perform this basic human function, the inevitable response from someone like her father if she came forward (*You know who doesn't have any hang-ups about eating? The rural African poor*).

She thought about her mother. Francine Alter, she of the round breasts and sturdy legs and solid comportment. The woman had substance. She was robust. In an evening dress she was unapologetically herself, irrepressibly female, a body that announced itself, broadcasting maternal authority. But in those last few months, in her bed at Barnes-Jewish, she'd weakened, withered, become small. "Look at me," Francine said, "I want to see you," the tears in Maggie's eyes obscuring the impossible image of her mother in such a diminished state. By then Maggie's appetite had begun to wane, the stress of her mother's illness precluding pleasure of any kind, estranging Maggie from her body, from food and sun and sex. Maggie had diminished in solidarity.

The funeral obliterated whatever control Maggie had left over her life. Her grief squeezed into the rigid strictures of ritual, Arthur a complete mess, Ethan locked up and inaccessible. All was disorder and Maggie was left to cope on her own. What was she to do?

How was she to live? But food, the simple question of what she put inside her body—that was Maggie's. She regulated what she ate like a dictator rationing grain and milk in a time of war. Food was in her control, and no one could take that away.

Maggie surveyed the café. Diners sat in pairs, stuffing their faces without hesitation or remorse. She spiked a sausage with her fork. The guard had insisted she eat, hadn't he? Maggie took a deep breath, shuddering on the exhale, and tucked in.

After her meal she found a shaded bench by the reflecting pool and sat. She could feel the food working through her. She envisioned it dissolving in her stomach into energy. She felt overstuffed and heavy, and could smell the meat on her breath, but the edges of her consciousness had sharpened. Ornamental lily pads of opalescent glass floated on the surface of the pool.

A few more weeks and it would be May. St. Louis would become unbearable. Maggie, with her pale skin and allergies and frizz-prone hair, had never felt suited to the summers here. She had a high-maintenance body, ill fit for the humidity of Missouri in August.

A splash; a scream. Maggie looked up from her lap as a boy hit the water. "Help!" cried a woman to Maggie's right. "Bradley, get out of there! . . . Help!"

The boy, Bradley, looked to be roughly nine years old and was, by Maggie's calculation, in no immediate danger. He was playing in the pool, slapping the surface of the water. Laughing. He seemed to be standing on his tiptoes. The water reached only as far as his collarbone.

His mother continued shouting. Calling out, "Please, someone!" She stood at the edge of the pool, above him.

It reminded Maggie of something a girl at one of her internships once told her. It was a thought experiment, a famous one, the girl said. It goes like this: You're walking to class and you pass a shallow pond. You see a kid has fallen in. He's drowning. You have the choice of rescuing the kid and missing class due to muddy and wet clothes, or else leaving him to die. Obviously you rescue the kid. The question is, what if the drowning kid is far away? Say, half a mile?

You'd probably still rush to his aid. But what about two miles? An ocean? The other side of the world? Let's say he's drowning on the other side of the world. Or, not drowning, but dying of something just as bad—disease, war, famine. And you can still help the kid, save his life by donating money or whatever, at extremely little cost to yourself. Well, guess what, the girl had said. That *is* happening. That *is* our reality.

Now it was playing out before her eyes. A boy was drowning. Except that he wasn't. This boy was all right. This boy was okay. He was having fun. Splashing and playing. But you wouldn't know it from the way his mother wailed.

"It's not that deep," Maggie told her. "He'll be okay."

The woman paused to scowl at Maggie before continuing to shout. It was all playacting, Maggie thought. Shameless theater.

The boy backstroked across the surface of the pool.

"It's not that deep," Maggie said again.

SEVENTEEN

D r. Saad Malouf was the best-looking ob-gyn in Boston. That he was a good doctor was almost, but by no means entirely, beside the point. His hair was thick and neatly parted. His heavy eyelids gave the impression he was squinting, which in turn gave the impression he was smiling. He had flawless teeth beneath a virile, salt-and-pepper mustache.

Dr. Malouf was a busy man. Patients invariably referred their friends to him. They arrived at his office in lipstick and mascara, hoping to leave a good impression. They usually walked out feeling as though they had. He was attentive, and his warm voice seemed incapable of delivering bad news. Francine was one of those patients, referred by a friend who'd advised her to make herself up before the appointment. This struck Francine as ridiculous, but when Dr. Malouf entered the examination room, she was glad she had taken the tip.

"Francine Alter?"

Her cheeks flushed. "That's me."

"A pleasure." He smiled, dimples framing his moustache like parentheses. "So, listen, I've looked at the ultrasounds and I'm going to recommend an elective C-section."

Francine bit her lip. "I had a C-section last time and it almost killed me."

"I won't let that happen," he said, in the confident tone of the very handsome.

"How can I be sure?"

"Well," he said, "last time you didn't have me."

When Francine was pregnant with Ethan, six years earlier, there was so much she'd been unprepared for: her ankles, swollen and dark like burnt puff pastries; her bizarre cravings for strange foods she'd never wanted before, like burnt puff pastries. Her labor was so terrible that when Arthur brought her to the hospital, and the chipper maternity ward nurse asked if she was ready to have a baby, Francine howled, "No! I'm ready to have an epidural!"

She had not been prepared for the pain. Ethan's head was large and he was coming out headfirst. All Francine could see was red red red.

She was in labor all night. She felt like someone was standing behind her with a chisel, hammering the blunt end while the sharp edge split her skull. "Mmmfghthmmtsthmm!" she screamed. The anesthesiologist had botched the epidural. Her face was numb, and Francine was unable to move her lips. The rest of her body, however, was awake to every shock. She could feel it all. She thought, *If I survive this, I am never doing it again.* She had never considered suicide, no matter how many French novels she'd read and French films she'd seen—the notion had always seemed romantic and distant—but now the darkness was descending. She felt ill. Nauseated. She thought that if she had a knife on hand she would open herself with it. On top of this, the worry that her impulses were corrupting the child. Could one think black thoughts, of suicide by knife, and still preserve the person in one's belly? Or would death seep from her mind, through her breasts, and contaminate the milk?

By two a.m., Ethan's heart began to fail. It took the expertise of the attending, a godsend whose name Francine vowed never to forget—Phil Walsh, Phil Walsh, Phil Walsh!—to properly re-administer the epidural and orchestrate the emergency C-section that saved her and Ethan's lives. When Francine came to, she was in the NICU. She closed her eyes, and opened them—not dreaming. She felt herself coming into consciousness, sound and light trickling in through the gauzy curtain of the drugs. The first image she registered was Arthur, leaning against the wall opposite her bed, holding their child, rocking him back and forth. Her vision was soft-lit and foggy. Her hands shook. She didn't have the energy to speak. She closed her eyes again and let herself return to sleep, finding solace in her husband's handling of their son.

But when she woke, an hour later, she was struck with fear.

"Can we stay here?" she asked Phil Walsh, cradling Ethan in her steady hands. Arthur was in the hallway, kicking a vending machine. "One more night. I don't want to go home yet. I don't know what to do."

"You'll be fine, just fine," Phil Walsh said.

"I'm . . ." She had to tell someone. "I'm *scared*." Tears welled in her eyes. "Don't say anything to my husband. He's probably more terrified than I am. I have to be the brave one. But I'm not, Dr. Walsh. I'm terrified."

"You'll be okay," said Phil Walsh. "You're extremely capable." Francine drew a deep breath. "Listen. If the baby cries, it can only mean one of three things. He needs to eat, he needs his diaper changed, or he needs to be held. You can handle all of that, yes?"

She nodded as Arthur reentered the room.

"Then you're all set."

Francine looked at her husband. "Nerves?" he said. She nodded. "We can do it. I know we can." He extended his hand toward her. "Almond Joy?"

She was glad to see her husband so confident. After Zimbabwe he'd been depressed for months. The wedding was a disaster, and he was not exactly thrilled about the prospect of child-rearing. But Francine had always wanted kids, and harbored hope that he would rise to the occasion when the day arrived. For once, it seemed as though he might not disappoint her.

When they got back to their apartment—early in Francine's pregnancy they'd moved from Kenmore to a brownstone near Jamaica Pond—Francine took Ethan in her lap while Arthur went to brew some coffee on the stovetop. She had expected to feel maternal, and she did. She had expected to feel protective, and she did.

But she had not expected to feel as she felt now, staring into her son's astonished eyes, that they were not only mother and child but *friends*. That Ethan was a kindred spirit. There was a kind of amity between them. Francine recognized him as a Klein. They were linked, these two. Not a full day old and she could already sense that they had something essential in common. He started to cry, and so did she. When Arthur walked into the living room to see what was the matter, he saw, to his confusion, then relief, that his wife was smiling. Eight days later, colleagues and cousins squeezed into that room, where cantor Arnold Peseroff raised a knife and welcomed Ethan into the vexing world of Jewish men.

To call Maggie a mistake would miss the point. Though unplanned, she was conceived in love during a tender weekend at a lodge outside of Hartford, Vermont, where Arthur took Francine for a vacation after six unrelenting months of work and parenting. They left Ethan with the neighbor, a Holocaust survivor Francine trusted implicitly.

The weekend was everything they'd hoped it would be, all forests and farmhouses and covered bridges. They walked through snow-trimmed woods and poked their heads into antiques shops. At night they slept close to one another under four layers of blankets.

Before Vermont, the Alters had considered themselves "done" with children. When Francine discovered that she was pregnant a few weeks later, the news rumpled the peace they'd reached on top of the wool comforter in the motel room with the window view of Quechee Gorge.

"To be honest, I always envisioned myself with two kids," Francine said back in Boston, setting the pregnancy test on the bathroom sink.

"I don't know. We've got our hands full, as far as I'm concerned. Money's okay now, with one, but *just okay*. And, you know, he's going to want to go to college someday."

"We'll make it work."

"And the time commitment. We don't have the *time* for two kids."

"If you chipped in a little more, we'd have plenty of time to—"

"'Chipped in'! I'd chip in if I didn't think you were overparenting him already."

"*Overparenting?*"

"It's true. He's going to grow up soft and mealy."

"If *I* overparent," she whispered, "it's because *you* underparent. I'm only trying to pick up *your* slack."

"I parent plenty!"

"*Shhh.*"

"Oh, he can't hear us. Even if he could, he wouldn't understand."

"Don't underestimate him."

"He's five years old!"

"He's a good listener. I can tell. Don't you dare underestimate him."

In the five years between Ethan's birth and Maggie's conception, Francine had lost a bit of faith in her husband. He still performed his parental duties, albeit the bare minimum, and showed little interest in the boy *as a person*. Arthur's engagement with his son declined around year three, as Ethan grew into himself. He seemed to feel as though his job was done once Ethan's personality achieved some semblance of consistency. He was good with infants, but not developed people. He was equipped to provide food, water, safety, and security to his son, but bowed out as the boy climbed Maslow's pyramid, unable to assist with the love, esteem, and self-actualization that Ethan came to need as he grew up. These were perhaps not ideal circumstances for the rearing of a second child, but Arthur wasn't going to press the issue. He had gotten her pregnant, she wanted to keep it, it was her body, she had won. "Fine," he sighed, but his tone said something else: *You owe me.*

Marriage was a barter economy. Domestic obligations were currency. Parenting, the active kind, could be currency. Currency was currency. *I'll cook if you buy groceries. I'll do both if you read to Ethan.* Everything was, in a way, for sale. In those years Arthur's salary was greater than Francine's, and that had implications. Francine spent more time with their son, which also had implications, but they were of a different kind, both more and less meaningful than Arthur's material contributions. Debts accumulated. Some were forgiven. None were forgotten. The money Francine had inherited from her father, the money that Messner invested for her, was never far from her thoughts, particularly when it came to these negotiations. She hadn't told her husband about it because he'd never asked; that is, he'd never asked about Messner in the first place. She'd been grateful for that at the time, but now it bothered her. Didn't he want to know what she'd been up to that whole year? Wasn't he curious about the man he had found in their apartment? *Have it your way*, she thought from time to time. *I won't tell you—any of it.*

Francine managed to keep her financial secret by paying all the family's bills and taxes. Whatever Messner had done was working. The value—Francine's net worth—continued rising, given a substantial lift by the state's economic Miracle. When things were going well with Arthur, and the kids, the money brought her nothing but guilt. What kind of person was she, concealing something like that from her husband, especially when they lived as many parents of their class did, investing everything they had in their children? But on bad days—the days she and Arthur had it out—the money was all she had to lean on. The thought that she'd be financially secure if ever they split up. The thought that her children would always be safe. And then there'd be a good day again, Arthur showing Ethan how to fix his kiddie alarm clock, Ethan staring in wonderment at the plastic parts laid out before him, and she'd think, *What do I need it for, anyway?*

It was different the second time around. In preparation for her time in the hospital, Francine got her nails done, slept ten hours for five consecutive nights, and delivered Maggie Ruth Alter in one crisp October hour with relative ease and comfort. Francine knew what she was in for this time. She asked all the right questions about the anesthetic. And having Dr. Malouf around made the delivery room a place she didn't mind being, a place where she felt like putting forward her best self, cosmetic concerns being a surprisingly effective distraction in the face of physical pain.

"She's a beautiful girl," winked Malouf, "like her mother."

"Easy, now," said Arthur.

Despite his iffy track record, Francine once again put her faith in her husband. She had no other choice. Arthur rose to the occasion. On the day Maggie was born, he presented Ethan with a set of small metallic Egyptian figurines from the Museum of Fine Art's gift shop. "They're from your sister," he told his credulous six-year-old son. "She says thank you for letting her into our family."

Francine wasn't bothered that the move came straight from one of her parenting books. It meant that he had read the parenting books! She even forgave the gift itself, the copper pharaohs small enough for a child to swallow. It made her happy to see him being thoughtful. It made her happy to hear him say the words *our family*. On the night they brought Maggie home, Ethan crawled into bed, and, as the radiator sputtered, trapped air clanking inside the pipes, the four of them kept each other warm.

Francine loved having a girl, and felt a similar affinity toward her daughter that she'd experienced with Ethan on that first day home. Two, she thought, was the right number after all. Though Ethan had already developed the habits of an only child, now the kids had each other. Nothing made Francine smile like the sight of Ethan pushing his sister in her stroller around Jamaica Pond. "Doing laps," he called it.

But there was no ignoring the differences. As she got older, it became clear that Maggie was much more combative than Ethan. Though she fell in line behind Francine, she took great pleasure in testing boundaries with her father, and was wily where Ethan was amenable. In this way, Arthur was forced to take a more active role with her. Ethan was self-sufficient, could sit still for hours with nothing but his thoughts, but Maggie wouldn't leave Arthur alone. She was forever needling him, asking, "Why?" in response to everything he told her—not with a child's curiosity, but in an effort to expose him as a fraud. Where some children believe their parents to possess a godlike omnipotence (and Maggie seemed to think this about her mother), she made it her goal, even as a girl, to journey to the limits of her father's knowledge. If Arthur met the challenge, he did it begrudgingly, but Francine was content just to see them together.

Differences aside, she was careful to instill her grandmother's philosophy in both her kids. Chores, allowance, sugarcoated cereal: everything was split evenly, despite the years between them. It took until Ethan's eleventh birthday before he asked, not unreasonably, what sense there was in sharing a bedtime with a six-year-old. Grandma Ruth's presence was so strongly felt in the Jamaica Plain apartment that when Arthur received the invitation to St. Louis, her ghost seemed to insist that since Francine had gotten the children that she'd wanted, she must consent to move the family back west, as always, in the name of fairness.

They drove halfway across the country, towing a rented trailer. Francine stared out the window, overcome by a creeping dread as landscape flattened around her.

"Mom?" asked Maggie, from the backseat.

"Yes, love?"

"What's this thing?"

Francine turned around. Maggie was holding a framed, bubble-wrapped diploma that was deemed too fragile for the trunk.

"It's her degree," said Ethan. "From graduate school. Right?"

"That's right, sweetie."

"What's graduate school?" Maggie asked.

"Nothing you need to worry about yet," said Arthur. "We're still working on the college fund."

"It's where you go to become an expert," Francine said. "To become the best at something."

"So you're the best at something?"

"Sort of. I went to graduate school to study psychology. You could say I'm an expert in that field."

"Do you know more than Daddy?"

Francine laughed. "Yes. In this subject, yes."

Arthur snorted.

"What if someone else went to graduate school?" Maggie asked.

"Then they'd be an expert too."

"Do lots of people go?"

"Some. Not many."

"Ten?"

"More than that."

"A hundred?"

"More."

Maggie's forehead wrinkled. "That's a lot of people to be the best."

"I suppose it is."

The highway stretched before them, empty and long.

"You know more than me, though."

"That's true. For now."

"And Dad."

"Yes."

Maggie considered this. "Okay," she said. "Good."

They split the drive into two days, spending the night at a motel in Columbus, Ohio. Arthur complained about the expense—it was ridiculous, when Francine's mother lived so close—but she refused to make the call home. It was hard enough, moving back to this part of the country. She was born there, and had spent her childhood dreaming of escape. Life was long, and unpredictable, but somehow, as they crossed into Missouri the next morning and through the city limits, Francine had the chilling thought that she was going to die there too.

EIGHTEEN

For the Alters' last dinner together in St. Louis, Arthur prepared vegetarian white bean chili, a thoughtful gesture compromised by his repeated mentions that the recipe actually called for chicken, which he'd been considerate enough to exclude. *This is perfect,* Maggie thought to herself. *He can't do one nice thing without making sure the whole world knows about it.* She was eager to raise the issue with Ethan. She saw him softening to their father's advances—it was lecherous terminology, but there was no other way to describe it; fatherhood was a creepy, ill-fitting look on Arthur, like a cape or a Speedo—and Maggie wanted to remind her brother that the man could not be trusted. Even if he'd behaved himself at the shelter. But when Ethan showed up around sunset, Renaissance clouds smuggling the last of the day's light, the state of his face precluded any other conversation.

"What the *fuck.*"

"Is that Ethan?" Arthur called from the kitchen. "Tell him about the chili." He stepped into the dining room, a tea towel draped over his shoulder. "Oh, Christ." The ladle dropped from his hands and clanged against the floor.

"What?" asked Ethan.

Arthur and Maggie responded in unison. "Your *face.*"

"Oh. I was . . . um . . ."

Maggie's eyes bulged. "You were . . ."

". . . spurned."

"What?" said Arthur.

"*Spurned.*" Ethan lowered his head. Cobalt smudges shadowed his eyes. His nose was crooked. His voice had a nasal pitch.

"What are you talking about?" said Maggie. "Your nose is all messed up."

"Does it hurt?" asked Arthur.

"It's okay."

"But what *happened?*" she said.

"It's not a big deal."

Maggie threw up her hands. "Do you need to see someone? A doctor or something?"

"It'll heal."

"Yeah, but what if it heals *wrong?*"

"If he says he's fine, he's fine," said Arthur, his voice wobbly and uncertain. Then, hopefully: "Maybe he doesn't want to talk about it?"

Ethan shrugged. "If it heals wrong, it heals wrong."

"I made dinner," Arthur said, bending to retrieve the ladle. "So . . ."

"This is too weird," said Maggie, shaking her head.

"I think," said Arthur, "it's ready to serve."

Ethan went to the bathroom and returned with florets of toilet paper stuck up his nostrils. They gathered around the table. Maggie sat with her back to the photographs. Arthur placed the pot on a trivet and ladled chili into their bowls.

"This is good," said Ethan, spooning some into his mouth.

"It'll clear up your nasal passages, maybe," said Arthur. "I'm glad you like it. Maggie?"

"Yeah," she sighed. "Not bad."

After dinner, Arthur insisted that they pile in the car.

"Where are we going?" Maggie asked. "Tell me we're taking Ethan to the hospital."

"I'm okay."

"See? He's okay," said Arthur. "No, no. We're going somewhere a little cheerier than that."

"Fine," said Maggie. "But I'm sitting in the back with him. I'm not okay with this whole situation. He looks like he got knocked in the head. I want to take a closer look."

Arthur drove south, his children whispering behind him. They had unwittingly assembled into a family pose: Dad in the front, kids in back. It was only the empty passenger seat that pointed to something missing.

Maggie was prodding Ethan, trying to inspect his nose. He fought her off with Don't Worries and It's Fines. But as Arthur turned down Arsenal Street, crossing the bridge above the rail yard and the drainage channel, the bickering ceased and he swore he saw their mouths fall open in the rearview mirror. Something was understood—they knew where they were going. He pulled onto Historic Route 66, past the Catholic Supply and the tanning studio, and into the parking lot of the proud little shack that sold frozen custard.

How many times had he driven this exact route? This fifteen-minute stretch, repeated over and over, back and forth, to and from? It was their routine, each Monday night. Francine's idea, to make the return to school and the workweek bearable.

Thousands of times he'd driven this way. It was almost incredible to think about. The world was large and vast, with much to explore and many kinds of people, but somehow Arthur had spent a good chunk of life tracing the same stretch of highway. Skinker, McCausland, Arsenal, Jamieson. Jamieson, Arsenal, McCausland, Skinker. Open sky, spare trees, parking lots. Blocky concrete overpasses. Think of the cumulative hours. The time invested. Think of the things you could have done with all that time. What you could have accomplished. Think of what you could have seen instead of that four-lane blacktop, those brutalist passes and artificial hills for the millionth time. So much of adulthood, of parenthood, was comprised by the same four or five repeated actions, over and over and over again. Why? Why did anybody do it?

"Race you."

Arthur had hardly parked before both kids sprung from the car.

The hours between ten p.m. and five a.m. were a source of anxiety for the residents of Chouteau Place, who were charged with the luckless task of regulating their neighborhood. Nights were controversial, the rules in constant flux. Decade-long grudges persisted over noise codes: How many decibels were allowed after sunset? Did that standard apply to domestic disputes as it did the playing of recorded music? Could that even be enforced? What about garden parties? Neighbor went to war with neighbor for the right to control one another's sleep. A long-standing dispute had recently come to an end, no thanks to Arthur, who was absent at the neighborhood association vote, in which competing concerns regarding safety and light pollution were resolved with the abolishment of lampposts and the installation of twenty-six blue-light emergency telephones, which emitted a rich cerulean glow into the dark.

Arthur leaned against the headboard, feeling, for the first time in a long while, a kind of relief. Satisfaction. Spring break was finished, the weekend at its end. His children were scheduled to leave that evening. All told he felt good about the state of things at this stage. His day with Ethan had gone well, if for reasons still unknown to him—Arthur didn't think he'd done anything that begged forgiveness, but, okay, he'd take it—and Maggie . . . It was harder to tell with her. She'd enjoyed herself at the no-kill, he was fairly sure of that, and he suspected that the photographs were reaching her. He was glad for the opportunity to tell her about Zimbabwe. Even if she'd known already, there was value in his telling it himself. The optimism and the hope, that was part of it. The desire to do good. To *be* good. He had a lot in common with his daughter. Or he had, once, before she'd existed. It was a special kind of tragedy that these two people—Arthur in his early thirties, Maggie in her twenties—never had the opportunity to meet.

He imagined a life after the mortgage was paid. He would move Ulrike in, resign himself to the life of an untenured professor, and profit off her successes as she ascended the byzantine ranks of the Danforth hierarchy. He plucked his cell phone from its charger and called her.

"Hello?" she groaned, her voice wrapped in a film of phlegm. "Arthur? What is wrong?"

"This house. I can't believe I ever left," he said. "It's so *big*. It's nothing like your place. I could work in one room, and you could work in another, and we would never know the other one was even home."

"Arthur . . ." She yawned. "It's four thirty in the morning."

"The sunroom is all yours. You could have a personal home office."

"Is that what you want?" she asked, clearing her throat. "To hide from me? To pretend I am not there? If I am going to live with you, you cannot hide from me."

"No, no! I'm saying, we could go days without seeing one another, to illustrate the point."

"Do you think it will work, Arthur? Will it?"

"Of course it will. I figure between the two of them I'll have enough money to beat the grace period and use what's left to buy off the remaining—"

"Arthur, no. I mean *us*. Will *we* work. I worry sometimes, I admit it. I worry about us. I want to see you. I need to see you, to talk, to see if we will work. Will we, do you think? Tell me, please, I am going crazy! Will we? Will we?"

The question didn't interest him. He was more concerned with the conclusion of his children's visit. The fate of the house. He couldn't see more than a few hours ahead. "Sure," he'd said, hoping this would calm her down. "Why not? Why wouldn't we?"

He woke on Monday to an undecided sky. Thunder, rain, hail—something was coming, though it wasn't clear what. Midwestern weather could turn without warning.

Before showering, he prepared an outfit. He had to look the part. Nonthreatening. The sympathetic father. As his irritating colleague Joan Vellum in media studies put it, "The twenty-first century has advanced the twentieth's preoccupation with surfaces," or something. But now, Arthur realized everything he owned was either gray or brown. Umber cords. Tweed blazers. His palette was a goulash of amber, beaver, beige, and buff. Smoky topaz, desert sand. Why had no one told him? Surely this was the kind of thing someone should have made him aware of. He laid clothes on the bed. A Kirkland Signature shirt from the Costco off I-55. Cords and a blazer. Too dark. Jeans—he had some somewhere. He found a pair in the back of the closet and swapped them in. Arthur stood back in underwear and socks, auditing the outfit. It wasn't ideal. The airless garments lay depressed on the bed like their owner had been sucked up to heaven, or down to hell, as in the kind of apocalyptic scenes represented on billboards all around the city limits.

With spring break finished, life returned to campus. Students reunited with their best friends like the week apart had been a century. All across Danforth's main and extended campuses, they greeted one another with all-encompassing hugs that Arthur had read for years as melodrama. Now he wasn't certain. The spectacle made him insecure. What was his deficiency? For years he'd imagined the students to be acting, performing happiness, dramatizing relief at seeing one another after separate vacations to Florence or Punta Cana. But there was something touching in the way they wrapped their arms around each other like family members separated by some catastrophic global conflict, reunited after believing each other dead.

Mondays he had one lecture, plus office hours. The lecture was for his advanced section, MECH ENG 400: Special Topics: Computational Forensics and Failure Analysis. The upperclassmen-only course was intended, according to Arthur's catalog copy, to introduce students to

1. the finite element method,
2. accident investigation,

3. fractography/fractured components,
4. computational fracture mechanics, and
5. the role of ethics in failure analysis.

He could've done the lecture blindfolded. Hands-free. This was familiar territory. It helped that 400-level engineering majors were the easiest students to teach, timid kids, seen-but-not-heard types, attentive seniors schooled in high-level fluid mechanics who had not solved the simple math of their virginities. Back from spring break, they remained conspicuously untanned.

He was leading the class through a case study in which a carbon steel pipe carrying raw gas has malfunctioned, causing a disruption in a supply chain. "Or," said Arthur, "if it helps to raise the stakes, think of the gas as poisonous. Toxic. And it's your job to figure out why the pipe broke. Not to fix the pipe, or design a better pipe. No. To simply understand why it broke." He walked them through their options. He suggested visual testing, penetrant testing, magnetic particle testing, and microstructural analysis. He floated the possibility that, in the light of what the tests revealed, the leak might be attributed to, say, a crack, most likely longitudinal, in the pipe. And that this fissure might be growing in size.

An arm extended upward from the auditorium seating.

"Yes?" said Arthur.

The arm lowered. From where he stood, Arthur couldn't make out whom it belonged to. One of his anonymous virgins. "I have a question."

He knew what the question was. Someone posed it every year. The predictability was a comfort to him. He could not envision a future in which he wasn't annually asked this idiotic question.

"Hit me."

"How would the, um, fracture—how would it get bigger by itself?"

"Think about it. You've got a crack in the pipe. And you've got the jet momentum of the gas still flowing through."

"Right . . ."

"The pressure of the gas pumping through the fissure increases the size of the fissure itself. Allowing more gas through, which means more pressure, which means an even larger break."

"So the gas pressure and the fracture—"

"They feed off each other. The pipe breaks down because of their cooperation."

"The pipe breaks itself."

"In a sense, yes. Exactly."

After class he stepped out onto the ripening quad, mentally preparing some remarks to deliver to his children before they left. He crossed the campus to his office, pausing to admire the lotioned legs of a passing freshman clique. "Woof," he said, and wiped his forehead.

Arthur's office was situated in Cornell Haynes Hall on Main Campus. Haynes was in the middle of renovations as part of Danforth's "Leap Forward" campaign, a multimillion-dollar endeavor aimed at gutting some of the university's older structures; a Damoclean crane loomed over the building. As Arthur approached he noticed Dean Gupta standing by the double doors, wielding his umbrella like a royal scepter. Arthur pivoted, ducking behind a bicycle rack. He stayed in a crouch, inching along a row of shrubs and entering the building through the rear. He walked the long, circuitous route to his office, thwarted by the roped-off passageways and stairwells that were still under construction.

Arthur's officemate was a gender studies adjunct with a septum piercing. But the adjunct was nowhere to be found, and Arthur had the place to himself. He sat at his desk and woke the monitor in front of him with a slap to its side. Shafts of noirish light cut through the blinds behind him, casting bars across the screen. Cocking his head left, then right, he began to type.

A man in crisis, Arthur typed, is compelled to act. He must do what he can to protect himself, and his family. He cannot hesitate. It is with this incontrovertible fact in mind that I will ask you

He deleted what he'd written. The cursor winked.

> A man in crisis is compelled to act. He must do everything in his
> power to protect his family, for as a man it is his responsibility to

Again he deleted the text.

> What is a home? A home is a place

It wasn't working.

> Webster's defines "home" as

Arthur could lecture a class of a hundred students—why not his
children? *Say it*, he thought. *Say what you mean.* He tried once more:

> A man in crisis must act
> A man in crisis
> A man in crisis
> Faced with a crisis, a man
> mh;lkd
> bkdjgh34i
> as;lk fhpiu
> As you know, houses cost money
> Let's talk about the mortgage
> I'm coming to you asking
> I come to you in need
> As a man in crisis
> I need your help
> Only with your support
> I'm coming to you asking
> In a time of need
> The thing about a man in crisis is
> A man in crisis is

A man in crisis is
A man

Arthur punched the keyboard, cursing under his breath. It was one thing to know what he wanted. It was much more difficult asking for it.

Ethan dressed and walked to campus, hoping to get one last look before he left. He climbed the tiered stone steps and crossed beneath the towering archway of the admissions center, emerging onto manicured Main Campus, the lime-green turf sectioned by three redbrick walkways. Ethan took the center path, which guided him to the Seidel Library. Danforth was prettier, more welcoming, and altogether more habitable than he'd remembered. The school had changed—or Ethan had. Farther up the path, someone had affixed a huge bouquet of heart-shaped balloons to a sign outside the Schlafly Chapel. He made his way to investigate.

The doors to the chapel were shut, but unlocked. Ethan stepped cautiously inside.

The chapel was packed, wall to wall, pew upon pew. The sheer density on the ground was astounding—never in his four years as an undergrad had Ethan seen the room so full, not when an ex-president's daughter came to campus, not when the Russian chess grand master spoke there, not when the Jewish magic realist read from his second novel—but the walls were high and grand. The chapel was characterized by a deliberate and mysterious emptiness. A young man's voice floated through the vacuum.

". . . People will feed you all kinds of lines," the voice said. Ethan, at the back of the chapel, standing beside other latecomers in the overflow, couldn't see its source. "'You are not your past.' 'Don't let your suffering define you.' What they are saying—what they *mean*—is that you should move on. *Get over it.* And hey, I understand that. No one wants to relive all that stuff forever. Betrayal. Addiction.

Body-shaming. Who would want to be defined by that? Who wouldn't want to overcome it?"

A murmur throughout the chapel.

". . . But what I'm here to say is this: Why *not* let it define you? Why cover up the past? See, it's as simple as this—and I know that it's an unpopular opinion: But what if our traumatic experiences *do* impact us? More than anything else? What if we really *are* the things we've suffered through?"

"Brilliant," the girl next to Ethan whispered.

"Who is he?"

She flashed Ethan a judgmental look that withered as she registered his broken nose. "Um," she said, turning away. "He used to go here. Now he's rich."

"I'll tell you a little story about myself," said the voice. "I wasn't the most popular kid in high school. I know, I know—hard to believe, right? That the comp-sci geek had trouble getting dates to the prom?" Ripples of laughter. "I didn't have a lot of friends. I certainly didn't have a girlfriend. You might say I was bullied. I'll spare you the details, but it wasn't pretty. It wasn't particularly unique either. The usual high school stuff. I didn't have the most *creative* bullies, but then again, bullies aren't known to be creatives." More laughter. "But there I was, confused, awkward, and certain things would never improve. I had to watch my back in the hallways. I ate in empty classrooms to avoid being teased at lunch. There's simply no other word for what I was: a victim.

"For years I wanted to pretend it hadn't happened. When I matriculated at this same institution, I was practically bursting with joy. I could start again. No one would know me, or what I'd been through. But sometimes our pasts follow us. I couldn't have predicted that a certain someone, not my high school bully but a member of his friend group, his social network, was *also* a matriculating freshman . . ."

Ethan looked around him. The room was rapt. Quiet save for the creaking of the pews and the confident, practiced voice delivering the speech. Sunlight poured in, colored by the stained glass, swaths of blue and red and yellow crowning the heads of the audience.

". . . I was left to make a tough decision. Spend four years in hiding, avoiding this kid from my high school? Reinvent myself beyond recognition? And then it hit me. I didn't have to hide. I didn't have to change. I could be *me*. Regular old me. The geek. The victim. Why not *own* my trauma? As I started to make friends, I learned quickly that I wasn't the only one. Like, after all, gravitates to like, and soon I found myself trading stories of high school terror back and forth with my hallmates and study groups. We *bonded* over them. I remember late nights in Seidel, fighting it out over who'd had it worst. It was great. It was a *relief*. But it wasn't until my junior year, in Mobile App Development, that I realized: all this suffering, all this data, could be put to use . . ."

Ethan stepped outside into the sun. He closed his eyes and let it warm his face. When he opened them, he saw his father scrambling across the quad. Ethan raised his arm and thought to call out to him, but didn't. He thought of his mother. He'd inherited from Francine a weakness for men who couldn't love him back. As he watched his father hurry across campus at the same embarrassed velocity at which Charlie had left him, not once now but twice, he stopped to wonder why it was that he wanted only what he couldn't have, while all around him a million unseen insects shuttled pollen to the ready stigmas of expensive flowers.

NINETEEN

A man in crisis," Arthur began, "is compelled to act."

The Alters had congregated in the living room. The unfortunate irony of this particular part of the house was that it was so tied to death. It was here that Arthur and Francine broke the news of Arthur's mother (stroke), Francine's great-uncle (heart attack), the white-haired Survivor who'd lived next door to them in Jamaica Plain (natural causes, Parkinson's-accelerated). It was here that Francine delicately explained the suicide of her close friend and former college roommate, who'd been living far away in Marin County with six guinea pigs and bipolar disorder. And it was here, the couch on which Ethan and Maggie sat awaiting their father's presumably bad news with Pavlovian apprehension, where Francine had squeezed Arthur's hand until it paled, explaining to the kids her diagnosis. "And when that crisis threatens his family," he continued, "he cannot hesitate—"

"Hey, Dad?" said Ethan.

Arthur paused.

"Before you go on . . ."

"What?"

"I wanted to say. Before you go on with your—before you get to whatever it is you're getting to . . . I wanted to say, thanks for having us."

"Th—oh. Okay. Well, yes. Good. You're welcome."

"I mean it," Ethan said. "I wasn't sure about this. But it was nice. To be home."

"Even with . . ." Arthur drew a circle in the air around his nose.

"Even with that."

Maggie looked up. "Seconded."

"You too?" said Arthur.

"Yeah. I don't know. I like being back. Seeing the city and everything. Last night, something in me just . . . I haven't had frozen custard in, I think, a decade. You used to take us all the time."

"I did." Arthur felt his insides quiver.

"So, anyway. Thanks, I guess. Like Ethan said. It was a good weekend."

Well, fuck.

He couldn't do it. He couldn't make the ask. Not now. The goal had been to win them over, but now that he had, he was paralyzed. He'd become accustomed to failure. Success confounded him. He squeezed the arm of the green wing chair where he sat. There they were. His children. They'd come back to St. Louis to see him. They were thanking him for it. He swelled with goodwill.

He drew a long breath and exhaled slowly, his shoulders sinking as the air left his body.

"You have no idea," he said quietly. "You have no idea."

"No idea about what?" asked Ethan.

Arthur shook his head. "Nothing," he said. "Nothing." He arched his back and laughed a small, private laugh. "You know," he said, "I'm glad you came back too. You didn't have to. You could've ignored my letter. Lots of kids would have done that. You didn't owe me anything, you really didn't."

"It's all right, Dad," Ethan said. "We were happy to."

"No, no. It's important that I get this off my chest." He felt drunk with gratitude, warm cheeked and loose tongued. "I've wanted to say this for a long time. Here goes: I don't feel like I *know* either of you. Does that make sense? It pains me to admit it. But it's true. I don't know you. I bowed out of parenting at some point. I stopped paying attention." He leaned back and crossed one leg over the other, nodding to himself. "See, the problem was, once I'd bowed out, I felt—I didn't know how to bring myself back. The longer I waited, the harder it was to get involved again. I felt like I'd already missed my chance. That's what it was. A feeling of having missed out. I couldn't start to know you because it was too late. I never stopped feeling that way. And the problem, when it's always too late, is that it's always too late, and getting later."

"This is nice of you, Dad," said Maggie, "but we're okay. We don't need—"

"Let me finish . . . let me finish." He uncrossed his legs and leaned forward, resting his elbows on his thighs. There was so much left to say. "For years," he continued, "for years I felt like I lived with strangers. People I didn't know. I hid. Retreated! It may have seemed like I was absentminded, out of the loop, but make no mistake. I knew what I was doing—and what I was not. I was not parenting. I hid in my office, not working. I hid in libraries, not reading. The long middle of my life was spent not-doing. Avoiding you both. My adulthood was defined by all the things I did not."

"We'd rather not hear—"

"What I'm saying is, I failed. I have been needy, reckless, and vain. I have been neglectful and self-centered. And I'm ready. I'm ready to acknowledge that now. What a relief! I can't even tell you. It amazes me, honestly, to think of how I acted. But I suppose it takes a moment of reckoning like this. Because before, there was always something to fall back on. There was always a safety net. When I ran out of ambition I had my job. When my career stalled I had your mother. When I lost your mother I had you. When I lost you I had the house . . . Now, without the house I'll have nothing."

"Without the house?" asked Ethan.

"Yes," said Arthur. "Yes. This is what it's all about. This is why you're here. Listen—I'm sorry to tell you, but we are going to lose the house."

"Wait," said Ethan. "What happened?"

Arthur shrugged. "Can't afford it."

"So what, then?" Maggie said. "We pack up? Is that what happens next?"

"The funny thing is," Arthur said, quietly enough to be heard, "I was going to try to save it."

"Save it? How?"

Arthur smiled. "Maggie. Ethan. I am *so* looking forward to getting to know you."

"Why is he talking like this?" Maggie whispered to her brother.

"I don't know."

"It's funny," Arthur said, again quietly. "I had this whole idea. This plan . . ."

"What are you talking about?" she asked.

"Let's just say I could have ended this weekend on a different note."

"Dad." Ethan cocked his head. "I don't think either of us knows what you're getting at."

"It's nothing. It's nothing . . . You know, I really spared you a good amount of discomfort."

Maggie shut her eyes. "Explain yourself, please."

"I was going to sit you down," he said, "right here, and ask you to save the house for me."

"Save it how?" said Maggie.

"I was going to ask," laughed Arthur, "for your help in buying back the house. Hell, I had a speech!" He dug into his pocket and removed a folded piece of paper. "But now—now I see how foolish that would have been. Now that I have you here, talking to me, I realize there's no point. This, right here, is what's important. I'll figure it out, I'll find a place to live. You don't have to worry about me." He returned the speech to his pocket.

"You were going to what?" asked Maggie.

"Save it? With what money?" said Ethan.

"Well. With your mother's money."

"Mom's?" Ethan asked.

"Yes. Come on. Don't kid me."

"No, honestly," said Ethan. "What money?"

"Your mother's money. The inheritance."

"But I'm broke," said Ethan.

"You're what?"

Maggie slapped her thigh. "I knew it!"

"I spent it," Ethan said. "I don't have it."

In the silence that settled, Arthur heard, for the first time, the rain. It had been raining all along, since he started talking, probably, cold drops battering the windows of the house.

"I don't understand."

Ethan shook his head. "What is there to say? I spent it. Real estate in New York—an apartment in Carroll Gardens. And I left the firm."

"Where are you working?"

"I . . . don't."

"You haven't been working?" Now Arthur was doubly perplexed. The natural order of things was upset when a son retired before his father.

"I quit."

"But . . ."

"Not 'but.' 'And.'"

Arthur leaned forward. "And . . ."

"And I'm in debt."

"Debt." He stared at his son in disbelief, zeroing in on his swollen purple nose.

"Yeah. A bit. The apartment is historic. Not cheap. I can go back to work, I mean I'll have to, soon, I was kind of biding my time until—well, I don't know what. Nothing, anymore. I was actually going to maybe ask you, if you had a minute . . . for a loan . . . although now . . ."

Confusion brewed in Arthur's heart. He was not accustomed to managing more than one feeling at a time. Tenderness boiled into shock. Rage. And relief, if only for the fact that his son now needed him at least as much as he needed Ethan.

But mostly rage.

"How could you spend it all? *And* quit work? What were you thinking? How do you live?"

"I live."

"That city is *expensive!*" Arthur spat. "How did you—how did you *eat?*"

Ethan hung his head. Arthur watched his son slump forward, bent over himself like a lowercase *p* for *pathos*. He turned to Maggie. "And you?"

"Me what?"

"Don't tell me you spent your money."

"Mom's money?"

"Yes, the fucking *money!*"

"Oh, no. No, no."

A thick vein throbbed on Arthur's neck. "Good," he said, wiping his forehead. "Fine. Good. . . . I don't suppose you want to put it toward the old mortgage, do you?"

"I'm renouncing it."

"*Excuse me?*"

"Yeah. Gonna give it all away."

Rage proliferated. Begat and sired more rage. He kept it bottled, eked out one careful word.

"*Why.*"

Maggie threw up her hands and let them fall with a patter on her lap. "It's not doing us any good! Look at Ethan. He's a mess." She turned to him. "No offense. But you're bleeding on the couch." He dabbed at his nose. "And you, Dad! I don't want to end up like this, trying to buy up a house that's way too big in the first place. In this walled-in neighborhood. What do we need it for? Listen. Chouteau Place has nothing to do with the world."

"Maggie—"

"Do you even like it here? You hate your job, I know that. Look. I don't know what I'm going to do with Mom's money but I know I can't spend it on myself."

"Then spend it here!"

"I'm sorry."

"You don't understand," Arthur protested. "You. Could. Save. Our. Home. Jesus Christ, I wasn't even going to *ask!* I was going to *spare you the discomfort!*"

"This isn't my home. I don't live here anymore. Neither does Ethan."

Arthur's stomach somersaulted and a wave of nausea rose and sank within him. In the late nineteenth century, his forebears fled tacitly sanctioned pogroms in Odessa and survived the arduous voyage to America with nothing. Arthur's great-grandfather had pushed a cart full of stinking fish around the Lower East Side so that his son could open a small shoe store so that his son could practice dentistry so that his son could build things so that what? So that *his* son could plummet into debt? So that his daughter could give away her inheritance?

"That's it?" asked Arthur. "That's where we are now? Ushering in our decline? Hm?"

"You're not going to renounce it," Ethan told his sister.

"Yes I am."

"Saying it is one thing."

Maggie fumed. "Why does everybody think I won't?"

"Maggie," said Arthur, heaving, "you don't understand what you're doing."

"I think I do," she said.

And then it all made sense. The photographs. The no-kill. The ballet. The whole weekend, each piece in its place. The weird smell that hung over everything, she could locate it now. Name it. As her pulse quickened, Maggie was reminded of something that her father used to do when she was young. The Daddy Tax. What began as a harmless Halloween joke—*hand over that Almond Joy, Maggie, I'm collecting my Daddy Tax*—had grown, over the years, into a pathological perversity. Her father levied Daddy Taxes on everything she earned or won. When she house-sat for the neighbors' kids, Arthur charged her a finder's fee for putting them in touch. He skimmed 15 percent off her paycheck during the summer of her first real job, working the register at a children's toy store, because, he'd said, she owed him gas money for driving her to work. He ate food off her plate when there was plenty for the taking on the table as a constant reminder of who'd put it there. And throughout her four years at Danforth, until Francine's death, he'd reminded Maggie that as soon as she graduated she could start paying him back for the tuition. With interest. His exact words: "Put it on your bill." As if parenthood was something to be paid back! As if children were an investment to be returned, doubled, in cash.

"Hold on," she said. "Is this why we're here? It is, isn't it? Mom's money—that's why. The whole trip. That's what this was all about."

"Maggie. Maggie, hold on—"

"Oh my god."

"Not the *whole trip*, Maggie. Not the whole thing—"

"It wasn't enough to *imprison* Mom in this house? In this city? It wasn't enough to cheat on her? While she was on her *deathbed*? You have to try to take her money too?"

"I did not *imprison* anyone."

"Do you even want us here? Do you even want a relationship with us?"

"Is someone knocking?" Ethan asked.

"*No*," snapped Maggie. "It's the rain."

"Someone's knocking."

"It's the *rain* . . . Dad?"

Arthur stared into the empty space between his children's faces. With a weary gasp, he said, "It's both."

"Dad, what the hell is going on?"

A knock echoed through the house. A screen door opened and closed with a pneumatic wheeze.

"Dad?"

A woman was standing under the arched molding.

She was not Francine.

Of course she wasn't.

But to the Alters looking upon her, the woman's most distinguishing feature appeared to be the extent to which she was not Francine. Tall, straight haired, crow eyed. Boyish above the waist and muscular below. Not Francine at all. Something, someone, entirely different.

"I am going to Boston," she said, quivering. A German accent swam through her watery voice.

Arthur ground his palm into his forehead. "What are you doing here?"

"Who's this?" asked Ethan. A drop of blood fell from his nose.

The woman spoke again. "I am taking the fellowship in Boston. I still have time. I deserve to find someone who—oh, Arthur. We cannot live here. You know that. Us, together, in the house of your family? Arthur, I am not your wife. I do not know what I am to you. But I know that I cannot waste my time anymore. You have a duty to stay and sort yourself. There is much for you to sort."

"What is happening here?" asked Ethan.

"You are sixty-five, Arthur," she said. "What will happen when you are gone?"

"I'm not going any—oh, Christ. Can you give me a minute here?"

Maggie's mouth hung open. She could not believe what she was seeing.

The watch.

The diamond-studded cocktail watch.

Her mother's watch. Wrapped tight around this woman's wrist.

"You. Have. To. Be. Kidding. Me."

"Okay," said Arthur, standing. "Kids? Excuse us for a minute. This is not—we are not—she is not—"

"Do you see?" said Ulrike. "With me it is just 'not, not, not.' You do not want me, Arthur. You want company. But I am more than company." She began to weep.

Maggie looked at the crying woman, then her father, then the woman.

She marched into the dining room, shoulder-checking the German as she blew past. She lifted one of Arthur's photographs off the nail from which it hung. *Man Kneeling with Arm Around Boy*. She brought the image crashing to the ground.

"Maggie," Ethan said.

"It doesn't belong to you!" Maggie shouted, and smashed the second photograph. *Man with Boy on Shoulders*. Glass scattered at her feet.

"Stop that!" Arthur called.

"What?" said Ulrike.

Man and Boy Standing Back-to-Back. Smash. *Boy in Man's Lap.* Smash. The frames lay broken at Maggie's feet.

Ethan and Ulrike hurried over.

"Are you insane?" Ulrike asked.

"The watch! Give it!" Maggie shouted, and grabbed the woman's wrist.

"This is mine," Ulrike pleaded, trying to wrest control of her hand. "It was a gift from your father!"

"It wasn't his to give!"

"You cannot take back a gift!"

Ethan looked around. "Where's Dad?" he asked. But the object of his sentence, the object of his sister's ire, was gone.

He's running against the foul weather, the rain blowing horizontal, each stinging drop a distinct irritation, a unique punishment. See him now, hurrying out the gates that describe Chouteau Place and on through splashing traffic, his mind blank, time smearing like the water on the windshields racing past. The neighborhood blurs. Main Campus is close ahead. He smashes past a student couple conjoined at the palm, splitting them in two, and scurries up the stairs of Greenleaf Hall. Temporary respite under a covered passage as he slides across the university seal imprinted on the stone walk—bad luck for those who tread on it, that's what campus tour guides say—and back into the rain until he's through the doors of the African Studies Library. One thing in mind.

He turns over shelves, tosses books underfoot. Entire subjects, peoples, plagues, histories, and languages are chucked aside and trampled. *Afrikaans. AIDS. Algeria.* Where is it? He can't find it. He will burst if he can't find it.

"Professor?"

He turns, soaked through, growling under his breath, and sees a student librarian. Standing eagerly before him. Masking concern beneath a shaky smile. A kid whose nervousness belies the Gothic-lettered tattoo on his left bicep: LOREM IPSUM. A design major.

"I thought it was you. I took your survey last year," he says, "Social Change!"

"Okay."

"Yeah," he continues, "really cool stuff. Applied engineering, 'the social responsibility of building things,' definitely interesting. A solid elective. Got me thinking, you know?"

"Well," says Arthur, "that's the idea." A shadow crawls across the stacks, swallowing a file of light. "Where is it?"

"Where's what?"

"I'm looking for a book and I can't fucking *find* it."

"Oh! Right. Well, come on back to the checkout desk and I'll see what I can do."

The kid guides him to the desk and slides over the counter. His right foot snags and brings a stapler down with it. "Shit. Argh."

"It's a small book . . ."

"Right right. Title?"

Arthur huffs. *"Toward a New System of Sanitation in the New Nation of Zimbabwe."*

The kid clacks away at his keyboard. "Author?"

"The author is . . . it's—"

"'Arthur Alter . . .' Hey . . . this is *your* book, Professor!"

"Yes."

"Weird!"

"Tell me where it is."

"I was only saying—"

"Do it."

"Okay, okay, well, actually, hold on—it looks like it's been flagged." The kid looks up all innocent, all sorries.

"Flagged?"

"Like, reported missing."

"So, not *flagged*, but *missing*."

"Flagged as missing, yeah."

"Fuck." He's pacing. "Fuck."

"Hey, Professor?"

Sweat drips from his brow. A fly buzzes circles around his ear.

"Why do you need a copy of your own book?"

"Excuse me."

"I mean, it's a little weird. Right? I mean. *Your own book.*"

Arthur bristles. Unthinking, he bends his knees. Spring-loads himself. "Listen to me. Listen. I need it. I need it now."

"Don't you have other copies? Like at home?"

"There was a fire. They burned."

"What fire?"

"Just find the book."

"I'm sorry, Professor," said the kid. "I don't think I can help you out."

Flattens his palms, thumbs out and hooked. Pleading. "It was just here weeks ago. You must know who last checked it out."

"I wish I knew," says the kid, "but I don't! It wasn't checked out. It was either lost, or . . ."

"Or . . ."

"Stolen."

By now he knows it's hopeless. By now he knows this is the end. Nothing good can come of this. This being Arthur. Nothing good has ever come of him.

"I only wish," the kid says, "that I could help—"

But before he can finish, Arthur lunges.

It must have looked strange to the students crossing campus on that April afternoon, sloshing to and from their libraries of choice, their protests, their treasury meetings, their improv shows, their study groups: a professor of mechanical engineering, tweed blazer draped across his shoulder, sitting on the rain-drunk grass outside the African Studies Library. There was something perverse about the sight of a grown man—a *scholar*—on the ground. Especially one in the exhausted but defiant pose of a child in the final act of a tantrum, on the slow path to acknowledging defeat. His legs were crossed. His head was in his hands. From a distance it might have even looked like he had fallen. But this, it was clear, to anyone who deigned to peer a little closer, was a man who had decided to sit down.

A semicircle formed around him. Ethan, Maggie, LOREM IP-SUM, and one thickset member of the Danforth Campus Police Department. Poised like a firing squad.

After much pleading, and with a pledge to sponsor new uniforms for the officer's squad, Ethan talked the cop out of detaining Arthur. The design major had emerged unscathed, miraculously free of bruises and scrapes and any other bodily proof of what had just transpired. A little jittery was all. A little shaken. Arthur muddled his way through apologies, first to the boy for their misunderstanding and then to the officer for the inconvenience of riding his Segway over from Main Campus. Above him hung the disapproving face of his late wife as performed by his only daughter.

Ethan pulled his sister aside while Arthur wallowed on the lawn. "What do we do?" he said. "I mean, where does this leave us?"

"You and me?"

"Yeah. Us."

Maggie furrowed her brow, planted her hands on her hips, and scanned the grounds of the university that was the focal point of her family life—the university that wanted nothing more than recognition, on the national level, that it was a decent school. "We leave," she said.

"We leave."

"That's right."

"What about Dad?" Ethan's crooked nose whistled.

"He'll be fine."

Their heads turned in tandem toward their father, still seated, the soggy soil saturating his jeans. Maggie shook her head.

"He'll pick himself up," she said. "He has to, eventually."

PART III

TWENTY

University City was not immune to the temperaments of the institution for which it was named. May at Danforth was a month of making plans, of humblebrags, of anxious inbox checking. Graduating seniors disappeared into boozy reminiscences. Couples broke up or decided, with the morbid optimism of a doomsday cult, to give long-distance a shot. Every sidelong look, every fickle change in the weather, was understood to accommodate great meaning. It was a heavy-handed month. Metaphor flourished. There was no shortage of open weeping: from emotions, from pollen.

For the nonwealthy children of this midwestern Ivy, the years of back-patting and positive reinforcement had come to a swift and salient end. Without the investment bank connections of their East Coast counterparts or the Silicon Valley hookups of the West, the majority of Danforth grads hunkered down and prepared to inherit the broken economy they'd spent four years hearing so much about. Where their parents once advised, "Shoot for the stars," they now said, "Manage expectations." When it came to the job search, passion was no longer a prerequisite. Health insurance was. Still, hopefulness prevailed with the promise of a new start. The intrigue of the nine-to-five. The magic of a paycheck: for the English major who'd lucked into an entry-level gig at the Poetry Foundation, the starting salary of $30,000 seemed like more money than would ever be possible to spend. Positions were applied for, letters of recommendation secured. Fulbright. AmeriCorps. Thirty students found work in the Danforth Office of Admissions, interviewing hopeful high school juniors and teaching phone etiquette to the work-study undergrads who rang up donors. The clinically depressed, a demographic that constituted 15 percent of the student body—and those were the diagnosed cases—began to feel the dead-weight lifting.

Days before commencement, a well-liked member of the Jewish fraternity slipped and fell from his frat-house roof, nearly sinking all of Danforth into a state of public mourning. He thwarted death and sprained his wrist instead. His brothers and sisters in the Greek system wrote well-wishes and addressed them to the great hospital complex by the park where he was being fitted for a cast, before returning to their own concerns. When graduation came, they shivered out into the world on the backs of one detestable family friend or another. The future, it seemed, was closer than it had ever been.

The student newspaper, the *Danforth Register*, picked up the story of Arthur and the librarian. The headline ran in all-capped distinction: PROF ASSAULTS FINANCIAL AID STUDENT. To Arthur's horror, the altercation had been labeled an "assault." The tattooed librarian was now a "financial aid student"—as though economic class had anything to do with Arthur laying the kid out.

Before he could harangue the editor in chief of the *D-Redge*, as the paper was informally known, he received an email from an admin at Dean Gupta's office. A reminder of their impending meeting. *What day this week is best for you?* Arthur slammed his keyboard, marched across the Main Campus quad, and barged into the dean's office.

"Don't tell me he's suing."

Gupta looked up from his desk. "Pardon?"

"The kid came away fine," Arthur said. "Unscathed. Not a bruise on him."

A young woman in a pencil skirt and heels followed him into the office, taking the longest strides her outfit would allow. "I'm sorry,

Dean Gupta," she said breathlessly, her breasts bouncing under her blouse as she halted in the doorway. "He walked right in—"

"It's okay, Lola. Arthur, come sit."

The woman glared at Arthur. She spun on her heels and exited the room. *Christ*, he thought, averting his gaze from the two half-moons under her skirt to the vaulted ceiling above, inadvertently taking in a whiff of the dean's powerful cologne, his nostrils filling with cedar and cardamom. *Lola.*

Gupta hardly looked up, his arms tentacling around the surface of his paper-strewn desk. A pince-nez straddled the bridge of his nose.

"Did you know my book is missing? From the library?"

"Arthur, Arthur," the dean said. "Sit down. Breathe."

Arthur sat, trembling with righteous frustration. He watched Gupta, framed by the tall wooden bookshelves behind him, taking his time to organize the items laid in disarray before him. After forty infuriating seconds—Arthur counted—Gupta procured a manila folder from the mess and handed it to Arthur.

"What's this?"

"Read it."

Unease rippled through him. Arthur's stomach seemed to know the contents of the folder before he did. He opened it slowly, squinting at the text so as not to take it in all at once, then pinched the folder shut.

"You don't have to do this," he said. "I'll teach anything. Any class. I'll work for nothing. I won't be a burden."

"Arthur, please."

"You can't fire me. Not after all I've done for this place."

"You're not fired. We're simply choosing not to renew your contract at this time," the dean said dryly.

"Read the article, Sahil. 'No visible scarring or bruising.' The kid's *fine*."

"It's not just that, Arthur. Although we do encourage faculty not to tackle members of the student body, when possible."

"What's the problem?"

"Arthur. You must have seen this coming. You were teaching, what, two courses this semester? For the same money we pay graduate students. Surely you didn't think this could continue forever. Frankly, I'm surprised you hung in this long."

"All these years . . ."

"Your position was never permanent."

"All the time I invested."

"I expected more from you. Time is one thing. You never published, Arthur. Not one paper in all the years you were here."

"I was focused on teaching!"

"Your student evaluations were in the sewer. Truly, Arthur, I never saw so many one-star reviews."

"I'm an acquired taste. And what's with the star system, anyway? We're entrusting eighteen-year-olds with people's livelihoods? Reviewing human beings like they're movies?"

"The students love the star system. We get many more evaluations this way."

"Sahil. Listen to me. You're making a terrible mistake."

"I'm sorry, Arthur. There's nothing I can do for you. And with this recent . . . incident . . ." The dean picked up a copy of the *D-Redge* from his desk and waved it in front of him. And then he slapped Arthur with the most terrible slur that can issue from the lips of a university administrator.

"Professor Alter," he said, "I'm afraid you've become a liability."

Arthur cursed his career. He cursed the politics of tenure, the years spent under the hanging sword. He cursed a thin-skinned and entitled student body, enabled by obscene tuition fees and the consumer mind-set they engendered to act out in whatever ways they pleased. He cursed Henrik Vergoosen, Nobel laureate in chemistry and tenured Danforth professor, who (it was well-known) had fucked five of his last six office assistants, consequence-free, students and townies both, whether he was in loco parentis or out. He cursed the sushi flown in for the dining halls and the Tempur-Pedic mattresses in the freshman dorms. He cursed the Board of Trustees, a conspiracy of coal and biotech billionaires who opposed a minimum wage of $15 per hour for the food service staff making hour-long commutes to campus from East St. Louis at dawn. He cursed the hypocrisy of a school that boasted female STEM recruitment on the one hand and bestowed an honorary degree upon Phyllis Schlafly with the other. He cursed the Chinese and Nigerian elite who bought their kids admission to a university hungry for multicultural brochure photos. He cursed an institution that killed a once-great sociology department because the instructors had a Marxist bent. He cursed the emergent "Campus Left" for their militant closed-mindedness and the administration's utter cowardice in dealing with them, second only to their gutlessness in handling the scandal-prone fraternities. He cursed Danforth's inflated sense of self, its obsession with public relations and image. He cursed and cursed until there was nothing left to condemn and he was dragged, raving, from the administrative offices and instructed not to return to campus again.

His dismissal from Danforth spelled the end of hope for Arthur. He resigned himself to his fate. He put the house on the market. Three weeks later, it sold. To Arthur's surprise, the buyers—a handsome young couple with triplets—were not, as he'd expected, affiliated with the university.

"What do they do?" Arthur asked.

"They're in the private sector," the real estate agent explained. Like that was some kind of an answer.

Ethan and Maggie flew out once again to help with the arrangements and observe the anniversary of Francine's death, which coincided with the sale of the house. Maggie said they were on hand to provide "moral support," a phrase Arthur had always found objectionable. What he needed was actual, physical help. In times like these, there was no substitute for manual labor. The few colleagues with whom he was on speaking terms had gone silent after word spread about his outburst in Dean Gupta's office. He didn't receive a single message of condolence or an invitation to debrief over a beer, to say nothing of an offer to help pack up the house. One of the perils of moving, he thought, is finding out who your friends are.

He asked for manual labor and he got it. His children moved through the house with a cold professionalism that made Arthur uneasy, talking to him only about logistical matters. But whether they'd forgiven him or not, they had come back, and he supposed he should be grateful.

One afternoon, he ran out of masking tape. He followed the muted sound of his children's voices up the stairs and into Maggie's bedroom. The room was empty, but the red-runged ladder cut diagonally from the ceiling to the shaggy rug. He could hear them in the attic above.

"I worry about him." Ethan's voice. "What's he supposed to do now?"

"That's his problem."

"Maggie . . ."

"See, this is the thing. You always let him off the hook so easily. Like he's a child who doesn't know better. He's a grown man, Ethan. More than that. He's an anachronism."

"I'll grant you that he's out of touch. But what's he supposed to do with that? Don't we have a responsibility to him? To see that he makes it out of this okay?"

"I don't."

"You do. We both do."

Maggie scoffed. "Whatever."

"You decided at some point that he was going to be your enemy. It's pure ideology with you. Anything that doesn't fit with your idea of him, you dismiss out of hand. But he's more complicated than that. You know he is. And how do you think I feel? You're the one he paid the most attention to."

"Me? Are you kidding?"

"He fights with you because he respects you. You're a worthy opponent. Whatever I am to him, I'm not worth taking seriously."

"And you're still defending him!"

"I'm not defending him. I'm asking you to look at everything he's done for us. Not only the slights. The whole picture . . ."

Arthur stood in the doorway. He knew he should back away but he couldn't. His heart leapt anxiously with every eavesdropped word. He stood there as the minutes piled up, listening, with defensiveness and hurt—and no small sense of self-importance—as his children debated his legacy.

The following day, Maggie brought Ethan to the Climatron to commemorate Francine's yahrzeit. Together they walked through the international gardens, all of them in vigorous bloom. They strode solemnly beside dogwoods beneath the English garden's canopy of oaks. They traced the dragon-rippled walls of the Nanjing Friendship Garden. They walked in silence, out of respect for the dead, though the piercing squeals of children and the red- and blue- and yellow-speckled greenery insisted that life was happening here.

St. Louis burns in May—absolutely roasts. Even in the gardens, where the seasonal fever was partially mitigated by tree cover, a gummy heat slid between skin and clothing, limb and torso, leaving a slug trail of dampness where it settled. Ethan's arms shimmered with sweat as they passed the reflecting pool where Charlie had rubbed his earlobe and the geodesic dome came into view.

The automatic doors closed behind them, and all at once they found themselves transported to another world. Leaves spilled over one another in the dense accumulation of bushes that lined the footpath. Mist machines spritzed on a timer. Maggie led her brother through a thatched-roof hut near the entrance, past the pleated palm leaves of a coco-de-mer and an overgrowth of passiflora, sidestepping the buttress roots of a looming tree. She pulled off the path and pointed to where she'd poured the remains. "You dumped them in the water?" Ethan asked, with a note of concern. Maggie nodded. "I wanted her to circulate." Ethan traced her gaze downstream to the edge of the dome, then looked up at the triangular panes and the aluminum network of pipes that supported them. "Okay," he said. They kneeled by the stream and sat awhile in the spring-green grove, girded by ferns and boscage and the odd Chihuly, the sounds of prerecorded wildlife distilling into one prolonged caw, the two of them sheltered, for the time being, under the great glazed-glass enclosure.

The sale covered the mortgage balance and left Arthur with enough money to take a room at the Chase Park Plaza and buy himself that most valuable commodity, time. There was an unexpected satisfaction in unloading the house, a decompression of anxiety, as when a person dies after a prolonged struggle with illness. His satisfaction was doubled by the realization that he was now free of teaching duties, committee meetings, all the caprices of an academic institution.

His room at the Plaza was furnished, the minibar stocked, and each morning he took brunch in the Chase Club. The lobby was his living room, the swimming pool his bathtub. He had his hair cut at the barbershop in the basement of the hotel, where a woman in a crop top with an obscenely appealing navel draped a hot towel over his face and put a cold glass of whiskey in his hand. He enjoyed himself for four wonderful weeks before the monthly bill arrived and the stress returned. Men of Arthur's age were pioneers, the first generation to consistently live into their eighties and nineties. There were many years ahead to account for.

The neighborhood had changed since he'd first moved to St. Louis. The new Central West End, with its vodka bars, all-night cookie delivery service, art galleries, and athleisure retailers, catered to the reprehensibly young. The undeservedly wealthy. He watched them from his window like a hunchback in a bell tower. College students and regionally attractive professionals. Buying things. Eating things. Surely, he thought, this cannot be what they do all day. Surely there is more to life than this. He shivered with loathing. On more charitable days, however, Arthur forgave them their consumer goods and blamed the systems that encouraged their behavior. On days like that he wondered what it must cost to be young and upwardly mobile in America.

Back in Ridgewood, Maggie continued her good work with the Nakahara boys, but summer found them restless. She kept them occupied as best she could. They ate pizza in a refurbished garage in Bushwick and wandered Mt. Hope Cemetery in Glendale. Twice, day-trips to Coney Island were foiled by the MTA. First, a sick passenger caused their train to be taken out of service. The following week there was a fire on the tracks.

When a long-stalled bill to legalize professional cage fighting in New York finally received the okay from Albany, Bruno begged her to take him to a fight.

"Come on, Maggie, please. This summer has been boring as *fuck*."

"Language. Jar. Now."

"He's not wrong," added Alex. "I, for one, have been feeling understimulated."

In August, Maggie caved, repurposing the jar into a field trip fund. With Oksana's permission (and a cryptic nod from her husband), Maggie brought the boys to the Barclays Center. It seemed like all of downtown Brooklyn was under construction that night. Huge swaths of pavement had been jackhammered into rubble. Unmanned tractors cast eerie shadows across vacant lots marked off with warning signs and tape. Cranes loomed above mid-rise condos, clawing at the blue-black sky. Coming out of the subway the boys walked with their jaws slack, awestruck, toward the arena and its huge glowing donut overhang.

Theirs were nosebleed seats, dizzyingly elevated and extremely far from the stage. Maggie surveyed the crowd. It was very . . . male. These were people, she thought, with riot thresholds of zero and one. The kind of people that made you wonder: What's the difference between a skinhead and a regular bald guy with tattoos? She didn't want to have to find out. She already knew this was too much testosterone for one room. This was a mob on the verge.

But Bruno and Alex were enjoying themselves, unfazed by their surroundings. Too far from the action to get a glimpse of anything happening in real time, they stared at the Jumbotron as the first fighter, a broad-shouldered white guy, made his way down an illuminated aisle, removed his shirt to much applause, and stepped into the chain-mesh enclosure. A kick drum thumped throughout the arena, anchoring the promethazine-and-Sprite-soaked voice of a rapper whose music Maggie recognized, finally, as the soundtrack to Emma's birthday party months earlier. The second fighter was darker skinned and sported a beard. He entered from the opposite end of the arena, booed the whole way down. He stuck out his tongue and sneered at the audience, waving a big red flag in step with the remixed Berber drums now throbbing through the speakers.

The emcee had frosted tips and took his time introducing the fighters. Their win-loss records were read aloud, as were their respective weights and countries of origin. "A good lesson on 'the other,'" Maggie whispered to the boys. "Or, I mean, a bad one."

They didn't hear her, lost as they were in the spectacle. She watched them shout and cheer, excited as she'd ever seen them, and all at once it dawned on her that they would soon be too old to need her. She dabbed at her eyes with her T-shirt.

Bruno elbowed her in the ribs. "You okay?" he asked.

"Yeah." She winced. "I'm fine." She reclined in her chair, gradually lowering her shoulders and watching, with begrudging amusement, as the fighters waled on one another.

In September, Ezra Goldin celebrated his bar mitzvah. Three hundred friends and family members were invited. Arthur wasn't one of them.

Maggie was not so confident in her brother's attendance as to eliminate the need for a plus-one. Though Ethan had assured her he was coming, Maggie knew he still might bail, leaving her to navigate

the Goldins' minefield of conspicuous consumption and unsolicited career advice. In the end, she decided to bring Mikey. Not as
her date—she was clear on that point—but as a friend. She figured
she'd been hard on him these past few years. His politics weren't
ideal, but she could work on that. Lean on him a little. Besides, he
cared about her. He was in her corner, and she was coming to feel
that that was worth something.

Bex greeted Maggie at the entrance to the sanctuary—"Mwah,
mwah, you're gorgeous"—while Levi subjected Mikey to a vigorous
handshake. The Goldins had come out in full force, the patriarchs
exchanging kisses like made men, the women wrapped in mink.
Maggie sat among the Kleins, who fidgeted in their tallitot and kept
checking the score of the Jets game on their phones. Floating congregants, unaffiliated with either family, occupied random seats,
murmuring prayers and davening at their own pace.

Ezra was meant to share the occasion with another boy in his
class, but that was before Levi bought the congregation a new Torah
and the rabbis bumped the poor kid back a week. Ezra chanted from
the scroll, speeding through his portion, cracking his voice on the
ancient cantillations. Those melodies, meaningless to Maggie but
warm and familiar, fell over her like a blanket and coaxed her to
sleep. When she came to, the temple's sisterhood was presenting Ezra
with a sterling silver Kiddush cup, and there were three individually-
wrapped Sunkist Fruit Gems on her lap. The sound of crinkling
plastic rose throughout the sanctuary as hundreds of Fruit Gems
flew through the air. Maggie chucked hers with a bit too much enthusiasm; a moment later she heard Ezra shout, "Ow! Fuck! My fucking eye!" Mikey scowled at Maggie. *"Don't look at me like that,"* she
whispered. *"The whole point of a firing squad is that you don't hold one
person responsible."*

As the service reached its end, the rabbi led the congregants in
prayer. On Ezra he bestowed the priestly benediction before implor-
ing the congregation to join him in blessing the United States Armed
Forces as well as the IDF. Maggie kept her mouth shut in protest.

All rose for the Kaddish, the hymn for the dead. Those in

mourning were asked to remain on their feet after the prayer so that the congregation could identify those grieving around them. Maggie stood. She raised herself up on her toes but couldn't spot her brother.

That night, before the party, Maggie lingered beside Mikey in the lobby of the Teaneck Marriot. Maggie wore a blue fit-and-flare dress with a pashmina shawl around her shoulders that Mikey had given her in college.

She'd gained back a few pounds in recent months. She was pleased with her new density. It felt good to be grounded again. She had been grieving her mother for ages, starving herself in a protest whose aims were unclear to her now, making herself ill in the process. It was time to get on with her life.

Independent of these developments, Mikey had embarked on a ridiculous home-workout regimen recently popularized by the ultraconservative Speaker of the House. He looked dapper in the charcoal suit he'd chosen after Maggie explicitly forbade pinstripes, his pale blue shirt accented by a red power tie and cufflinks.

"Come on," she gestured, hastening toward the ballroom.

Bex spared nothing when it came to her children. The orthodoxy of the morning had given way to the excess of a nightclub in Tel Aviv. Blue and red LEDs steeped the foyer in neon. A bar had been erected in the middle of the anteroom. A crystal pyramid of upside-down martini glasses shone in rows of saturated backlight.

"This is the scene," Maggie said, "where the underclass smashes through the gates and we all get what's coming to us."

Two women on stilts in glitter-flecked suits directed them inside. Maggie saw a familiar silhouette by the bar, shoulders high and tense, leaning on the table that supported a bust of Ezra's head carved in ice.

"Ethan!" Maggie called. "My brother," she told Mikey. "I'm going to say hi. You stay."

She skipped over and hugged him. His nose had recovered from the blow. It was only the faint smudges of darkness at the corners of his eyes that gestured to lingering damage. "You look good," she said.

"Thanks." He downed half of the drink in his hand.

"What's that?"

Ethan swirled his glass. "Club soda. Trying to kick some habits."

Maggie nodded. The glittering women made their way through the room on their stilts, posing for pictures with guests.

"Hey," she said. "Where were you this morning?"

"I almost didn't come. I don't know how to talk to anyone here. I'm thirty-one years old. I'm jobless. I'm broke."

"Half the people in this room are in debt," Maggie said, "and a whole lot worse than you. They've learned how to live with it."

"To live despite it."

"To live with a big fat middle finger to it."

"You're probably right."

Maggie nodded. "Thanks for not asking me to bail you out, by the way."

Ethan laughed. "I wouldn't dare."

A gaggle of tweens tumbled past, spilling bright red virgin cocktails in pursuit of a boy who'd swiped a pair of heels.

"I'm heading back to school," she said.

"No kidding. For what?"

"To be a teacher. Middle school, I was thinking. In some states you don't need a master's or anything."

"You're leaving New York?"

"I've had enough of this city. It's too expensive."

Ethan cocked his head.

"You pretty much have to be a petrogarch to live in Manhattan," she continued, "and I don't plan on sticking around to see Brooklyn fill up with skyscrapers."

"Where then?"

"Vermont. That's the plan, at least."

Ethan nodded. "I was thinking about school too."

"You were?"

"Yeah—or, well, I already thought about it. And applied. And I'm going."

"Ethan! Wow! What's the program?"

"Pratt has a graduate degree in interior design. An MFA."

"Ah," she said. "An MFA. That famously practical degree."

"Funny. Dad said basically the same thing."

Maggie rolled her eyes. "Whatever."

"I'll have to sell the apartment," he said.

"Where will you go?"

"I'll be a resident advisor. They let you live in the dorms if you keep an eye on the undergrads."

"You're going to have to do more than keep an eye on them."

"I know."

"They're gonna come to you with problems, you're gonna have to—"

"I know, Maggie. I know."

The gauzy lights harmonized into a rich lilac. A tuxedoed man passed the bar carrying a wood block on which three metal chimes were strapped. He tapped them gently with a mallet. "Ladies and gentlemen," he said, "if you'll follow me now to the main hall."

"This isn't the main hall?" Ethan asked.

"Save me a seat," said Maggie. "Two of them."

She found Mikey with a plate of Japanese food. "I ran into some guys from work," he told her through a mouthful of sashimi. "Inhaling what appeared to be top-shelf cocaine in the men's room. Small world, right?"

"Too small. Come on, let's find our table."

In the ballroom, Ezra's name was projected onto the ceiling in italic script. Motivators in disco vests shimmied across a grid of faux wood laminate tiles. One side of the dance floor was bordered by a herd of white leather couches, and across the room a pair of strobe-lit bartenders dispensed drinks with choreographed skill. Above them, a violinist and a saxophonist flanked a DJ on an elevated platform. Ambient electronica pounded throughout the ballroom. Voices fizzed and sparkled above the bass.

Maggie pushed through a crowd of people and found her brother seated at a long table. She introduced him to Mikey.

"Nice to finally meet you," Ethan said.

"You too," said Mikey. "Maggie's told me loads."

The music swelled. "Hatikva" overdubbed with synths and snare rolls. A motivator had miked his headset and was barking at the guests. *"Zaides and gentlemen, goys and girls,"* he called. *"Please find your way to the dance floor. That's right: it's time to horah!"*

A circle of interlocking hands formed on the dance floor. Levi appeared behind his niece and nephew, yanked their chairs out, and pushed them onto the floor. They were swept into the spinning circle, torquing like a flywheel, orbiting Ezra at the center of the room. Dollar bills began to fall from the ceiling, flitting through the air like confetti, and it wasn't until they began to accumulate on the dance floor that Maggie saw they had Ezra's face on them. She soon lost sight of her brother and her date as the ring became recombinant, permitting everyone, parents and children and cousins and business partners. For a moment, before Ezra was hoisted in a chair above adoring friends and family, Maggie, then flanked by two commercial real estate moguls, felt herself begin to rise, a centrifugal wonder, her toes skirting the floor.

The party got Maggie thinking. About money. She would never be able to spend as freely as her uncle's family did. But she didn't love the idea of her mother's inheritance sitting in a cold bank vault, either, doing absolutely no good for anyone. Then again, it wasn't really sitting there, was it? It was being traded, withdrawn from, speculated on, and invested with by boys like Mikey's coke-addled colleagues, traveling at breakneck speed through the sketchy passageways of global commerce.

She hated the idea of "fictitious capital," insofar as she understood it. The "fictitious" part needled her. Were the people in charge just making this stuff up? As they went along? ("Economics," she recalled a senile Danforth professor lecturing her class, "is a fiction. Narrative interpretation. Exegesis.") It was disquieting. The longer her mother's wealth occupied the realm of the imaginary, the longer someone savvier than she could profit from it. As long as she was going to keep the money—and she was, for the time being, going to keep it, until she officially renounced it—she thought it should exist in real life. The material sphere. Not that she was turning into one of those lunatic, paleocon, back-to-the-gold-standard syndicated-radio head cases. But for the first time in her life, she understood the limits of her understanding.

In October her application with the Vermont Agency of Education was approved. She was to begin her coursework in the spring. Following the decision, she liquidated the trust and bought a ten-acre lot outside Woodstock, Vermont, on a hilltop called Harmony Ridge. The property boasted a three-bed, two-bath, two-story home; a furnished barn; a rustic outhouse; and five fenced acres of pasture with a run-in shed for a horse.

Before moving north, she put aside a year's worth of living expenses to sustain her while she worked toward her teaching license, and donated the remaining funds in the trust to Danforth's Student Health Services. She gave the money in her mother's name, under the strict terms that it be used to supplement the organization's anemic mental health funding. She knew that Student Health was overburdened. And if the university wasn't going to channel its endowment toward something worthwhile, the responsibility would have to fall to private donors like Maggie. "Use this grant in whatever way you like, per the conditions above," she'd written in the letter accompanying the donation. She felt like a person of influence, using *per* like that. "But if you're having trouble coming up with something, I'd recommend bringing on additional qualified, permanent staff." There were plenty of kids, she figured, whose survival might depend on whether they had access to a woman like her mother.

Managing an estate as large as the one she'd purchased, especially when she'd soon be in class all day, proved difficult. Maggie hired a local Birkenstocked vagrant named Bo to look after the property. But Bo didn't have a cell phone, or a landline—he believed the government was listening in on him—so Maggie could get in touch with him only when he was at the house.

She never thought she'd be anyone's boss. Now that she was, she wanted to be the kind of employer who was put off by perfect attendance and unquestioning obedience. She wanted to take it easy, to rule not with an iron fist but a laissez-faire high five. This proved difficult in practice. Bo was unreliable, and there was so much work! What with the taxes, the fallen trees, and the termite infestations. Boiler trouble, water pressure malfunctions. A lot could go wrong on that much land. In late November, a sugar maple on the property was struck by lightning. It toppled, crushing a ground-level pipeline that joined the main house with the septic system. Maggie got a call the following day. "It's kind of a disaster," Bo said, sounding entirely unconcerned. "Fecal matter everywhere. Bubbling up in the grass . . . Want me to call in a professional? Take a look?"

"Hmm." Maggie thought about it for a moment. She ran a hand through her curls. "No," she said. "I think I know a guy who can fix it."

Arthur arrived at Harmony Ridge on a blustery December night, snow sifting down from a single gray cloud, powdering his daughter's estate. He inched along, the yellow headlights of Francine's Spero illuminating a few feet of road ahead of him. He maneuvered the car up the winding drive, guided by the low stone fence on either side of him, until the stones disappeared and the path became indistinguishable from the field, the land dressed in uncanny white, leaving Arthur with little guidance but the glow from inside the gigantic house ahead, arched and shining through Palladian windows, and the winged light of the fixtures mounted on the house's stone facade. He approached it, slowed, and cut the engine.

He sat inside the sagging station wagon, the trunk heavy with duffel bags and bubble-wrapped breakables. He could feel the heat slowly filtering out of the car, and the cold creeping in. He had overestimated himself again. He'd been on the road for almost nineteen hours and was delirious with exhaustion. A crumpled paper bag was pinned between the windshield and the dash, speckled with greasy liver spots from the French fries he'd picked up in Columbus, the only food he'd eaten on the road. He'd impressed himself at the time, the fries a pleasant reminder of how little he needed to subsist on, but now his stomach roiled with a savage hunger.

It was easier to leave St. Louis than he'd expected. Anxiety belonged to the future, not the past, and he didn't see the point in wasting time with regrets. To dwell on all that he'd abandoned there—not only the house but those insidious, immaterial, American ideals: his dream of status and security, the pride of homeownership, the expectation of professional advancement—would surely bring on a heart attack of the type that killed his father. Still, it was hard to look upon the isolated, rustic chateau before him and know that it belonged to his daughter, while he could claim nothing in this world but the contents of the Spero. He reminded himself that it was not an unheard-of arrangement, the aging father sent to live with the adult child. But how many of those fathers had minds as sharp as his? And how many were expected to work for their room and board? He steeled himself and stepped out into the cold.

Maggie answered the door in black leggings and hiking socks, an oversize sweater draped over her torso. "Dad," she said, leaning forward for a hug. "I almost thought you wouldn't make it."

"I-90 is a deathtrap in this weather."

"Yeah, yeah. Come inside."

He followed her into the house.

The living room was high-ceilinged, the stone walls framed by beams of varnished timber mottled with knots. "Some of this was Ethan's idea," Maggie said, nodding up at the iron ring chandelier. She led Arthur through the abutting dining room. "I'll give you the grand tour tomorrow. As you'll see, the main problem is the septic system, which is ancient. But there's plenty more for you to do once that's fixed. Falling trees are going to be the least of our problems, especially now that it's winter. How do you feel about horses, by the way? I'm toying with the idea."

He was queasy with excess. The house was too big, his status too compromised, the arrangement too bizarre. He hadn't expected the place to be this grand. He hadn't expected Maggie to be so readily at home there.

"It's a bit . . . enormous, isn't it?" he said.

"It's just a farmhouse."

"It's a ski lodge, is what it is."

Maggie smiled. "You'll sleep in the barn."

"Like an animal."

"Hardly. It's furnished and heated. I left out towels, the bed has sheets, et cetera. It'll be more private that way. I'll let you get settled."

They looped back to the foyer. Arthur glanced down at the trail of brown water his squeaking sneakers had left behind.

"Maggie," he said.

"Yeah?"

He looked her in the eyes then, for the first time, it seemed, since she was an infant, flailing and defenseless. He opened his mouth to speak, but no words came out.

"Whatever it is, don't worry about it," she said. "Make yourself comfortable."

He nodded and walked out into the snow.

He trudged to the car and popped the trunk, hoisting a heavy duffel bag over his right shoulder. It would take multiple trips to get all his things out, three to four at least—unless he pushed himself, took up a heavier load. Leaning over, he grabbed a second bag and threw it over his left shoulder. His knees almost buckled, but they held. His thighs shook under the weight. He saw the barn across the field and set off toward it. Step after step he walked slowly, deliberately, hauling his load through the dark. Flakes alighted on his scalp.

The barn was designed in the same style of the main house, all smooth knotted wood, one great room like an overturned ship's hull. The straps on the duffel bags dug burns into his shoulders. He followed a row of dim Edison bulbs to the far end of the cavernous space, where a large bed with a wrought-iron headboard was flush with the wall.

Make yourself comfortable. He could imagine no slicker slogan for these times, no better clarion call for a species in surrender. But he was not like other people. He would not succumb to comfort and complacency. Not yet. Not when there were debts to be repaid.

It wasn't until after he dropped his luggage, stretched, and sat on the edge of his bed that he saw what Maggie had left on his pillow. A book. A slim red volume, his name stamped across the cover. The sight of it startled him. This was not the old comfortable feeling. Something prickly and hot came over him. His cheeks flushed. He stuffed it in the drawer on his bedside table.

Five months later, on the third anniversary of Francine's death, Ethan took a bus up from the city. He slept in the guest room he'd designed for himself. The mattress was a king, sized aspirationally for two. On the bedside table was a photograph he'd found in the attic while clearing out the St. Louis house, developed from a 35 mm slide. Francine lay in a hospital bed, her head haloed by burnt-red hair. She held a squirming pink baby in her hands. Arthur crouched to fit into the frame, clothed in blue scrubs, one gloved hand on Ethan's shoulder.

Where civilization does not exist, you must invent it. Out in the sticks, surrounded by pasture and, beyond that, acres of maple trees in leaf, the Alters were feeling their way toward a new arrangement. That night, the family gathered around a fire pit in the clearing behind the house. When the fire dimmed, and Ethan offered to grab some kindling, Arthur stopped him, removing the little book from his back pocket and tossing it without reservation into the flames. Under the cloudy sky, it was the only light for miles.

Acknowledgments

The author is indebted to Erin Sellers, Oliver Munday, Nicholas Thomson, Peter Mendelsund, Jennifer Olsen, Sonny Mehta, Dan Frank, Michal Shavit, Ana Fletcher, Peter Straus, and Allison Lorentzen for their help with this book.